Ex Libris

A GOOD FRIEND IS LIKE A BOOK I WOULD KEEP FOREVER

Lani Dado

DHARMA OCEAN SERIES

In a meeting with Samuel Bercholz, the president of
Shambhala Publications, Ven. Chögyam Trungpa expressed his interest in publishing a series of 108 vol-
umes, to be called the Dharma Ocean Series. "Dharma
Ocean" is the translation of Chögyam Trungpa's Tibetan teaching name, Chökyi Gyatso. The Dharma
Ocean Series consists primarily of edited transcripts of
lectures and seminars given by Chögyam Trungpa during his seventeen years of teaching in North America.
The goal of the series is to allow readers to encounter
this rich array of teachings simply and directly rather
than in an overly systematized or condensed form. At
its completion, it will serve as the literary archive of
the major works of this renowned
Tibetan Buddhist teacher.

Series Editor: Judith L. Lief

Chögyam Trungpa, Gold Hill, Colorado, 1970

Transcending Madness

THE EXPERIENCE OF THE SIX BARDOS

Chögyam Trungpa

Edited by Judith L. Lief

Shambhala • *Boston & London* • *1992*

SHAMBHALA PUBLICATIONS, INC.
Horticultural Hall
300 Massachusetts Avenue
Boston, Massachusetts 02115

SHAMBHALA PUBLICATIONS, INC.
Random Century House
20 Vauxhall Bridge Road
London SW1V 2SA

© 1992 by Diana J. Mukpo

9 8 7 6 5 4 3 2 1

First Edition

Printed in the United States of America on acid-free paper
∞
Distributed in the United States by Random House, Inc.,
in Canada by Random House of Canada Ltd, and in the
United Kingdom by the Random Century Group

Library of Congress Cataloging-in-Publication Data

Trungpa, Chögyam, 1939—
Transcending madness: the experience of the six Bardos /
Chögyam Trungpa.
p.   cm.—(Dharma ocean series)
ISBN 0-87773-637-5
1. Intermediate state—Buddhism. 2. Death—Religious aspects—
Buddhism. 3. Eschatology, Buddhist. 4. Meditation—Buddhism.
5. Buddhism—Psychology.   I. Title.   II. Series.
BQ4490.T78, 1992   91-50879
294.3'423—dc20   CIP

Frontispiece photo from the Vajradhatu Archives. Photographer unknown.

Contents

PART TWO
THE SIX STATES OF BEING
Karme-Chöling, 1971

Acknowledgments

I would like to thank the many people who helped in the preparation of this book: Carolyn Rose Gimian, Sherab Chödzin, Emily Hilburn Sell, Lilly Gleich, Hazel Bercholz, Alma Carpenter, and Helen Berliner. In addition, the recording, transcribing, and preservation of these materials has taken the work of countless volunteers, to whom I am most grateful.

I would like to thank Mrs. Diana Mukpo for her continued support of the Dharma Ocean Series and for her kind permission to work with this material.

Most especially I would like to thank the Vidyadhara, Venerable Chögyam Trungpa, Rinpoche, who dedicated his life to making such precious teachings available to North Americans.

Judith L. Lief
Editor

Editor's Foreword

In 1971, the Vidyadhara, Chögyam Trungpa, Rinpoche, gave three seminars in rapid succession on the topics of the six realms, the bardo experience, and *The Tibetan Book of the Dead,* one in Colorado and the other two in Vermont. At a time when there was great fascination with the notion of reincarnation and life after death, Trungpa Rinpoche emphasized the power of these teachings as a way of pointing to the traps and opportunities of present experience, rather than as fodder for intellectual speculation. At that time, he was also working on a translation of *The Tibetan Book of the Dead,* which he described as a detailed and sophisticated map displaying the potential of confusion and awakening in each moment of experience. These three seminars, two of which form the body of this book, were to be pivotal in the development of the Vidyadhara's early students.

In the early seventies, Trungpa Rinpoche had attracted many students with a background in higher education, psychology, and the arts. These early students were strongly interested in integrating their Buddhist training with their practice of Western disciplines. Those with background in the arts studied "dharma art" teachings, which explored the connection between meditation experience and the creative process. The Vidyadhara worked with these students in a number of ways, ranging from holding theater conferences, creating theater exercises, and writing and producing plays, to establishing the arts programs in the newly formed Naropa Institute in Boulder, Colorado. At that time, the Vidyadhara's two bardo seminars were the core teachings studied by students preparing to establish a therapeutic community. The community he established, called Maitri, or "loving-kindness," later evolved into the clinical psychology program at the Naropa Institute.

The Vidyadhara presented teachings on the realms and bardos as a way of understanding madness and sanity and learning to work directly and skillfully with extreme states of mind. Based on direct observation of mental patterns, these teachings provide a way "to see our situation along with that of our fellow human beings." As is usual in the Buddhist approach, such a study is not done as though one were studying rats in a laboratory, but begins with oneself and one's own state of mind. By familiarizing ourselves with our own insanity and making friends with mind in all its variety and extremes, we can learn to accommodate others and work with them without fear. So the process begins with a detailed exploration of our own mental states and of how we color our world through our preconceptions, expectations, hopes, and fears.

When we have developed the courage to look at ourselves without blinders, we can also begin to see others more clearly. We can connect with people, because we learn not to fear our mind, but to work with it through the practice of meditation. It is an approach based on nonviolence and acceptance, rather than on struggle or the overpowering of others. The acceptance of our experience with all its complexity and uncertainty provides the basis for any real change.

This volume could be considered a practical guide to Buddhist psychology. It is based on the interweaving of two core concepts: realm and bardo. The traditional Buddhist schema of the six realms—gods, jealous gods, human beings, animals, hungry ghosts, and hell beings—is sometimes taken to be a literal description of possible modes of existence. But in this case the schema of the six realms is used to describe the six complete worlds we create as the logical conclusions of such powerful emotional highlights as anger, greed, ignorance, lust, envy, and pride. Having disowned the power of our emotions and projected that power onto the world outside, we find ourselves trapped in a variety of ways and see no hope for escape.

The six realms provide a context for the bardo experience, which is described as the experience of no-man's-land. The bardos arise as the heightened experience of each realm, providing at the same time the possibility of awakening or of complete confusion, sanity or insanity. They are the ultimate expression of the entrapment of the realms. Yet it is such heightened experience that opens the possibility of the sudden transformation of that solidity into complete freedom or open space. So even within the most solidified and seemingly hopeless accomplishment of ego's domain, the possibility of awakening is ever-present.

The two seminars included in this book approach the topic of the realms and the bardos in two very different ways. The first seminar associates each realm with a characteristic bardo state. In this case, the realms are pictured as islands and the bardos as the peaks highlighting each island. In contrast, the second seminar emphasizes the process of continually cycling through the bardos. (It should be noted that the second seminar introduces the bardo of dharmata, thereby increasing the list from six to seven.) From this perspective, each realm contains the full cycle of bardos, which serves as a means to strengthen and sustain its power. By looking at the same topic in two contrasting yet complementary ways, we can begin to understand and appreciate the richness and complexity of these teachings.

In general, Trungpa Rinpoche placed great emphasis on dialogue and discussion with his students. In order to preserve that flavor, the extensive discussions following the talks have been included in this volume. In that way, readers who wish to follow the flow and development of the teachings through the two seminars may do so. Others may prefer to concentrate on the talks themselves.

May these subtle and practical teachings strike home and thereby help to alleviate the confusion and suffering of these current times. May they spark humor and gentleness in dealing with our states of mind and those of others.

ONE

The Six States of Bardo

ALLENSPARK   1971

Bardo

There seems to be quite a misconception as to the idea of bardo, which is that it is purely connected with the death and after-death experience. But the experience of the six bardos is not concerned with the future alone; it also concerns the present moment. Every step of experience, every step of life, is bardo experience.

Bardo is a Tibetan word: *bar* means "in between" or, you could say, "no-man's-land," and *do* is like a tower or an island in that no-man's-land. It's like a flowing river which belongs neither to the other shore nor to this shore, but there is a little island in the middle, in between. In other words, it is present experience, the immediate experience of nowness—where you are, where you're at. That is the basic idea of bardo.

The experience of such a thing also brings the idea of space, of course. Without seeing the spacious quality, which does not belong to you or others, you would not be able to see the little island in the middle at all. The living experience of bardo could only come from seeing the background of space. And from that, within space or an understanding of space, a brilliant spark or flash happens. So generally, all bardo experiences are situations in which we have emerged from the past and we have not yet formulated the future, but strangely enough, we happen to be somewhere. We are standing on some ground, which is very mysterious. Nobody knows how we happen to be there.

That mysterious ground, which belongs to neither that nor this, is the actual experience of bardo. It is very closely associated with the practice of meditation. In fact, it *is* the meditation experience. That is why I decided to introduce this subject. It is also connected with the subject of basic ego and one's experience of ego, including all sorts of journeys through the six realms of the world.

Beyond that is the issue of how we happen to be in the six realms of the world; how we find that experience is not seen as an evolutionary process, as it should be, but as extremely patchy and rugged, purely a glimpse. Somehow, things don't seem to be associated or connected with each other—they are very choppy and potent like gigantic boulders put together. Each experience is real, potent, impressionable, but generally we don't find that there is any link between those potent experiences. It is like going through air pockets—emotionally, spiritually, domestically, politically. The human situation passes through these highlights or dramas, and on the other hand, the absence of drama, and boredom—which is another aspect of drama. We go through all these processes. And somehow these isolated situations, which from our confused way of thinking seem to have nothing to do with the basic quality of continuity, are the continuity itself. So the only way to approach this is to see the evolutionary process.

I can't lay heavy trips on people to understand that or accept that purely on blind faith. In order not to lay heavy trips on people, we have to have some concrete thing to work on. That is where the six experiences of bardo come in—in each moment, each situation. Each of the six types of bardo is individual and unique in its own way. They are isolated situations on the one hand, but on the other hand they have developed and begun to make an impression on us, penetrating through us within that basic space or basic psychological background. So the bardo experience is very important to know. And in fact it is much more fundamental than simply talking about death and reincarnation and what you are supposed to experience after you die. It is more fundamental than that.

I know people would love to hear about undiscovered areas: "Do Martians exist?" In a lot of cases, when we talk about karma and reincarnation and life after death, we tend to make assumptions or logical ideas about them. And people often get quite emotional about it, because they would like to prove that there are such things as life after death or reincarnation. But the subject we are going to work on is not based on trying to prove logical conclusions. I mean, it is not really that desperate, is it? What difference does it really make whether we are going to come back or not? The question of whether we are what we are or whether we are on some ground seems to be more realistic and more important.

In discussing the experience of the bardos we are working on that realistic aspect of the process of changing from birth to death, the intermediate process between birth and death. We are not trying to prove logically or by theology that life after death is important and that you must accept that on faith. In many cases, particularly in the West, people try to prove the existence of life after death, saying: "Such and such a saint or sage was a great person when he lived, and his example of being is beyond question—and he also says that there is such a thing as life after death." That is trying to prove the notion of life after death by innuendo: "It is true because he was an enlightened person as a living being and he said so!" When we try to prove the point of view of life after death in that way, we have no real proof. The only thing we could prove is that he was an awake person and that he said so.

There is almost a feeling of rediscovery: Eastern traditions have managed to present to the Western world that nothing is fatalistic but everything is continuously growing, as an evolutionary, developing process. In many cases, Westerners find this view extremely helpful and hopeful. They no longer just wait to die, but there's something hopeful—the message of continuity, that you have another chance. But I think all of these views and attitudes on the idea of rebirth and reincarnation and karma are very simple-minded ones. As well as that, we begin to feel we can afford to make mistakes, because surely we will have another chance. We are going to come back and we might do better. Often people who are afraid of dying have been saved by hearing the idea of reincarnation. They are no longer afraid of death, or even if they are afraid of death, they try to contemplate the idea of rebirth, which saves them from that. I don't think that is a complete way of looking into the situation.

The fatalistic quality of life and death depends on the present situation. The present situation is important—that's the whole point, the important point. Whether you continue or whether you don't continue, you are what you are at the moment. And you have six types of psychological thresholds, or bardo experiences, in your lifetime. We will go into details if you don't find this too heavy an intellectual supposition. You might ask, "Is it worth speculating about all these six types of bardo experiences? Why don't we just sit and meditate and forget all this jargon?" Well, it is much easier said than done. To start with, when we begin to sit down and meditate, these collections do come up. They happen continuously in the thought process. Discursive thoughts, argumentative thoughts, self-denial thoughts—all sorts of thoughts begin to come up. So it seems to be important to know something about them. In other words, you could make use of these thoughts instead of pretending to be good and trying to suppress thoughts, as though you don't require them anymore or they don't require you anymore.

It is good to make use of speculative mind. That is exactly why the whole idea of studying scriptures and going through disciplines or practices is extremely important. It is a way of us-ing these living materials that we have. Whether we try to quiet ourselves or not, these things come up constantly and do happen. Therefore, making use of such thought processes as a way of learning is extremely necessary and good and helpful and important—unless you develop "gold fever," believing that you have found some argument, some logic which you're excited about, and you spend the rest of your life arguing, trying to prove it logically all the time. If this begins to happen, then the intellect is not being properly cared for. It begins to take on a self-destructive quality, as in gold fever, where you're constantly willing to sacrifice your life looking for gold, gold, gold, and you end up destroying yourself. It is the same thing when you're trying to look for something, trying to prove something purely by intellectual speculation, beyond the ordinary level of thought process. The ordinary level of thought process has been transformed into a more ambitious one. Being able to click with your thought process and work something out is good, but beyond that goodness, you begin to get a faint idea of satisfaction—just a teeny-weeny bit to start with and then it begins to grow, grow, grow, and grow. It becomes addictive and self-destructive.

So that seems to be the limitation. If one's experiences, discoveries, and intellectual understandings coincide simultaneously, like putting together a jigsaw puzzle, that's fine. That doesn't mean that you have to have an absolute understanding or a complete command of the whole thing necessarily at all. But you could have a basic glimpse or understanding of the situation and you could go along with it, without indulging in the experience as a new discovery of an exciting thing. And I hope, in any case, to introduce in my lifetime, working with people in the West, all the teachings that are available and have been studied, practiced, and experienced in Tibet and elsewhere. And I have tremendous confidence that people in the West will be able to grasp them if we are not too rushed, if no one has caught gold fever halfway. That would be too bad.

I'm sure that such studying, such learning, means sacrificing intellect when it goes beyond, to the pleasurable point of intellectualization. It also means sacrificing the emotional, impulsive quality of wanting to exaggerate by tuning in to your basic neuroses and trying to interpret them as discoveries. That is another problem. You see, there are two extremes: one extreme is indulgence in the intellectual sense and in intellectual discovery; the other extreme is using the impulsive, instinctive level of the ego as camouflage to prove your state of mind in terms of the teachings. The two of them could work side by side with some people, or else there could be a greater portion of one or the other with others. It could work either way.

Our task is not purely trying to save ourselves alone—whether you are ninety-nine years old or whether you are ten years old doesn't make any difference. Our task is to see our situation along with that of our fellow human beings. As we work on ourselves, then we continuously work with others as well. That is the only way of developing ourselves, and that is the only way of relating with the six experiences of bardo. If we relate our experience with the dream bardo, the bardo between birth and death, the bardo of the before-death experience, or the bardo of emotions—all of these have a tremendous connection with our projection of the world outside. Other persons, animate and inanimate objects, the apparent phenomenal world, also play a great and important part. But unless we're willing to give in, give way, and learn from these situations, then our prefabricated learning—either by scripture or by the constant close watch of our instructor—doesn't help. It doesn't mean anything very much.

I think I've said enough. This much introduction is quite a handful. At this seminar, a lot of us, all of us actually, are brought together by individual convictions. That individual conviction means a great deal. We were not brought up in Buddhist families; our parents did not pay our fee and push us here. Everything here is based on individual conviction. We are free people; we have the right to use our freedom, our insight, for our own benefit as well as for sharing and communicating with others as compassionately and openly as possible. Perhaps we should have a short question period.

STUDENT: You said one should not try to save oneself alone, and then you used the expression "projections." But in another talk you said that in order to be able to communicate you have to respect the existence of the other person. This is more than projection, isn't it? It's a recognition.

TRUNGPA RINPOCHE: Well, you see, that is a very interesting point. And actually, to tell you the truth, nobody is quite certain whether it is one hundred percent projection or whether it is only partially a projection. Things do exist independent of you, outside you, and you exist independent of them in some ways. But occasionally you need their help to reaffirm yourself. If you are a fat person, somebody will say you are fat because they are thinner than you. Without their comparison you wouldn't know what you were, because you would have no way of working with yourself. And from that point of view it could be called a projection. But projection in this case does not necessarily mean purely your hallucination; things outside *do* exist as they are. But that's a very dangerous thing to say.

Things do exist as they are, but we tend to see our version of them as they are, rather than things as they really are. That makes everything that we see projections. But one doesn't have to make a definite and absolute reassurance of that necessarily at all. You just go along with situations, go along with dealing with them. If you are going too far, they'll shake you. They'll beat you to death if you're going too far. If you're going well, if you are balanced, they will present hospitality and openness luxuriously to you. I mean, that much of a situation is there anyway; some kind of rapport between this and that goes on all the time. As long as a person is sensitive enough to experience it, that rapport goes on. That's the important point. One doesn't have to make it definite and clear-cut as to which is not projection and which is projection. It is sort of a gradual understanding. Until the attainment of buddhahood, this experience goes on—and nobody is able to answer it because they themselves don't know.

STUDENT: When was *The Tibetan Book of the Dead* written?

TRUNGPA RINPOCHE: According to tradition, it was about the fourteenth century, or about two hundred years after the introduction of Buddhism into Tibet from India. At that time, a particular teacher called Karma Lingpa discovered this teaching—he did not actually compose it, but it is as though he discovered, or rediscovered, this teaching. The actual teaching existed in the seventh century. He rediscovered the idea of bardo and the death experience out of his own experience as well, in the death of his very beloved child. He had watched the death of his child, and after he had conducted the funeral service and the child had been buried, he came back home to find that his wife was also just about to die. So he watched and he worked through this experience of the death process. From that experience he discovered that the process of birth and death is continual, taking place all the time. And therefore the six types of bardo were developed.

I think it had something to do with the local situation in Tibet at the time as well, because generally people regarded death as extremely important as well as birth. People often gathered around their dying friends, dying relatives, and tried to work with them and help them. That was the common tradition. It seems that in the West, people make birth more important. You congratulate someone for having a child, and you have parties for birthdays. But there are no parties for dying.

STUDENT: In Ireland there is the wake, or party for the deceased, which happens down South as well.

TRUNGPA RINPOCHE: I hope so. I'm pleased. That is probably connected with ancient ideas, which is very right, very good.

I think it is extremely important to a dying person that he or she receive proper acknowledgment that he is dying, and that death plays an important part in life as well as birth—as much as one's birthday parties. It's an important thing.

STUDENT: I didn't understand the distinction between intellectual and instinctual.

TRUNGPA RINPOCHE: In instinct, you don't use any logic. To put it very bluntly, extremely bluntly, if you're studying and practicing the teachings of some religion, and you have some pseudo-experience of the spiritual path—sort of a shadow experience of what has been described in the scriptures—you'll go along with it, but you are not quite certain exactly. You would like to believe that these experiences are true experiences. And at a certain point, you have to make up your mind whether all this experience and development have been pure hypocrisy on your part or not—you have to make a decision. Either you have to renounce your discoveries as being false up to that point or you have to make another leap of building yourself up.

That very peak point becomes extremely important to a person—whether he will confess everything completely, or whether he will latch onto some continual buildup. If a person has decided to continually build up and to latch onto that, then he begins to realize that he can't keep up with the speed of what's going on, with his experience. In the scriptures, the analogy for this is a street beggar who's been enthroned as a universal monarch. There is a sudden shock, you don't know what to do. You never had a penny; now you have the rest of the world, from your point of view. And you automatically freak out because of such a change. You act as though you are a universal monarch, although in mentality you are still a beggar. A beggar doesn't make a good millionaire. If there's no gradual experience of the transition, things will become chaotic and emotionally disturbed as well in such a relationship. That is, of course, the emotional or the instinctive.

The scholarly approach is less violent than that, less dangerous than that, but at the same time it is extremely contagious in the sense of bringing you down. Continual bondage is put on yourself, all the time. You become heavier and heavier and heavier. You don't accept anything unless it is logically proven, up to the point that the logic brings you pleasure, the discovery brings you pleasure. In certain neurotic intellectual states of mind, *everything* is based on pain and pleasure. If your discovery brings pleasure, then you accept it as a masterpiece. If that discovery or logical conclusion doesn't bring you pleasure, or victory, then you feel you've been defeated. You find this with certain college professors: if you discuss their sore point in their particular subject, if there's the slightest usage of certain words, since their whole world is based on words, the structure of words, they become extremely upset or offended. The whole thing is based on pleasure and pain, from the point of view of getting logical conclusions. But the scholar doesn't claim that he or she has spiritual experiences, as the other person would claim. In fact, the scholar would be afraid of any actual experience of what he's teaching; he wouldn't actually commit himself at all. He may be a professor of meditation, but he wouldn't dare to take part in sitting meditation because that doesn't bring pleasure or any logical conclusions for his work or research.

STUDENT: If you really start to study very hard, do you have any conscious control over the experiences you receive? Doesn't it just happen to you? Can you really push it too fast?

TRUNGPA RINPOCHE: Well, you can push too fast, of course, but that doesn't mean the whole thing should be ruled out. I mean, there is a balanced pattern happening all the time. It's a question of how open you are. The minute you set foot on the path, if there's room for suggestion and if you are flexible and not too serious or sincere, there is, of course, room for study. But once a person begins to make up his mind that whatever he is doing is a matter of death or life, kill or cure—as they say, "publish or perish"—then it could become self-destructive. It is very individual; you can't make generalizations.

S: Is it possible to check yourself when you start on the path so that you're not deceiving yourself all the time about your seriousness, your sincerity, and so that it doesn't just become a trap?

TR: Generally, if you allow some space between the action and the thinking, it is a natural process, always predictable. In this case, there will be a definite experience of genuine understanding of yourself as you are and as what you're trying to do—in other words, your hypocritical aspect and you as an innocent child. That will be quite obvious, provided you allow room or space between action and thinking. It will be quite a natural process.

A person might be convinced that he has gained something which he actually hasn't gained. And if you talk to such a person, he might behave as if he has no doubt about himself at all. He overrides your doubts about him: there's no question about his attainment; it's absolutely valid; he is a bank of knowledge and he knows what he's doing. But the very fact of the way he overrides any doubts means the subtlety of something is not quite right. It could happen that if we were really honest with ourselves, if we allowed space for ourselves, we automatically would know that the subtlety of self-hypocrisy is always there, without fail. Even if you had great power, great will power to override these obstacles, still you would know. There still will be a very faint but very sharp, very delicate and penetrating understanding that something is not quite right. That is basic sanity, which continues all the time, without fail. That basic sanity really allows you to engage your speed and your pressure, so to speak. It happens all the time, continuously.

S: I want to know how it works, the space between action and the thinking process. Is it that you think of an action, then do it?

TR: When I talk about space, I don't mean you have to delay yourself between thinking and doing things. It is a fundamental understanding that, to start with, what you're doing is not warfare. No one is losing and no one is gaining. There's time to be open. It doesn't mean you have to slow down your footsteps and be half an hour late for your interview necessarily; it is not that literal. But there will be some feeling of spaciousness or roomy quality, that you can afford to be what you are. Really, you can afford to be what you are. You may think you're alone and nobody's with you, but that in itself is good enough. The aloneness is good, because you are definitely what you are, clear-cut what you are. Your area has not been intruded on or taken advantage of by others. You have your space; you have your place. It is a definite thing: you are alone and you can afford to be what you are, and you don't have to rush into it. It is fundamental space, basic space—extreme, fundamental space.

STUDENT: Usually in real life one cannot afford to do or be what one wants to be for oneself because it involves many other people, so it can be very selfish.

TRUNGPA RINPOCHE: The point is not that you have to centralize yourself. If you can afford to be what you are, then that automatically means you could receive others as your guests. Because the ground your guests are treading on is safe ground, nobody is going through the floorboard. It is a sound, well-built house, your own house, and people could be welcome in it. That makes other people more comfortable and welcome, so they don't have to put up their portion of resistance anymore. It is mutual understanding. You see, generally people pick up some kind of psychic vibrations that you put out, and before you exchange words there is a kind of meeting of the two psyches. That takes place continuously.

STUDENT: Could you elaborate on the importance of studying the six states of bardo in connection with meditation experience?

TRUNGPA RINPOCHE: You don't have to try to put them together; they are the same experience. However, the six types of bardo are postmeditation experience, the meditation-in-action aspect. Sitting meditation is *being,* a way of being in open space, providing a clear white canvas in order to paint pictures on it. So they are complementary to one other.

STUDENT: As Evans-Wentz mentions in *The Tibetan Book of the Dead,* [1] there are various books of the dead in various cultures. Are the experiences they describe inspired parables, or have they actually been experienced and can be experienced by us, too?

TRUNGPA RINPOCHE: You see, all ancient traditions—such as the Egyptian, the Pön tradition of Tibet, the Shintoism of Japan, the Taoism of China, and others—all paid a great deal of attention to the process of growth. The process of growth means birth as well as coloring, blooming, decaying, turning into a seed, dropping on the ground, regenerating as another plant, and going through the cycle of the four seasons continuously. Because of that, because it is of the same nature, human life has been dealt with in exactly the same way. So much sacredness has been imposed on the idea of the birth and death process. I don't think it is so much an intellectual, philosophical, or religious phenomenon, but it is much more earthy—being one with the facts of life, with this growth process.

For instance, in Pön, the Tibetan pre-Buddhist tradition, they say the time of death and the time of birth should coincide. That brings a conclusion to that process of birth and death—which includes the climate, the time, the location, the direction the dying person is facing, the particular collection of parents and relatives, and how many people are gathered there, how many men, women, or children. That whole collection brings a total picture of complete conclusion. So they are very earthy people. It is quite different from how modern occultists work with the same thing. It is very earthy; nobody allows room for hallucinations or imagination. Everything is dealt with completely within the tradition and the actual experience of the moment.

From that point of view, in all the traditional civilizations of many different cultures, the death experience is regarded as an important point. And on top of that, the Buddhist discovery was to see all those colors, directions, temperatures, and climates of the dying person as a psychological picture. So it is seen completely differently but in exactly the same way.

S: Are the deities which appear during the forty-nine days following death just visions, or are they actually experienced?

TR: Nobody knows. But as an experience of a given situation develops, it has a feeling around it as well. That could be said of anything, like the meeting of two friends—the situation of the meeting, the nature of the conversation, the particular kind of prelude to the meeting the individuals had before they met the other person, what kind of state of mind you are in, what kind of incidents you have gone through, whether you just got up and felt high-spirited when you met this person or whether you were just involved in a car accident and you happened to drag yourself into a friend's house and met this person—I mean, such situations make *real* life, the living quality. From that point of view it is a definite thing, an experiential thing. But as far as the death process is concerned, nobody knows. It is left to individuals to work through it from their living experiences.

S: If you have decided to return to earth, the soul sees visions of copulating males and females. Well, this is a marvelous simile, but does that vision really exist?

TR: It could exist, sure. If you are without a home for seven weeks and you see somebody decorating a beautiful apartment . . .

STUDENT: Through meditation I get myself together. But can I use it to help other people, all those who are oppressed?

TRUNGPA RINPOCHE: I think so, definitely, yes. It wouldn't become true meditation if you couldn't help other people. That is a criterion of meditation—meditation experience is not only an introverted experience, but it is also associated with the experience of life in general. You see, the idea of meditation is complete sanity, a completely balanced state of mind. If you are a completely sane person, even your example will be inspiring to others, that you are a balanced person, beautiful to be with.

STUDENT: Is it helpful to study *The Tibetan Book of the Dead?*

TRUNGPA RINPOCHE: Sure, of course. But you have to understand the symbolism, all the subtleties, because the people who wrote such writings were very earthy people. They saw things as they really are. When they say *water,* they really mean it. When we say *water,* we might see it as something coming out of taps, in terms of cold and hot. It could be misleading.

DISCUSSION NEXT MORNING

STUDENT: We were talking this morning about ego, and we seemed to have trouble defining it. Could you say what it is?

TRUNGPA RINPOCHE: Well, there seem to be different ways of using the word *ego.* To some people, the ego is that which sustains them. That which gives some kind of guideline or practicality in dealing with things is referred to as ego, being conscious of being oneself. And you exert effort through it, so any kind of self-respect is referred to as ego, which is a general sense of the term.

But ego as we are discussing it is slightly different from that. In this case ego is that which is constantly involved with some kind of paranoia, some kind of panic—in other words, hope and fear. That is to say, as you operate there is a constant reference back to yourself. As you refer back to yourself, then a criterion of reference develops in terms of hope and fear: gaining something or losing one's identity. It is a constant battle. That seems to be the notion of ego in this case, its neurotic aspect.

You could have a basic sound understanding of the logic of things as they are without ego. In fact you can have greater sanity beyond ego; you can deal with situations without hope and fear, and you can retain your self-respect or your logical sanity in dealing with things. Continuously you can do so, and you can do so with much greater skill, in a greater way, if you don't have to make the journey to and fro and if you don't have to have a running commentary going on side by side with your operation. It is more powerful and more definite. You see, getting beyond ego doesn't mean that you have to lose contact with reality at all. I think that in a lot of cases there is a misunderstanding that you need ego and that without it you can't operate. That's a very convenient basic twist: hope and fear as well as the notion of sanity are amalgamated together and used as a kind of excuse, that you need some basic ground to operate—which is, I would say, a misunderstanding. It's the same as when people say that if you are a completely enlightened being, then you have no dualistic notion of things. That is the idea of ultimate zombie, which doesn't seem to be particularly inspiring or creative at all.

STUDENT: What do you mean by basic sanity?

TRUNGPA RINPOCHE: It is relating with things which come up within your experience and knowing experiences as they are. It's kind of the rhythm between experience and your basic being, like driving on the road in accordance with the situation of the road, a kind of interchange. That is the basic sanity of clear perception. Otherwise, if you wanted to reshape the road in accordance with your excitement or your wishes, then possibly, instead of you reshaping the road, the road might reshape you and you might end up in an accident. This is insane, suicidal.

S: How about vajrayana, crazy wisdom?

TR: Well, crazy wisdom—that's a very good question—is when you have a complete exchange with the road, so that the shape of the road becomes your pattern as well. There's no hesitation at all. It's complete control—not only control, but a complete dance with it, which is very sharp and penetrating, quick precision. That precision comes from the situation outside as well: not being afraid of the outside situation, we can tune into it. That's the fearless quality of crazy wisdom.

STUDENT: What do you mean when you speak of "the simple-minded attitude toward karma?"

TRUNGPA RINPOCHE: Well, there seem to be all sorts of different attitudes toward the idea of karma. One is that if you constantly try to be good, then there will be constant good results. That attitude to karma doesn't help you to transcend karmic creation. The ultimate idea is to transcend sowing the seed of any karma, either good or bad. By sowing karmic seeds you perpetually create more karma, so you are continuously wound up in the wheel of samsara.

Another attitude to karma is that it is connected with rebirth, life after death—which is pure blind faith. That approach brings a certain amount of psychological comfort: this is not the only life, but there are a lot more to come; other situations will come up so you don't have to feel fatalistic any more. That kind of attitude to karma is not dealing with the root of the karmic situation but is purely trying to play games with it or else trying to use karma as a comforter. It is based on distrust in oneself. Knowing that you are making mistakes, you think that even if you do make mistakes, you can afford to correct them, because you have a long, long time, endless time to do so.

S: I understand that an enlightened person doesn't carry a trace of what happens, but the rest of us do.

TR: In terms of an enlightened being, his attitude to karma is that either of the two polarities of good and bad is the same pattern—fundamentally a dead end. So there's no fear involved. In fact, there's more effort, more spontaneous effort of transcending sowing karmic seeds. In the ordinary case, you are not quite sure what you are doing, and there's fear of the end result anyway. So there's the constant panic of losing oneself, the ego.

STUDENT: Could you discuss what it is that reincarnates, especially in relation to the Theravadin doctrine of *anatman,* egolessness?

TRUNGPA RINPOCHE: Well, from the point of view of an-atman, nothing reincarnates. It is more of a rebirth process rather than reincarnation. The idea of reincarnation is that a solid, living quality is being passed on to the next being. It is the idea of some solid substance being passed on. But in this case, it's more of a rebirth. You see, something continues, but at the same time, nothing continues. In a sense we're like a running stream. You could say, such and such a river, such and such a stream. It has a name, but if you examine it carefully, that river you named three hundred years ago isn't there at all; it is completely different, changing, passing all the time. It is transforming from one aspect to another. That complete transformation makes it possible to take rebirth. If one thing continued all the time there would be no possibilities for taking rebirth and evolving into another situation. It is the change which is important in terms of rebirth, rather than one thing continuing.

S: Doesn't that happen moment to moment within a lifetime?

TR: Yes, exactly. You see, the ultimate idea of rebirth is not purely the idea of physical birth and death. Physical birth and death are very crude examples of it. Actually, rebirth takes place every moment, every instant. Every instant is death; every instant is birth. It's a changing process: there's nothing you can grasp onto; everything is changing. But there is some continuity, of course—the change *is* the continuity. The impermanence of the rebirth is the continuity of it. And because of that, there are possibilities of developing and possibilities of regressing. Certain new elements and inspirations could insert themselves into that process of continual change. You can enter yourself into the middle of the queue, if you are queuing, because this queue is made out of small particles, or people, rather than one thing.

STUDENT: Doesn't *alaya* consciousness provide the ground of continuity?

TRUNGPA RINPOCHE: In order to have alaya consciousness, you have to have change taking place all the time. This common ground idea, or alaya, is not ground in terms of solid ground, but perpetually changing ground. That's why it remains conscious-ness—or the unconscious state—it is a changing process.

STUDENT: This morning there was some confusion in our discussion group about the place of technique in dealing with the problems of everyday life and in meditating, and whether there should be any techniques at all.

TRUNGPA RINPOCHE: Whether there shouldn't be any techniques or there should be techniques, both remain techniques in any case. I mean, you can't step out of one thing because you have gotten a better one, you see? It's a question of what is needed. Any kind of application becomes a technique, therefore there is continual room for discipline.

S: Is the technique of "no technique" a fiction? In fact, do you always have to apply some technique?

TR: When you talk about "no technique" and "technique," when you begin to speak in terms of "yes" and "no," then that is automatically a polarity. And however much you are able to reduce your negativity into nothingness, it still remains negative as op-posed to positive. But at the same time, being without the sophis-ticated techniques of everyday life, the practice of meditation is in a sense more ruthless. In other words, it is not comforting and not easy. It is a very narrow and direct path because you can't introduce any other means of occupying yourself. Everything is left to a complete bare minimum of simplicity—which helps you to dis-cover everything.

If you present the simplicity of nothingness, the absence of technique, the so-called absence of technique, then that absence

produces a tremendously creative process. Nothing means everything in this case. That helps you to learn not to be afraid to dance
and not to be afraid of too many things crowding in on you. It
helps keep that guideline of simplicity. Whereas if you already
have complex techniques and patterns, if you already have handfuls
of things, then you don't want to pick up any more. Any new
situation that comes in becomes overcrowding. But all of these
tactics, so to speak, are fundamentally still acts of duality, of
course.

S: Is that all right? Is that the best we can do at this point, to
act within that duality?

TR: Well, there's no other thing to work on; the best we can
do is just work on what we have.

STUDENT: Some people reach a sort of meditative state without knowing it. I met somebody who was emphatically against
even hearing about meditation, and yet he was often in a meditative state. But if I told him, he would be furious.

TRUNGPA RINPOCHE: Well, that's always the thing: even
if you start with the bare minimum, complete nothingness, it
tends to bring you something anyway. You end up practicing some
kind of teaching; that automatically happens. Before you realize
where you are, you have technique; before you realize where you
are, you have religion, so to speak, you have a spiritual path. You
see, you can't completely ignore the whole thing, because if you
reject everything completely, that means there is still a rejecter.
As long as there's a rejecter, then you have a path. Even if you
completely ignore the road, there still will be a pair of feet, and
they have to tread on something. That automatically happens.
Things always work with this kind of logic. If you commit yourself
to collecting a lot of things, you end up being poor. But if you
reject—not exactly reject, but purely accept everything as bare
simplicity—then you become rich. These two polarities, two as-

pects, continue all the time. It is a natural thing. It doesn't matter whether you are studying Christianity or Buddhism. Whatever technique or tradition it may be, it's the same thing as far as ego is concerned; it's still stuff that you are collecting. It doesn't matter what this stuff consists of, still you are collecting something.

The Six Realms of Being

Generally there is the basic space to operate, in terms of creative process, whether you are confused or whether you are awake. That basic space acts as the fundamental ground for the idea of bardo. Many of you may also have heard about the development of ego, which is exactly the same pattern as the operation of bardo. The experience of bardo is also operating on the basis of that evolution of ego. But the discovery of sudden glimpse, or the experience of bardo, is a momentary thing, impermanent. So fundamentally we might say that the teaching of bardo is closer to the concept of impermanence.

Bardo is that sudden glimpse of experience which is constantly developing. We try to hold on to it, and the moment we try to hold on to it, it leaves us, because of the very fact that we are trying to hold on to it, which is trying to give birth to it. You see something happen and you would like to give birth to it. You would like to start properly in terms of giving birth, but once you begin to prepare this birth, you realize you can't give birth anymore. You lost your child already by trying officially to adopt it. That is the kind of bardo experience which happens in everyday life. It is operating in terms of space as well as in terms of ego.

Bardo is generally associated with samsaric mind, not necessarily with the awakened state of being. There is a background of bardo experience, which is like a river. A river does not belong to the other shore or to this shore; it is just a river, a no-man's-land. Such a no-man's-land, or river, has different characteristics: it may be a turbulent river or a gently flowing river. There are different categories and types of rivers—our basic situation, where we are at, our present psychological state of being—which make the bardo experience more outstanding. If there is an impressive little island, by being in the middle of a turbulent river, it becomes more outstanding. An island in the middle of a gently flowing river is also more impressive and outstanding. At the same time, the shape and condition of the island itself will be completely different, depending on the river and the background. Therefore it seems necessary to go through these patterns, which are called the six types of world: the world of the gods, the world of the jealous gods, the world of human beings, the world of animals, the world of hungry ghosts, and the world of hell. Before we get into the bardo experience, it is very important to know these particular types of worlds. They are not purely mythical stories or concepts of heaven and hell; they are also psychological pictures of heaven and hell and all the rest.

We could begin with heaven. The notion of heaven is a state of mind which is almost meditative. Heavenly psychology is based on a state of absorption in something, or spiritual materialism. It is complete absorption, which automatically, of course, means indulging ourselves in a particular pleasurable situation—not necessarily material pleasure, but more likely spiritual pleasure within the realm of ego. It's like the notion of the four *jhana* states. Traditionally, the thirty-three god realms are based on different degrees of jhana states, up to the point of a completely formless jhana state containing both experien*cer* and experien*cing*. But if there is an experiencer and also an experience, then that experience must be either pleasurable of painful—nothing else could exist beyond those limits. It could be an extremely sophisticated experience, seemingly transcending pain and pleasure, but there is still a very subtle and sophisticated experience of some *thing* going on. The thingness and the awareness of self continue. That is the realm of the formless gods—limitless space; limitless consciousness; not that, not this; *not* not that, *not* not this—the full state of absorption in a formless state. Other states as well are inclined toward that state of mind, but they become less sophisticated as the experience is on a more and more gross level. The first state, therefore, the realm of spiritual pleasure, is so extremely pleasurable that you can almost afford to relax. But somehow the relaxation doesn't happen, because there's an experiencer and an experience.

That is the realm of the gods. And in that god realm, as you can imagine, in such a state of spiritual materialism, there is a weakness. The intensity of your experience is based on collecting, possessing further experiences. That means that fundamentally your state of mind is based on give and take. You are developing immunity to temptation and fascination in order to seek pleasure and try to grasp hold of the pleasure more definitely.

As that state of mind develops in terms of the six realms of the world, we are talking about regressing from that sophisticated state of spiritual materialism in the world of heaven down to the world of hell—regressing. Such a state of pleasure in the world of heaven, that complete meditative absorption into the jhana states, automatically brings up temptations and questions. You begin to get tired of being extremely refined, and you want to come down to some raggedness. Jealousy or envy or dissatisfaction with your present state comes up automatically as an obvious next step, which then leads to the realm of the jealous gods, the asuras.

The realm of the asuras is highly energetic, almost in contrast to that state of spiritual absorption. It's as if somebody had been far away a long time from their civilization, in the middle of a desert island, and they suddenly had a chance to come down to the nearest city. Automatically, their first inspiration, of course, would be to try to be extremely busy and entertain themselves, indulging in all sorts of things. In that way the energetic quality of busyness in the realm of the asuras develops.

Even that experience of tremendous energy, driving force, trying to grasp, trying to hold on to external situations, is not enough. Somehow you need not only rushing, but you have to pick something up, taste it, swallow it, digest it. That kind of intimacy is needed. You begin to feel tired of rushing too hard, too much, and you begin to think in terms of grasping and taking. You would like to take advantage of the situation and the intimacy of possessing, the sexual aspect, the tenderness. You try to use it, chew it. That is the world of human beings. (In this case, when we talk of the world of human beings or the world of animals, it is not necessarily human life or animal life literally, as conventionally known. It's the psychological aspect.) So the human realm is built on passion and desire.

Somehow, indulging ourselves in passion and desire is again not quite enough—we need more and more. You realize that you can come down to a more gross level, a cruder level. And realizing that, you begin to yearn for much more real and obvious experience as a way of putting into effect your emotional need. But at the same time, you are tired of relationships. You are tired of relating to experience in terms of pleasure, and you begin to find all sorts of facets of your experience are involved with just that. You begin to look for something simpler, a more instinctive way of dealing with things, in which you don't have to look for the complicated patterns of that passion, that desire. Then you are reduced to the animal level. Everything is put into practice in an instinctive way rather than by applying intellectual or emotional frustrations as a way of getting or possessing something.

Then, again, such a state of mind, in which you are purely acting on the impulsive or instinctive level of the animal realm, is not gross enough. You begin to feel that there is a tremendous weakness in your state of being, in such animal mentality. You don't want to give away anything, but you would like to take more. So far, all experience—from the realm of the gods down to the animal level—has been a kind of exchange constantly, a balancing act or play. And somehow you begin to realize and come to the conclusion that exchanging or commuting between two situations, even at the blind level, is too exhausting. Then you look for a highly crude form of maintaining yourself. That is the world of the hungry ghosts. You don't want to give away anything, but you just want to take. And since you do not want to give anything away, since you would purely like to take in, the mentality of that world becomes an extremely hungry one, because unless you give, you won't get anything. And the more you get, the more you want to receive. In other words, you do not want to give or share any experience. There's so much hunger and thirst, me-ness, unwillingness to give an inch, or even one fraction of a moment, to relate with the world outside. So the hungry ghost realm is the height of poverty.

Ultimately that sense of poverty leads to aggression. You not only do not want to give anything away, but you would like to destroy that which reminds you of giving. That is the ultimate world of hell, or naraka, an instant and extremely powerful state of aggression or hatred.

All these six states, these six different aspects of the world, are the rivers in which the bardo experience is taking shape. In terms of the realm of the gods, it's a very dreamlike quality. The realm of hell is very aggressive and definite. It would be good to think about that process of the six types of world and become familiar with those different states of mind before we get into bardo experience itself. That would be very helpful. Having already developed that ground, we can pinpoint the different experiences of bardo and fit them into these different types of rivers, samsaric rivers. It would be much easier to work on at that level.

And strangely enough, these experiences of the six realms—gods, jealous gods, human beings, animals, hungry ghosts, and hell—are *space,* different versions of space. It seems intense and solid, but in actual fact it isn't at all. They are different aspects of space—that's the exciting or interesting part. In fact, it is complete open space, without any colors or any particularly solid way of relating. That is why they have been described as six types of consciousness. It is pure consciousness rather than a solid situation—it almost could be called unconsciousness rather than even consciousness. The development of ego operates completely at the unconscious level, from one unconscious level to another unconscious level. That is why these levels are referred to as *loka,* which means "realm" or "world." They are six types of *world.* Each is a complete unit of its own. In order to have a world, you have to have an atmosphere; you have to have space to formulate things. So the six realms are the fundamental space through which any bardo experience operates. Because of that, it is possible to transmute these spaces into six types of awakened state, or freedom.

STUDENT: Can you be in more than one type of world at the same time?

TRUNGPA RINPOCHE: With momentum the worlds always change. But it seems that there is one particular governing factor.

STUDENT: When you're in one of these worlds, can you remember another one?

TRUNGPA RINPOCHE: Well, you have the instinct of the other one. That's why you can move from one experience to another experience.

S: By your own will?

TR: Not necessarily by your own will, but you sense that you know something. For instance, dogs occasionally forget that they are dogs. They almost think they're human beings taking part in human society.

STUDENT: These worlds of the bardo, are they real, or are they mind-manufactured?

TRUNGPA RINPOCHE: That's a very heavy question: What is real? It is very difficult to distinguish one hundred percent real in any case.

S: Does it make any difference if these take place only in the mind or in reality?

TR: Well, mind operates realistically.

S: Does it make any difference whether they are actually acted out?

TR: Well, they are acted out, of course, but that activity is questionable—whether it is purely action for the sake of action or whether it is inspired by the mind. The point is that once you are in any of these realms, you are completely immersed in it. You can't help showing the internal impressions of it. You are completely submerged into that kind of experience. It is so living and so real. It is almost confusing whether the experience of hell, for instance, is external hell or internal hell, purely in your mind. At the time, you can't distinguish whether you are just thinking or whether you've been made to think that way. And I don't think you can avoid acting at all. If you are nervous, for instance, much as you try not to act nervous, there will still be some signs of nervousness.

S: But take passion, for instance: you can restrain your action, but you can't restrain your thinking.

TR: You can. At a certain gross level there are different ways of putting out passion. Passion is not sexual passion alone at all, there are many kinds: one particular desire can be replaced by all sorts of other things. You see, what generally happens is that if you don't want to reveal completely your full state of being, quite conveniently you tend to find ways of interpreting that in order to get satisfaction in all sorts of ways.

S: So whether you act on it or not, you're in that world?

TR: Yes, at that time you're in that world, and action happens.

S: And repressing it doesn't change the fact?

TR: No, you always find a way of doing it.

STUDENT: I sense, when you talk about transmuting the six realms of samsara into the six realms of the awakened state, that the six worlds are to be avoided or worked through into something else. Is that a good way to think about it?

TRUNGPA RINPOCHE: I don't think replacing them with something else would help. That doesn't seem to be the point. The point is that within that realm of intensity there is the absence of that intensity as well—otherwise intensity couldn't exist, couldn't happen, couldn't operate. Intensity must develop in some kind of space, some kind of environment. That basic environment is the transcendental aspect.

S: There's no sense in leaving the world of hell behind, transmuting it into something which excludes hell?

TR: No, then you go through the realms again and again. You see, you start from the world of heaven, come down to hell, get tired of it, and go back up to heaven. And you come down again and again—or the other way around. That's why it is called *samsara,* which means "whirlpool." You are continually running around and around and around. If you try to find a way out by running, by looking for an alternative, it doesn't happen at all.

S: Does it make any sense to look for a way out?

TR: It's more like a way in, rather than a way out.

STUDENT: Were you ever in the hell world yourself? Have you yourself ever experienced the hell world?

TRUNGPA RINPOCHE: Definitely, yes.

S: What do you do?

TRUNGPA RINPOCHE: I try to remain in the hell world.

STUDENT: What is the basic ground that allows one to enter completely into that state and yet be completely out of that state at the same time?

TRUNGPA RINPOCHE: The point seems to be that the hell realm, or whatever realm may be, is like the river, and the bardo experience out of that is the island. So you could almost say that the bardo experience is the entrance to the common ground.

S: Is it the key to that experience?

TR: You could say key, but that is making a more than necessary emphasis.

S: So it's like the high point or peak.

TR: Yes. Yes.

STUDENT: You spoke yesterday of the ground or canvas on which experience is painted. How does that relate to the river and the island?

TR: That's a different metaphor altogether. In this case, the canvas had never known colors yet, it's an open canvas. Even if you paint on the canvas, it remains white, fundamentally speaking. You could scrape off the paint.

S: I still don't see how it relates to the gulf between the ground and the experience.

TR: The experience is, I suppose, realizing that the turbulent quality purely happens on the surface, so to speak. So you are not rushing to try to solve the problem of turbulence, but you are diving in—in other words, fearlessness. Complete trust in confusion, so to speak. Seeing the confused quality as the truth of its own reality. Once you begin to develop the confident and fearless understanding of confusion as being true confusion, then it is no longer threatening. That is the ground. You begin to develop space.

S: Where hope and fear cease to exist?

TR: Of course.

S: And activity continues; each state continues. Nothing changes?

TR: Nothing changes.

STUDENT: If confusion persists, do you just let it persist? Don't you try to clear it out?

TRUNGPA RINPOCHE: You do not go against the force, or try to change the course of the river.

S: Suppose there are four exits, and in our confusion we don't know which is a good one?

TR: You see, the whole idea is not to try to calm *down;* it is to see the calm aspect at the *same* level rather than just completely calming down. These particular states of turbulence, the emotions or confusions, also have positive qualities. One has to learn to transmute the positive qualities as part of them. So you don't want to completely destroy their whole existence. If you destroy them, if you try to work against them, it's possible that you will be thrown back constantly, because fundamentally you're running against your own energy, your own nature.

S: There's still something undesirable I feel about confusion. You always think that you're going from some unenlightened state to an enlightened state, that if you stay with it there is this little hope or feeling that you will develop clarity sooner or later.

TR: Yes, there will be clarity. Definitely.

S: So you don't want confusion to be around, you want to get rid of it, but nevertheless you have to stay in it to see it?

TR: It doesn't exactly work that way. You see, you begin to realize that the clarity is always there. In fact, when you are in a state of complete clarity you realize that you never needed to have made such a fuss. Rather than realizing how good you are now, you begin to see how foolish you've been.

STUDENT: Does anything actually exist outside of the mind itself? Does anything actually exist?

TRUNGPA RINPOCHE: I would say yes and no. Outside the mind is, I suppose you could say, that which is not duality—open space. That doesn't mean that the whole world is going to be empty. Trees will be there, rivers will be there, mountains will be there. But that doesn't mean they are some *thing*. Still, tree remains tree and rocks remain rocks.

STUDENT: I wonder, in the human world is there any advantage over, say, hell for crossing over, or is it equal in all respects?

TRUNGPA RINPOCHE: I think it's the same. The karmic potential of the human realm seems to be greater because there is more communication in the human state. The human state is the highest state of passion, and the ultimate meaning of passion is communication, making a link, relationship. So there is a kind of open space, the possibility of communication. But that doesn't mean that the human realm is an exit from the six realms of the world. The experience of passion is very momentary: you might have a human state of mind one moment and the next moment you have another realm coming through.

S: But seeing as how we have human bodies, isn't the human world the one in which we have the best chance to accept ourselves for what we are?

TR: Yes, but we are talking about the realms as six experiences within the human body. We are not talking about the different realms as other types of worlds.

S: I understand that, but since we have human bodies and minds, isn't passion the basic framework of our lives rather than hatred? Don't we have the best chance of crossing over within that framework?

TR: I think so. That's precisely why we can discuss these six types of world in a human body. So as far as experience goes it is equal, but the physical situation of the human realm seems to be unequal or special. As I've said already, we are discussing these realms now, in our human bodies. However, all of them are human states of mind, one no more so than any other.

STUDENT: I'm not clear about the difference between humans and asuras.

TRUNGPA RINPOCHE: The asura realm is a kind of intermediate state between the intense passion of the human realm and intense bliss, which is the world of heaven. Somehow there's a discontentment with the blissful state; one is looking for a more crude experience. Then you begin to transform your experience into that of an asura, which is energy, speed, rushing, and a very sudden glimpse of comparison which is called jealousy or envy. But I don't think jealousy and envy are concrete enough words to express this state of neuroticism. It's a combination of jealousy with the efficient speed of looking for an alternative to the blissful state of the world of the gods.

Then in the human realm you begin to find some way of communicating, some way of making that experience more concrete. You begin to find passion instead of pure jealousy and comparison alone. You begin to find that you can get into it: you can dive into it and indulge, in fact. In the realm of the asura there's no time for indulgence because the whole thing is extremely fast and rushed. It's almost a reaction against the blissful state.

I would say that with all the realms you are not quite certain what you are actually getting and what you are trying to get hold of. So you try to find the nearest situation and reinforce that or change that. There's constant confusion.

STUDENT: If you drop all your usual patterns of relating, what holds on to giving logical answers?

TRUNGPA RINPOCHE: You can't do that in any case. Impossible.

S: You could go to the desert.

TR: Then there would still be the desert. If you try to give up patterns, that in itself forms another pattern.

S: But what if you're not trying?

TR: If you are not trying to drop anything, either pattern or without pattern, and you are accepting all of them as just black and white, you have complete control; you are the master of the whole situation. Before, you were dealing purely at the ground level, but in this case you are dealing from an aerial view, so you have more scope.

STUDENT: Does anxiety have anything to do with the asura realm, that rushing quality?

TRUNGPA RINPOCHE: I think so, yes.

S: It also seems that the rushing quality is very closely connected to the hungry ghost state.

TR: That's a good observation. The world of hell is ultimate crudeness, and the world of the gods is ultimate gentility. The hungry ghost and asura realms are the intermediaries between these two realms and the animal and human realms.

STUDENT: Sometimes the fear of losing oneself, of losing ego, is very overwhelming. It's very real. Is there any way to prepare the ground for dropping that, or do you just have to drop it one step at a time?

TRUNGPA RINPOCHE: I think the only alternative left is just to drop. If you are as close as that, if you're extremely close to the cliff—

S: You mean to the ground.

TR: To the cliff. [Laughter]

S: It almost seems as if someone has to push you over; you won't go yourself.

TR: Yes. [Laughter]

STUDENT: I was wondering, is there really any reality except the reality about which everyone agrees?

TRUNGPA RINPOCHE: You might find that everybody agrees on it, but sometimes people don't agree. To some people, one particular aspect is more real than the others. Somehow, trying to prove what is real and what is not real isn't particularly beneficial.

S: Is it possible that a real world exists, but that even if we all agree as human beings, a catfish or a gopher might see it differently?

TR: Well, it seems that reality, from a rational point of view, is something that you can relate to—when you're hungry you eat food, when you're cold you put on more clothes, and when you're frightened you look for a protector. Those are the kinds of real things we do. Real things happen, experiences such as that happen.

STUDENT: Rinpoche, are you going to discuss ego at all during this seminar?

TRUNGPA RINPOCHE: I suppose that subject will pop up. [Laughter]

STUDENT: Rinpoche, you said that you can't get out of a situation, you have to get completely into it.

TRUNGPA RINPOCHE: You have to be completely fearless. And there should be communication with the ground you're standing on. If you are in complete touch with that nowness of the ground, then all the other situations are automatically definite and obvious.

STUDENT: Which world are you in now?

TRUNGPA RINPOCHE: Woof, woof.

S: But you said these are not states of the awakened mind—they are only confusion!

TR: Yes, confusion. Sure. [Laughter]

STUDENT: Do the six bardos go around in a circle like the six realms?

TRUNGPA RINPOCHE: Somehow it isn't as methodical as that.

S: Is it one continuum? How does one move from one to the next?

TR: It's the same as the different types of emotions, which change from one to another, like temperament. Each bardo is individual, an independent thing, like an island; but each island has some connection with the other islands. The presence of the other islands allows us to see the perspective of any one island. So they are related as well as not related.

S: Is it the water that connects them?

TR: I think so, yes.

STUDENT: Could you say that each experience has its root in one or another of the bardos?

TRUNGPA RINPOCHE: Yes, definitely.

S: Is it a good thing, as one is experiencing, to try to hold that view?

TR: Well, one doesn't have to acknowledge them on the spot necessarily, not intellectually, but from an experiential point of view, this happens and one can acknowledge it, so to speak. It is not necessarily healthy to speculate or to try to put it into categories intellectually. You see, meditation is a way of providing a clear perception of these experiences, so that they don't become confusing or inspire paranoia. Meditation is a way of gaining new eyesight to look at each situation, to feel situations. And often the hidden aspect of these states or worlds is brought out by meditation. If there's a tendency to try to hide from yourself the suppressed elements of these worlds, then meditation brings them out. If your experience is constantly destructive, then meditation brings out the friendliness in these situations and you begin to see that you don't have to regard them as external attacks or negative destructive things anymore. Meditation is a way of seeing the perfect value of them, in a sense, the perfect relationship of them. The whole thing is that you have to work from within. Unless you are willing to go back to the abstract quality, the root, judging the facade doesn't help at all. So meditation brings you back to the root, dealing with the root of it.

STUDENT: Does meditation mean nothing but simply sitting still quietly for forty-five minutes?

TRUNGPA RINPOCHE: In this case, it is not necessarily only that. It's the active aspect of meditation as well as the formal sitting practice. All aspects.

STUDENT: Everybody seems to have different interpretations or opinions as to what you feel about drug addiction or alcoholism in relation to the Buddhist path. Can you relate drug use or heavy drinking to bardo experience?

TRUNGPA RINPOCHE: Well, it seems to be connected with the idea of reality, what is real and what is not real. Everybody tries to find what is real, using all sorts of methods, all sorts of ways. A person may discover it by using alcohol or by using drugs, but then you want to make sure that discovery of reality is really definite, one hundred percent definite. So you go on and on and on. Then somehow, a sort of greediness takes over from your discovery at the beginning, and the whole thing becomes destructive and distorting.

This happens constantly with any kind of experience of life. At the beginning, there's a relationship; but if you try to take advantage of that relationship in a heavy-handed way, you lose the relationship absolutely, completely. That relationship becomes a destructive one rather than a good one. It's a question of whether the experience could be kept an actual experience without trying to magnify it. At a certain stage, you begin to forget that the usage is not pure experience alone; it begins to become a built-up situation that you require. And then there will be conflict. In terms of LSD, for instance, a person has an experience for the first time, and in order to confirm that experience he has to take LSD again—a second, third, fourth, hundredth time—and somehow it ceases to be an experience anymore. It isn't exactly a question of middle way or happy medium, but somehow trusting oneself is necessary at that point. One doesn't have to be extremely skeptical of oneself. You have one experience, and that experience *is* experience—you don't necessarily have to try to make it into a clear and complete experience. One experience should be total experience.

STUDENT: In meditation, how does one get these glimpses of clarity?

TRUNGPA RINPOCHE: In a sense you can create a glimpse by being open to the situation—*open* meaning without fear of anything, complete experience. A glimpse just takes place; it takes shape of its own and sparks us. But in many cases, when a person tries to re-create that glimpse he or she had already, that sudden flash, it doesn't happen at all. The more you try, the less experience you get—you don't experience open space at all. And the minute you are just about to give up, to give in and not care—you get a sudden flash. It's as if a person is trying very hard to meditate for a set time—it could be in a group or it could be alone—and it doesn't go very well at all. But the minute you decide to stop, or if it's group practice, the minute the bell is rung, *then* the meditation actually happens, spontaneously and beautifully. But when you want to recapture that, to re-create that situation, it doesn't happen anymore. So it's a question of trying to recapture experience: if you try to recapture an experience, it doesn't happen—unless you have an absence of fear and the complete confidence that these experiences don't have to be re-created, but they are there already.

S: Supposing what you think you want more than anything is openness, but you don't know how to open?

TR: There's no question of how to do it—just do it! It cannot be explained in words; one has to do it in an instinctive way. And if one really allowed oneself to do it, one could do it.

STUDENT: People seem to want to be happy, but it doesn't work out.

TRUNGPA RINPOCHE: Happiness is something one cannot recapture. Happiness happens, but when we try to recapture it, it's gone. So from that point of view there's no permanent happiness.

STUDENT: Are the six worlds always happening, and do you attain them in meditation?

TRUNGPA RINPOCHE: Yes, the six realms seem to happen constantly; we are changing from one extreme to another and going through the six realms constantly. And that experience takes place in meditation practice also. Therefore, the whole idea of trying to create a fixed, ideal state of meditation is not the point. You can't have a fixed, ideal state of meditation because the situation of six realms will be continuously changing.

S: I mean, we've spent all our lives in these six realms, but through meditation we can learn to see which realm we're in, and how to deal with them?

TR: That isn't the purpose of meditation, but somehow it happens that way. Actual meditation practice is a constant act of freedom in the sense of being without expectation, without a particular goal, aim, and object. But as you practice meditation, as you go along with the technique, you begin to discover your present state of being. That is, we could almost say, a by-product of meditation. So it does happen that way, but is no good looking for it and trying to fit it into different degrees or patterns. That doesn't work.

STUDENT: When you just perceive something—smell, hear, see—and you don't have any thought about anything for a very brief time, what world is that?

TRUNGPA RINPOCHE: Any world. Sure, any world.

STUDENT: Are people born with a quality of one of the worlds as predominant?

TRUNGPA RINPOCHE: It seems there is one particular dominant characteristic—which is not particularly good and not particularly bad, but a natural character.

STUDENT: Would sense perceptions be the same in all six realms?

TRUNGPA RINPOCHE: The sense perceptions will be different. We are talking about the human situation, and in human life the six experiences of the world will be the same, of course, but your impressions of them will be different. Each thing we see, we see purely in terms of our own likes and dislikes, which happen all the time, and our associations. Certain trees, plants, and things may be irritating for some people; whereas for some other people they may be a good experience.

DISCUSSION NEXT MORNING

STUDENT: Would you discuss briefly the similarities and differences between Zen practice and *mahamudra* practice?

TRUNGPA RINPOCHE: Well, that has something to do with the evolutionary aspect of the teachings. The Zen tradition is the actual application of *shunyata,* or emptiness, practice, the heart of the mahayana teaching. Historically, the Zen method is based on dialectical principles—you engage in continual dialogues with yourself, asking questions constantly. By doing that, in the end you begin to discover that questions don't apply anymore in relationship to the answer. That is a way of using up dualistic mind, based on the logic of Nagarjuna. The interesting point is that the practice of traditional Indian logic used by Hindu and Buddhist scholars is turned into experiential logic rather than just ordinary debate or intellectual argument. Logic becomes experiential. In other words, the subject and object of logical discussion are turned into mind and its projections—and that automatically, of course, becomes meditation. Once you begin to follow the whole endless process, everything begins to become nothing—but nothing becomes everything. It's the same idea as the four statements of *Prajnaparamita:* form is emptiness, emptiness is form, form is no other than emptiness, emptiness is no other than form.[2] It's kind of using up the abundance of hungry energy. Or, it could be said, self-deception is exposed by realizing that you don't get any answers if you purely ask questions, but you do get answers if you don't ask questions. But that in itself becomes a question, so in the end the whole thing is dropped completely: you don't care anymore.

S: In Zen they talk about abrupt realization.

TR: That abruptness is referred to in the Zen tradition as the sword of Manjushri, which cuts through everything. It is symbolized in Zen practice by the stick (*kyosaku*) carried in the hall during meditation (*zazen*) practice. If a person wants to have sudden penetrations, or if a person is off his pattern, he's reminded by being hit on the back—the sword of Manjushri.

In the case of mahamudra, the application or the technique is not quite like the Zen approach of logic, questioning, or koans. It is, in a sense, a highly extroverted practice—you don't need inward scriptures, but you work with the external aspect of scriptures, which is the phenomenal world. Mahamudra has a cutting quality as well, but that cutting or penetrating quality is purely based on your experiential relationship with the phenomenal world. If your relationship to the phenomenal world is distorted or if you are going too far, then the sword of Manjushri—the equivalent of the sword of Manjushri, which is the phenomenal world—shakes you and demands your attention. In other words, the situation begins to become hostile or destructive for you if you are not in tune with it, if you are dazed or if you're confused. If you are not willing to put your patience and discipline into practice, then such situations come up. In this case, mahamudra is very much purely dealing with the phenomenal world aspect of symbolism. So mahamudra practice contains a great deal of study of events or situations, seeing them as patterns rather than using logical, koan types of questions—which brings us to the same point.

These two practices are not polarities. You have to go through Zen practice *before* you get to mahamudra practice, because if you don't realize that asking questions is the way to learn something, that the questioning process is a learning process, then the whole idea of study becomes distorted. So one must learn to see that trying to struggle for some achievement or goal is useless in any way. You have to start by learning that such a dualistic notion is useless; you have to start from the Zen or mahayana tradition. And after that, you realize that asking questions is not the only way, but being a fool is the only way. If you see the foolishness of asking questions, then you begin to learn something. Foolishness begins to become wisdom.

At that point, you transform yourself into another dimension, a completely other dimension. You thought you had achieved a sudden glimpse of nonduality, but that nonduality also contains relationship. You still need to relate yourself to that sudden glimpse of beyond question. That's when you begin to become mahamudra experience. In other words, the Zen tradition seems to be based on the shunyata principle, which is a kind of emptiness and openness, absence of duality. The mahamudra experience is a way of wiping out the consciousness of the absence: you begin to develop clear perceptions beyond being conscious of the absence. If you feel that absence, voidness, or emptiness is so, then you are dwelling on something, on some kind of state of being. Mahamudra experience transcends that consciousness of being in the void. In that way every situation of life becomes play, dance. It is an extroverted situation.

I suppose you could say that Zen and mahamudra are complementary to one other. Without the one, the other one couldn't exist. As experience, first of all you clear out the confusion of duality. And then, having cleared that out, you appreciate the absence of the blindfold in terms of appreciating colors and energies and light and everything. You don't get fascinated by it at all, but you begin to see that it is some kind of pattern. The whole process of mahamudra, in other words, is seeing the situation of life as a pattern. That's why the word *mudra* is used, which means "symbolism." It doesn't mean ordinary symbolism; it isn't a question of signifying something, but it is the actual fact of things as they are. The pattern of life *is* a pattern. It is a definite pattern, a definite path, and you learn how to walk on it. I think this particular topic needs some kind of actual experience or practice, you can't really explain it in terms of words.

S: If one is preliminary to the other, can you explain the emphasis in Zen meditation practice on posture and the lack of emphasis in mahamudra?

TR: Well, I think that the discipline which goes along with Zen practice is connected with the experience of being determined—being determined and willing to use up any dualistic notion. Therefore it is described in terms of struggle, or within the framework of discipline. Otherwise, if there were no framework around this notion of shunyata, or voidness, you wouldn't have anything at all; you wouldn't even have practice, because everything is nothing, absolute nothing. In order to bring out the notion of shunyata and voidness, you have to create a horizon, or some framework, which is discipline. That is necessary. That is what we all do in the practice of meditation: at the beginner's level, we have disciplines or techniques, something to do. In the case of mahamudra, instead of putting discipline into situations, the situations bring out discipline *for* you. If you are lax, the situation reminds you, jerks you, and you'll be pushed; if you are going too slow, if you are too careful, the situation will push you overboard.

S: Are we beginners, or are we advanced enough to disregard the techniques?

TR: It's much safer to say that we're all beginners, that we do need some act of sitting down and practicing. But, of course, the level of discipline in meditation practice is not only a conflict between mahamudra practice and the Zen tradition at all. It's also connected with different styles of teaching, such as the Theravadin tradition of Southeast Asia, Tibetan Buddhism, or the Chinese tradition. Each culture effects a different tradition and style of practice. Obviously, in the Zen tradition a lot of the formality is highly connected simply with Japanese culture rather than fundamental Buddhism. And the same thing could be said about Tibetan Buddhism as well—a lot of things came into it from the Tibetan cultural background, not from the actual teaching. Those cultural styles make a difference in some ways.

STUDENT: Do you have to have some preparation for working in a mahamudra way? Does one have to be particularly conscious of the transition point from Zen to mahamudra?

TRUNGPA RINPOCHE: Well, it happens as you grow. It would be too presumptuous for teachers to say that now you're ready for mahamudra—in fact, it would be dangerous to say it. But if a student finds himself in the situation of mahamudra under the pretense of practicing Zen, he'll find himself in a mahamudra situation automatically. Then of course he'll accept that as the next process. But there wouldn't be a big deal about relaxing from one technique to another technique at all; it would become a natural process for the student.

STUDENT: When you say "situations," do you mean the situations that arise in daily life?

TRUNGPA RINPOCHE: I mean individual meditation experience as well as daily life and your relationship to it. Many people have heard about the principle of *abhisheka* and the initiations that are involved with mahamudra teachings or tantric teachings in general. But initiations aren't degrees at all; initiations are the acceptance of you as a suitable candidate for the practice. There's really only one initiation, and that's the acceptance of your whole being, your whole attitude, as suitable to practice, that you are the right type of person. Beyond that, there's no change of techniques and practices. It's not like a staircase at all; everything's a very evolutionary process. When you are on the first level, as you go along, you begin to develop possibilities and qualities of the next step. And then, as you begin to lose the idea that the first step is the only way, you begin to discover something else. You begin to grow like a tree. It is a very general process, and therefore it is very dangerous to pin down that you belong to a different type of experience, a different level.

STUDENT: Both you and Shunryu Suzuki Roshi speak of the path as being dangerous. I always wondered what the danger is that I should be avoiding.

TRUNGPA RINPOCHE: They are numerous. Danger is really a relative term, in terms of the relationship of ego and the relation-

ship of being awake. The relationship of ego is regarded as a
danger—the extreme or the confusion. But danger also comes
from different levels of practice. Danger always comes with speed,
going fast—very rarely from going too slowly. And generally we
go very fast. There's the possibility that if you go too fast you will
get hurt. There's the danger of going too slow as well, being too
concerned and becoming ultraconservative. That's not the case in
the West, particularly; it is more the case in the East. Easterners
go too slowly; they don't go fast enough. In a lot of cases, according
to the stories of great teachers and their relationship to students on
the path, the teachers actually have to push their students overboard, kick them out. "If you hesitate to jump, then I'll push
you—let's go!" That sort of hesitation is a problem of the Eastern
mentality. And in the West, the problem seems to be one of going
too fast, being unbalanced, bringing up pain and confusion in
terms of ego.

S: If the danger is of going too fast, don't you intensify that
danger for us by outlining the mahamudra practice as a superior
one, because most of us tend to want to skip to a more advanced
practice without experiencing fully the preliminary level?

TR: Precisely. That's the whole point. I do feel that I'm respon-
sible for this. And precisely for that reason, in the practice of
meditation I try to present everything as extremely dull and un-
colorful. In fact, most people who practice meditation are going
through the process of discovering that meditation practice is not
a kick anymore; the whole practice is extremely dull and uninter-
esting. And I think we have to go through that process as well.
But I don't think there is anything wrong in mentioning mahamudra. It doesn't have to be introduced as a surprise. There is this
possibility if you go through it, but is needs patience and hard
work—that automatically brings up a person's inspiration, which
is a very great thing.

STUDENT: Concerning the idea of different levels or hierarchies of practice, sometimes it seems like we're in all these levels at the same time.

TRUNGPA RINPOCHE: Well, we are passing through the six realms of the world all the time. I mean, you pass through those different states of the world every moment or every other moment, on and off. But the gradual development we've been talking about is more definite than that. You may have an experience or mahamudra as well as an experience of Zen happening all the time, but as your Zen practice develops, your experience of mahamudra becomes more frequent, and you develop in that way. And beyond mahamudra, your experience of *maha ati* also begins to develop more. The flash of that experience becomes more and more frequent, stronger and more real.

STUDENT: All this seems endless.

TRUNGPA RINPOCHE: I think it is an extremely good thing to realize that the learning process is endless.

S: I thought you said the whole idea is to stop collecting things, but you're collecting more things.

TR: It isn't really collecting, but you're involving yourself in it. You see, the whole point is that mahamudra is not introducing a new thing or new theme, but if you reach an absolute understanding of the shunyata principle, then that *becomes* mahamudra. And when you understand completely the level of mahamudra, then that becomes something else. So it's a growing process. It's not collecting anything at all, but it's the way you grow. And each step is a way of unmasking yourself as well. You begin by realizing the shunyata principle and experience, and then you begin to see it as a foolish game. You begin to see the foolishness of it once you get to mahamudra experience. And once you transcend mahamudra experience, then you again begin to see that you unnecessarily fooled yourself. It's a continual unpeeling process, a continual unmasking process. So it's more of a continual renunciation than collecting anything—until there's nothing further that you have to go through, no journey you have to make. And then you begin to see that the whole journey you made was a foolish thing that you never made at all.

STUDENT: You speak of the original understanding of voidness as something that you transcend more and more, rather than giving up one thing to proceed to another, as though you were climbing a ladder?

TRUNGPA RINPOCHE: Each moment has possibilities or potentials of everything. Your experience of emptiness and form is empty at the beginning level as well, all the time, but somehow your experience becomes more and more deep as you go along. So in a sense it could be called a progressive process, but is not absolutely so—because all the possibilities or potentials of the various steps are present in one moment of personal experience.

S: Is it as if the circle of one's understanding keeps enlarging and includes more and more, rather than giving up one thing to proceed to the other?

TR: Yes. It's a process of going deeper and deeper. You are unpeeling, unmasking the crude facade to start with. Then you unmask the semi-crude facade; then you unmask a kind of genteel facade; and you go on and on and on. The facades become more and more delicate and more profound, but at the same time they are all facades—you unpeel them, and by doing so you include all experiences. That is why at the end of journey, the experience of maha ati is referred to as the imperial *yana* (vehicle or path) which sees everything, includes everything. It is described as being like climbing up the highest mountain of the world and seeing all the other mountains underneath you: you have complete command of the whole view, which includes everything in its absolute perfection.

STUDENT: I don't understand what is meant when it's said that forms are empty. I don't understand what emptiness means.

TRUNGPA RINPOCHE: When we talk of emptiness, it means the absence of solidity, the absence of fixed notions which cannot be changed, which have no relationship with us at all but which remain as they are, separate. And form, in this case, is more the solidity of experience. In other words, it is a certain kind of determination not to give away, not to open. You would like to keep everything intact purely for the purpose of security, of knowing where you are. You are afraid to change. That sort of solidness is form. So "Form is empty" is the absence of that security; you see everything as penetrating and open. But that doesn't mean that everything has to be completely formless, or nothing. When we talk of nothingness, emptiness, or voidness, we are not talking in terms of negatives but in terms of nothingness being everything. It's another way of saying "everything"—but it is much safer to say "nothing" at that particular level than "everything."

STUDENT: What is the relation of kriya yoga, the Hindu practice, to mahamudra?

TRUNGPA RINPOCHE: It's the same thing. Kriya yoga, or kriya yana, is the first tantric yana, or stage. In kriya yoga, the basic notion of absolute is presented in terms of purity. Because your discovery of the symbolism of mahamudra experience is so sharp and colorful and precise, you begin to feel that if experience is so good and accurate, it has to be pure. And that fundamental notion of purity in kriya yoga is the first discovery that such an experience as mahamudra is there. In other words, it is excitement at the discovery of mahamudra, the experience of a tremendously valuable discovery. An extra attitude of sacredness begins to develop because of your mahamudra experience. That is kriya yoga, the first step. It is the first discovery of mahamudra.

S: But kriya yoga is also a Hindu school.

TR: Buddhist and Hindu kriya yoga probably use different kinds of symbolism, iconography; but the fundamental idea of kriya yoga in the two traditions is very close, definitely close.

S: Is kriya yoga a definite technique?

TR: It is. In fact, you could almost say it is ninety-nine percent technique.

STUDENT: Couldn't one use the expression "truthfulness" instead of "purity," since in the experience you are talking about, all pretensions are suddenly missing?

TRUNGPA RINPOCHE: Yes, that's true.

S: So why should one get rid of it?

TR: Well, you see, there are different types of discoveries. The discovery that happens in kriya yoga is in some ways a sharp and absolute discovery, but it is still based on spiritual materialism, meaning spirituality having a reference to ego. You see, any kind of practice which encourages constant health, constant survival, is based on ego. And actually, any discovery of such a practice wouldn't be absolute truthfulness or an absolute discovery, because it would have a tinge of your version of the discovery rather than what *is,* because you're seeing through the filter of ego. Such discoveries, connected with spiritual development or bliss, are regarded as something that you should transcend.

I suppose we are talking about the definition of "absolute" and of "truth." You see, absoluteness or truth in the ultimate sense is not regarded as a learning process anymore. You just see true as true. It is *being* true, rather than possessing truth. That is the absence of ego; whereas in the case of ego, you still feel you possess truth. That doesn't mean that you have to start absolutely perfectly. Of course you start with ego and with confusions and negatives—that's fine. Ego is the sort of ambitious quality which comes up throughout all parts of the pattern, a kind of continual, constant philosophy of survival. Ego is involved in the will power of survival, the will power of not dying, not being hurt. When that kind of philosophy begins to be involved with the path, it becomes negative—or confusing rather, in this case. But that doesn't mean that you wouldn't have any of these notions at all. At the beginning of the path, you have all sorts of collections, but that doesn't matter. In fact, it is very enriching to have them, to work with them. So the point is, one begins with faults, one begins with mistakes. That is the only way to begin.

S: When I think of some possible terror or pain, I think, "That's my ego." At the same time, if I get very relaxed, then I think maybe I am heading for danger, that I am not taking any precautions.

TR: One doesn't have to rely purely on blind faith or guesswork alone. Whether it is going to be dangerous or not depends on how much of a relationship to the present situation you are able to make, how much you are able to communicate with the present situation. If your relationship with the present situation is vague or confused, then something's not quite solid; whereas if your relationship is quite clear and open, then that's fine. That seems to be the criterion and judgment—standing on the ground, the earthy quality, grounding quality. I often refer to it as the peasant quality—simple, but at the same time, solid.

The Bardo of Meditation

In order to understand bardo experiences, you also have to understand basic psychology. Yesterday we discussed the six realms of the world—the world of hatred, the world of possessiveness, the world of ignorance, the world of passion, the world of speed or jealousy, and the world of pride. These different patterns or worlds are the sources of particular emotional experiences—hatred, meanness, passion, or whatever. They are the basic background; they are the space. And within that, there will be the different experiences of bardo, which work with the thought process and with different types of emotions than the emotions that you were born with, so to speak, that you are made out of. The experience of the six realms is like having a body: you have involved yourself in the world of hell or the world of the hungry ghosts. But if you have a wound on your body, that is the experience of the different types of bardo, a flash of bardo experience.

To understand bardo, we have to understand the pattern of ego as well. Our basic involvement with situations, or the six realms, and the specific situation that we are facing, or bardo, have to have some relationship. The specific development of bardo experience—in the form of a dream, in the form of birth or death, whatever it may be—also has to come from the pattern of ego. I have discussed ego previously, but perhaps it is worth going over again, in order to bring out the bardo concept properly.

The Development of Ego

When we talk of ego, it is as if we are talking about a man with a body and limbs. It has a basic makeup and it has its tentacles, so to speak, as well. Its basic makeup consists of paranoia and confusion. But at the same time, its basic makeup started from some kind of wisdom as well, because there is the possibility that we don't exist as individual entities or as solid persons who can continue all the time. There is the possibility that as individuals we consist of particles or of lots of things—but those particles don't exist as individuals either.

When that possibility first flashes onto itself, there's sudden panic. If this is the case, we'll have to put up some kind of defense mechanism to shield out any possible discovery of the nonexistence of ourselves. We begin to play the game of deaf and dumb. We would like to be individuals who are continuously existing, continuously surviving, continuously being one person, not even making the journey through time and space. Time and space may be extra attributes, but the actual basic phenomenon of our consciousness of being has to be a solid thing—that's how ego tends to see it. So the whole thing is based on a kind of dream, wishful thinking. It is based on what we would like to be rather than what we are.

That leads to paranoia as to the possible discovery of wisdom. And that paranoia begins to develop: from that paranoia you begin to experiment with extending yourself. You can't just remain constantly deaf and dumb, you also have to learn to establish your ground as deaf and dumb. That is, you extend yourself into different areas, different realms, trying to feel the situation around you—trying to project yourself and then trying to experience that. It's kind of an experimental level of feeling. So first you have the basic ignorance of refusing to see what you are, and then you have the possibility of relating yourself through feeling.

The next stage is impulse: feeling begins to develop beyond simply trying to feel good or bad or neutral; feeling has to become more sophisticated and efficient. Therefore, impulse begins to develop along with feeling, as that efficiency, or automatic mechanism.

Next, impulse also begins to develop—into perception. You try to perceive the result of your impulsive actions. A kind of self-conscious watcher develops, as the overseer of the whole game of ego.

The last development of ego is consciousness, which is the intellectual aspect of the ego: trying to put things into categories and make intellectual sense of them. We try to interpret things and their basic meanings, and we begin to see in terms of consciousness, in the sense of being conscious in relating with situations. That is the last stage in the development of ego.

From that point of view of consciousness, the idea of bardo comes through. Bardo experience presents a case of surviving, occupation—in terms of subconscious thought patterns, conscious thought patterns, dreams, birth, death, being with oneself, or the meditative state. These are the types of thought that we begin to put out.

The next situation in the development of ego is that as we develop our personal state of being, up to the point of consciousness, that consciousness not only acts in terms of our own subconscious thoughts, dreams, and such things, but also puts out particular shapes or patterns or creeds, so to speak. It puts out a sense of belonging to a particular race or a particular family. Consciousness would like to associate itself with particular types of world. That is where the six realms we discussed yesterday begin to develop. Consciousness could either begin the six types of world from the world of hell, or it could start from the world of heavenly beings. It could begin either way. That process is like buying land;

we associate ourselves with a particular land, with one of the six lokas, six worlds.

Having bought that land—it doesn't matter whether the land is a hot land, the burning hotness of hell; the tropical land of human passion; the heavenly land with the clear and crystal air of pleasurable meditative states; or whatever land we associate our-selves with as natives—we still have to survive. You see, the point is, how are we going to survive? How we going to survive as hell beings? How are we going to survive as heavenly beings? We need some mechanism of survival, some method. And that survival mechanism, or survival policy, so to speak, is that of the six types of bardo.

The Bardo of Clear Light

We could begin with the world of heaven, for instance, the realm of the gods. The world of the gods is a state of complete bliss, a spiritual state of complete balance from a temporary point of view, a meditative state. In order to survive in that meditative state of the world of heaven, there is the experience of the clear light. In Tibetan it is called *samten* bardo. *Samten* means meditative state, in other words, complete absorption in the clear light, or the perception of luminosity. So in the world of the gods, in order to survive as they are, they have to have the highlight of meditation, like the island which remains in the middle of the river. You need this particular type of highlight of what you are, which is the clear light experience.

In terms of the ordinary experience of bardo, it has been said that the clear light experience can only happen in the moment of death, when you begin to separate from physical being. At the moment of separation between consciousness and the physical body, you begin to develop the idea of clear light as spontaneous experience. In that perception of clear light, if you are a meditator who meditated before, you begin to see the clear light and you begin to recognize it, as in the analogy of son meeting mother. But in the case of the world of heavenly beings, the clear light is a constant process.

This also brings another kind of bardo: the bardo of birth and death. When we begin to leave one kind of experience, whatever it may be, we look for the next experience to get into. And between birth and death, there is a sudden recognition that birth and death would never need to happen at all; they are unnecessary. We begin to realize that the experience of birth and the experience of death are unnecessary concepts. They just happen; they are purely perceptions, purely the result of clinging to something. We experience birth in terms of creative things and death in terms of destructive things, but those two things never need to have happened.

A sudden experience of eternity develops, which is the bardo of clear light. And this experience of eternity, beyond birth and beyond death, is the source of survival of heavenly beings in the meditative state. That's why they attain a pleasurable state in meditation, because each time their meditation experience begins to wane, the only possible kick they could get, the only possible way they have of latching onto their previous meditation experience, is to reflect back on that eternity. And that eternity brings a sudden glimpse of joy, the pleasurable state of jhana experience.

That's the bardo of clear light. In other words, the experience of the eternity of clear light is the ultimate meditative state of ego—and the ultimate state of nothingness. You see, the point is that when we see eternity from the point of view of the world of the gods, it is an exciting thing to discover. There is tremendous hope that it is going to be the promised state of being, that you're going to be all the time like that—there is tremendous hope. On the other hand, from the awakened point of view you see that eternity means constant nothingness as well, constant space. Eternity needn't really have existed, nor do birth and death need to exist. In the absolute clear light, in the case of the awake state, when you begin to feel solidness, you automatically begin to feel the loose quality of the space as well.

The experience of clear light is extremely subtle. It is like experiencing hot and cold at the same time, extreme hot temperature and extreme cold temperature simultaneously. You could appreciate either side. If you'd like, you could believe in hot, although you experience both hot and cold simultaneously; or if you want to believe in the cold, you could believe in that as well, because it is also intense. The whole thing is based on this: believing is, in fact, solidifying the experience of the bardo of clear light. So clear light could present itself as egohood, or clear light could present itself as the awakened state of mind.

This is described in *The Tibetan Book of the Dead* as the after-death experience of seeing peaceful and wrathful divinities. The pattern is as follows: you always get peaceful divinities as your first experience, and then wrathful divinities are the next experience. This, again, is the same analogy as the idea of experiencing hot and cold simultaneously. If you have experienced the more pleasant aspect, the pleasurable aspect of the eternity of clear light as peaceful divinities, then automatically, if you are too relaxed in that pleasurable situation, the next situation brings dissatisfaction and wakes you up. Eternity begins to develop an impermanent quality, or the voidness quality of open space. That is the first experience of bardo, which is connected with the world of heavenly beings.

The clear light bardo could also relate with our own experience of meditation as well. The perception of meditation becomes promising: that promise could become the equivalent of eternity as experienced in the world of the gods, or else that promise could mean that there's no goal anymore, that you are experiencing that the promise is already the goal as well as the path. That is a kind of shunyata experience of the nonexistence of the journey—but at the same time you are still treading on the path. It is an experience of freedom.

STUDENT: Does one have any choice at all? If you have some kind of eternity experience and then you feel satisfaction, is there anything you can do about that except recognize that you felt that satisfaction?

TRUNGPA RINPOCHE: Well, you see, the funny thing is that once you begin to recognize it, once you begin to be satisfied with it, that automatically invites dissatisfaction. Because you are trying to solidify it, that means that you feel some kind of threat, automatically. So you can't really secure that experience, but you can just experience it and let things develop in a natural process. As soon as you experience eternity as safe and solid, you are going to experience the other aspect as well.

S: That's when ego is involved?

TR: When ego is involved, yes. Ego's ultimate dream is eternity, particularly when eternity presents itself as meditation experience.

S: So where there's hope, there's fear?

TR: That, I would say, is the heart of the heavenly world, the world of the gods.

STUDENT: You said when *you* experience eternity—it seems to remain a subjective experience. How are you sure that this *is* eternity, not some game you are playing with yourself? Is there a verification, perhaps by you?

TRUNGPA RINPOCHE: There doesn't seem to be any way at all to prove it and to definitely make sure. The mirage is more vivid than the desert.

S: There seems to be no feedback—in *The Tibetan Book of the Dead* or in the way you explain it—that you really have anything other than what you imagine you have.

TR: In every situation of life, particularly the world of the mind, hallucinations and colors and temperatures are the world— that's all. If you're trying to look back and find real eternity, you find just mind, that's all. Just pure mind, that's all. That is why bardo is referred to as an in-between period. It's something you go through between two intervals rather than a permanent thing. That is why the whole idea of what I'm trying to say is no-man's-land rather than somebody's land, because you can't build a permanent residence on no-man's-land.

STUDENT: Rinpoche, what is a hallucination?

TRUNGPA RINPOCHE: Well, we could almost ask, what isn't a hallucination? I mean, the things we see and perceive are there because we see and perceive. So the real reassurance of absolute proof is because we saw it.

STUDENT: If one is completely absorbed in the eternity, then how could one remember that it's a passing experience?

TRUNGPA RINPOCHE: Eternity experience in this case is not eternal. It's a glimpse of eternity—then there will be a moment to appreciate the eternity, then there will be the eternity experience, and then there will be a gap to appreciate the eternity. It is like an artist painting, and then stepping back and appreciating it or criticizing it.

STUDENT: If everything is in the mind, yet we can have experiences of the truth occasionally of which we are absolutely convinced. That truth is an expression of one's own being.

TRUNGPA RINPOCHE: There is something to that. And that something has to do with the distance of the projections. You judge whether you're experiencing something or not by the distance of the projections. From this point of view, there's no such thing as absolute truth; on the other hand, everything is true.

STUDENT: Bardo seems to be the ultimate extension of ego— what's the relation of that to the awakened state? In your analogy of the water and the islands, what is the bridge to the awakened state—the mountain?

TRUNGPA RINPOCHE: That's a very important point, seeing bardo as the path to the enlightened state. On each particular
island, bardo is the highest point. In other words, it is the em-
bodiment of the whole experience of each different realm. For
instance, in terms of the world of the gods, eternity is the highest
point of ego's achievement. And because it is the highest point of
ego's achievement, therefore it is close to the other side as well, to
the awakened state.

STUDENT: When we're talking about the path to the awakened state, it is almost as if it is all something that has to occur
within *us*, as if what is happening with other people is somehow
less relevant and not really worth paying attention to. But you
yourself seem to maintain yourself on the path by perpetual response to *other* people, almost as if you're forgetting about yourself.
Can you describe the path in terms of your own experience, which
is more like constantly responding to other people? It seems as if
you don't pay much attention to developing yourself as you suggest
that we do.

TRUNGPA RINPOCHE: That's a good one. I think it's happening in exactly the same way in the case of others as well, because
it is necessary for you to relate with others or to relate with me. I
mean, you can't develop through the path without relationships—
that's the fundamental point. But meditation becomes the starting
point of relating; you learn how to create the right environment in
order to relate to yourself. In terms of my own experience, that
learning process takes place constantly, all the time, in terms of
working with other people. You see, that's the point when you
regard yourself as officially teaching other people. When you regard yourself as a student on the path, that student would gain
certain experiences and ideas by himself, through practicing meditation, going on retreat, being with himself, as well as by being
with his version of the world. But he wouldn't share his experience
with others as much as a teacher would. That's a very dangerous

point, when you begin to work with other people as a teacher. Unless you are willing to learn from students—unless you regard yourself as a student and the students as your teacher—you cease to become a true teacher. You only impart your experience of what you've been taught, a package deal. And having done that, there's no more to say—unless you just repeat yourself again and again.

S: Your life seems to be so concentrated, in terms of practicing in regard to other people's needs. But we seem to bypass that worldly side—we forget about practicing the perfections (*paramitas*) and just get into the meditation; whereas in your life you are always practicing the perfections.

TR: The whole point is that it would be dangerous purely to try to imitate me, and it would be dangerous for me to try to make other people into replicas of me. That would be a very unhealthy thing.

S: But aren't there fundamental teachings in Buddhism about how people can best relate to each other on a daily basis? Those teachings seem to be forgotten on account of the fact that they are so rule-oriented.

TR: You see, what we are trying to do here is to start purely with the practice of meditation. From that base, you begin to feel the need or the relevance of the other aspect, as you encounter all sorts of temptations. And then discipline based on individual conviction comes through.

S: I'm reading Gampopa's *Jewel Ornament of Liberation,* which you spoke of so highly in your foreword, and repeatedly he quotes the sutras as being step by step: you can't practice the perfections until you've found a teacher; you can't practice the second perfection until you've mastered the first, and at the end of those perfections he gets into meditation.[3] But you don't tell us much about the practice of patience in everyday life, or charity, or strenuousness.

TR: In actual fact, in following the path you have to have a commitment at the beginning, like taking refuge and surrendering yourself, and the basic practice of meditation always happens right at the beginning. The kind of meditation that Gampopa talks about is the fifth paramita, *dhyana,* or meditation. Dhyana is the highest meditative state the bodhisattvas achieve—which is different from the basic meditation of beginning practitioners. You see, in terms of patience and generosity and the other paramitas, the conflicts of life bring them out in any case. One doesn't have to make big speeches about them. People find that meditation is all the time painful or difficult, and then they look for something. They begin to realize that something is wrong with them or they begin to find that something is developing in them. And these kinds of meditation in action we've been talking about, the six paramitas or disciplines, happen as a natural process. The pain of meditation takes on the pattern of discipline—you find that you are running too fast and you need patience to slow down, and if you don't do that, automatically you are pushed back, something happens. A lot of people begin to find that they are facing a lot of problems if they've done something not in accordance with the pattern. And if you were a scholar, for instance, or a sociologist of Buddhism, you could try to match their experiences with the technical aspects of the teaching. But there's no point trying to prove such an interpretation, anyway.

S: Gampopa's *Jewel Ornament of Liberation* provides an outline of the bodhisattva's career. Is it helpful to us to study that, or is it a hindrance?

TR: What do you mean by *study?* Practicing?

S: Reading the book.

TR: It is definitely an inspiration. I have recommended that most people read Gampopa, and we have also discussed bodhisattva actions. And each time I have interviews with people, almost without fail some aspect of aggression which they find a conflict with always comes up. And the bodhisattva activity of generosity and compassion comes up automatically, as a natural process.

STUDENT: Is sex the human equivalent of eternity?

TRUNGPA RINPOCHE: Sex? I don't think so. Sex is somehow too practical. It is governed purely by physical experience, whereas eternity is connected with imagination. Eternity has a very dreamlike quality; it has no reality, no physical action, and no involvement with earth. It's purely living on imagination and dream world. I would say it is more like wish or hope.

S: How about when you're creating something, making a form or something? Is eternity something like that kind of creative ecstasy?

TR: I think so, yes. The pleasure of producing something. Meditation is something like that.

STUDENT: In the clear light experience, how does one recognize whether it is egohood or the awakened state?

TRUNGPA RINPOCHE: There's a very faint, very subtle distinction between the two. When you begin to see the sudden glimpse but it's not eternity—it's all-encompassing rather than eternity—then that's the awakened state of clear light. Whereas if you begin to see all this not as all-pervading but as something definite, solid and eternal, then that's the ego inclination.

STUDENT: In *The Tibetan Book of the Dead,* it seems that they talk about the clear light as reality, but you talk of it as the ultimate ego experience. Is seeing it as eternity like seeing something new, and seeing the awakened state like seeing something which is more familiar? That seemed to be in there too, in the description of clear light experience as being like a son recognizing his mother.

TRUNGPA RINPOCHE: That's beyond ego's range, the notion of son meeting mother.

S: Does the complete human ego continue after the experience of death and then go through the bardo states in the process of its disintegration?

TR: I don't think so. Somehow it continues through all those experiences. I mean, you might have an experience of egolessness, but at the same time, beyond that experience, ego continues.

S: Even past the bardo state?

TR: Past the bardo state.

S: And it's the same ego as right now?

TR: Well, that's difficult to say. It wouldn't be the same anyway, would it?

STUDENT: The distinction you made between the egotistical experience of the clear light and the awakened experience seems to me to be partially a difference in emphasis between time and space. The experience of ego involves the notion of endless time, and the awakened experience seems to involve all the spacious aspects.

TRUNGPA RINPOCHE: In terms of ego, it seems that space and time are very solid. In terms of awake experience, the time concept is very loose. In other words, in terms of ego there's only one center and the radiation from it; in terms of beyond ego, center is everywhere and radiation is everywhere. It's not one center, but it is all-pervading.

S: Is it a particular trick of ego to see things in terms of time?

TR: In the ordinary sense of ego, there's very little understanding of time. Ego's understanding of time is purely based on desire, what you would like to see, what you would like to develop. It's sort of wishful.

STUDENT: Is the clear light something you see? The way I see you now? Is it something you see with your eyes, or is that a metaphor?

TRUNGPA RINPOCHE: It should be quite obvious that when we talk of clear light as all-pervading, you can't see all-pervading. I know that there is a book on psychedelic experience and *The Tibetan Book of the Dead,* which talks about some kind of glimpse of light that you experience.[4] But in actual fact, when we talk in terms of the awakened state of mind, that doesn't mean that Buddha never sleeps. That he is *awake* doesn't mean he's devoid of sleepiness—he sleeps and he eats and he behaves like any other person.

S: It's easy to correlate the awakened state and clear light as verbal approaches to something that can't be discussed, but the subsequent lights which are described in terms of blues and reds and such sound so visual. I never had that kind of visual experience.

TR: They are metaphors. For instance, we talk in terms of a person's face turning red when he's angry, that doesn't just mean the color of his complexion turns crimson; it's a metaphor. It's the same thing in the text, which speaks in terms of colors: the color of emotions, the clear light, and many other experiences. It is very complicated. Particularly when you get further into *The Tibetan Book of the Dead,* it begins to describe all sorts of different divinities and iconographical details—and all these colors and shapes and symbolism are connected purely with one's state of mind. If a person is open enough to his own state of being, completely absorbed in it, you could almost say the experience becomes tangible or visual—it's so real, in that sense. It's that point of view.

S: For example, to experience these colors and forms, is it relevant whether or not your eyes are open?

TR: I don't think so. I don't think so at all. In any case, if you experience them in the bardo after death, you leave your body behind.

STUDENT: When you were talking about ego as having the experience of eternity as something solid and then nothingness afterward, you used the analogy of hot and cold. I started to think about the Chinese yin-yang symbol and the knot of eternity, trying to flash back and forth between the space, the light, and the so-called form.

TRUNGPA RINPOCHE: Well, I tried to explain the aspect of experiencing hot and cold *simultaneously,* the possibility of two experiences coming at the same time, both confused and awake. In fact, that seems to be the whole idea of bardo altogether, being in no-man's-land, experiencing both at the same time. It's the vividness of both aspects at the same time. When you are in such a peak of experience, there is the possibility of absolute sanity and there is also the possibility of complete madness. That is being experienced simultaneously—in one situation, one second, one moment. That seems to be the highlight of bardo experience, because bardo is in between the two experiences.

S: Does it have something to do with letting go in that instant when you decide which one you'll plop back into? In other words, when the thing is over, you either end up awakened or back in samsara.

TR: Yes.

S: So it seems like you're given a chance, and if you miss, somehow you're back in samsara.

TR: Your actual practice in everyday situations, when those peak experiences are not present, brings them into a balanced state. If your general pattern of life has developed into a balanced state of being, then that acts as a kind of chain reaction enforcing the bardo experience. In other words, you have more balanced possibilities of sanity because of your previous chain reactions.

S: It's like the base of a mountain—the broader and more solid your base, the stronger and taller you stand.

TR: Quite. Yes.

S: So that's what sitting meditation is all about.

TR: Yes. I mean, that's the whole idea of bardo being an important moment. I think that working on basic sanity provides tremendous possibilities. It is basic—there will be tremendous influence and power, needless to say.

STUDENT: Do you have to go through the bardo to get to the awakened state?

TRUNGPA RINPOCHE: There will be some moment of experience, peak of experience, before the awakened state of mind. That is called bardo. It is not particularly that bardo is special, but it's just that the gap is called bardo.

S: It may not be anything special, but when we see it coming, we say, "Wow, that's it."

TR: Well, I wouldn't make a particularly big deal of it—although we are holding a seminar on it.

STUDENT: There is something that continues after death, and I guess that something is the you that reincarnates.

TRUNGPA RINPOCHE: Nobody knows. But if you see it in terms of the present situation, experiences happen; they pass through continuously. Our physical situation can't prevent the psychological experience of pain or pleasure—it's beyond control. So if we work back from that level, there seems to be the possibility that even beyond physical death there will be continuity of consciousness throughout—but that's an assumption.

STUDENT: If you finally reach the awakened state, you're released from having to come back—I've heard this in Hindu thought.

TRUNGPA RINPOCHE: There is the same idea in Buddhism as well—if you use up your karmic chain reactions and if you use up your karmic seeds, then you are no longer subject to the power of karma, returning to the world. But then, of course, if you are that advanced a person, naturally the force of compassion forces you out, to come back and help other people. So in any case you come back, it seems.

STUDENT: In talking about time, you said that time was an invention, a wishful thought, that it was related to hope. But time is also related to fear, because time moves us up to death. Is it true, then, that if one manages to give up both fear and hope, one is also released from time?

TRUNGPA RINPOCHE: Well, time is a concept, obviously, and you transcend concepts. I would say so, definitely.

S: But one doesn't have to be awake to understand the concept of time, because in ordinary everyday life one sees that time is very unreal. Sometimes there are five days that seem like five years; other times there are five years that seem like five days.

TR: If you look at it from a rational point of view, it is determined by your preoccupations. They determine the length of time. But that isn't exactly transcending time in terms of freedom; that is simply the degree of your determination, your preoccupation. If something is pleasurable, it passes very quickly; if something is painful, it lasts an extremely long period. And certain people have a kind of noncaring quality, feeling that time doesn't matter; they are completely easy about it. But that again is purely habitual rather than a fundamental idea of time. You see, time means struggle, or wish. It's a demand for something—you have a particular concept or desire to achieve something within a certain limit of time. When you don't have this desire to achieve something or desire not to do something, then somehow the limitation of time doesn't become important. But you can't say that you completely transcend time, in terms of transcending karmic seeds or karmic patterns. Even the awakened state of mind of compassion and wisdom, in communicating and dealing with other people, still has to use the concept of time. But at the same time, *your* version of time doesn't last any longer; that fundamental, centralized notion of time doesn't exist anymore.

STUDENT: You spoke of compassion as being a force that brings us back, insists that we reincarnate again. Is that the same as when we are feeling bliss in meditation and we do not want to stop and go back to everyday activities, but out of our sense of duty to our friends, we do?

TRUNGPA RINPOCHE: Any kind of awake experience you have should have sharpness or intelligence as well. I don't think there will be possibilities of being completely dazed in the experience at all—if that's so, then something must be wrong. You see, when you are completely involved in the awake state of mind, you develop discriminating wisdom as well as the wisdom of equanimity.

S: You are here out of compassion. Are we here out of that same compassion?

TR: I hope so.

S: I never experienced any sharp, clear choice to stay in the world for the sake of others.

TR: Perhaps you feel that you are not ready to help others yet.

S: I feel I have no choice but to be in the world.

TR: That's generally how things operate: you have no choice. You are bound by karma; you have no choice.

S: Is there an alternative state where the awakened person constantly has the option of being in the world or out of it?

TR: Well, if an awakened person is not bound by karmic duties, so to speak, then of course there is that option, definitely. Even the arhants, who have achieved the equivalent of the sixth stage of the bodhisattva path, supposedly have the option of not stepping back into the world, because they have transcended certain karmic seeds. They remain for kalpas and kalpas (aeons) in the meditative state until a certain Buddha comes to the world. He has to send his vibrations to wake them up and bring them back to the world and encourage them to commit themselves to the bodhisattva path of compassion, not to stay out.

S: You mean you can leave if you don't feel a strong enough duty to others?

TR: That would mean that it was a partial kind of enlightened state. A fully enlightened state automatically would have compassion, whereas a partially enlightened state would have wisdom without compassion; and in this case, you quite likely would stay away.

S: Is remaining in nirvana for kalpas something worth shooting for?

TR: That's purely up to you.

STUDENT: I have a question about the difference between buddhahood and egohood in the six bardos. At certain times I've experienced leaving this situation, a kind of transcending, but there's still a center, a source of radiation. But at a certain point, if I'm willing to let go further, it seems to break loose into a more spacious quality without this center.

TRUNGPA RINPOCHE: Well, you get a potential glimpse of that constantly. All aspects are in individuals all the time, and you do experience that, yes. But that doesn't necessarily mean that one has reached higher degrees; more likely, a person is able to see the potential in himself.

STUDENT: How would you relate the déja-vu experience to the six bardos, the feeling that you have been someplace before?

TRUNGPA RINPOCHE: Before?

S: [Repeats]

TR: I suppose that experience is within the six realms of the world.

STUDENT: Would you translate *bardo* again?

TRUNGPA RINPOCHE: *Bar* means "in-between" or "gap" or "the middle," and *do* means "island," so altogether *bardo* means "that which exists between two situations." It is like the experience of living, which is between birth and death.

S: What is not bardo?

TR: The beginning and the end. [Laughter]

STUDENT: Can there be wisdom without compassion or compassion without wisdom? Can either exist independently?

TRUNGPA RINPOCHE: According to the teachings as well as one's own personal experience, it is quite possible you could have wisdom without compassion, but you couldn't have compassion without wisdom.

STUDENT: I know somebody who almost doesn't sleep at all, he sleeps sometimes one hour a day, and he leads a frightfully energetic life. He's not a Buddhist, but he's a rather enlightened person—is that at all relevant?

TRUNGPA RINPOCHE: Well, I don't know about that. You see, ultimately there are certain requirements for the physical being, as long as you have a physical body—like sleeping and food. It's a natural process. And of course there's the balance of whether you need a great deal of sleep or a great deal of food, which depends on whether a person is using sleep or food as an escape, or in some other way. I mean, from a rational point of view, one would presume that enlightened beings would eat balancedly, sleep normally. They wouldn't have to fight with the pattern of their life anymore, whether it was sleep or food. It just happens, I suppose. But that's pure guesswork on my part.

S: I think I've read somewhere that if one is really relaxed one sleeps more efficiently, so one doesn't need much sleep.

TR: Generally you need very little sleep. It depends on your state of mind. But you need some sleep anyway, and you need some food. On the other hand, there's the story of the great yogi Lavapa in India: he slept for twenty years, and when he woke up he attained enlightenment.

STUDENT: What do you mean when you say that no one knows about the after-death period? I thought all bodhisattvas would know, all those who have returned.

TRUNGPA RINPOCHE: I think they would have confidence, definitely, and they would have some definite intuitions about it, or quite possibly memories of their previous lives. But in the ordinary case, nobody knows; nobody has actually gone through it, like a journey.

S: In other words, for a bodhisattva, all his lives aren't just like one life, just one change after another?

TR: It wouldn't be as clear as that for a bodhisattva. A bodhisattva still works with situations; therefore he works with his own life and death, and his physical being as well.

4

The Bardo of Birth

Yesterday we discussed the world of the gods and the particular point of eternity—involvement with eternity. That whole idea comes from an approach to spiritual practice which is based on the principles of ego. In such a spiritual trip, you tend to reach a peak point in which you do not know whether you are following a spiritual path or whether you are going completely mad, freaking out. That is the point of the bardo of meditation, or samten bardo. You worked so hard to get something—eternal promise, eternal blessing—and you begin to feel that you are achieving something; but at the same time you are not quite certain whether that achievement is imaginary, based on self-deception. That doubt brings madness. Conviction is part of the pattern which leads you to the madness, conviction based purely on relating with ego. Whenever we talk about bardo principles, we can apply the same analogy that I used yesterday: experiencing both hot and cold water being poured on you simultaneously. That pattern, which is pleasurable and at the same time extremely painful, continues with all six types of bardo.

The second bardo is connected with the realm of the jealous gods, the asuras. According to the teaching, it is described as the bardo of birth or, in Tibetan, *kye-ne* bardo. *Kye* means "birth," and *nye* means "dwelling." So kye-ne bardo is the birth and dwelling aspect of bardo. This experience of birth and dwelling is based on speed and on our trust in speed. It is based on living and dwelling on that particular state of being, which is our own individual experience of speed, aggression, and that which brings speed, the ambition to achieve something. In this case, the bardo experience is not necessarily a meditative state of spiritual practice, but it is an ordinary everyday life situation. You put out a certain amount of speed constantly, yet you are not quite certain whether you are getting anything out of it or whether you are losing something. There is a certain peak point of confusion or hesitation, uncertainty. It is as if you are going too far. If you spin really fast, faster and faster—if you spin fast enough—you are not quite certain whether you're spinning or not. You are uncertain whether it is stillness or whether it is absolute speed that drives you. Absolute speed seems to be stillness.

This, again, is exactly the same point as in the bardo of meditation: that uncertainty as to sanity or madness. You see, we come to this same problem all the time—whenever we have some peak experience of aggression, hatred, passion, joy, pleasure, or insight. In whatever we experience, there's always some kind of uncertainty when we are just about to reach the peak of the experience. And when we reach the peak point, it is as though we were experiencing both hot and cold water at the same time. There is that kind of uncertainty between the fear of freaking out and the possibility of learning something or getting somewhere. I'm sure a lot of us have experienced that; it is a very simple and experiential thing. I would like you to have a clear perception of the bardo experience, both theoretically and experientially. Particularly those who feel they have experienced so-called satori have felt this experience. We are always uncertain whether we have actually achieved something or whether we are just about to freak out. And this very faint line between sanity and insanity is a very profound teaching in regard to the experience of bardo and Buddhist teachings in general.

According to history, at the very moment of enlightenment, Buddha experienced hosts of *maras* both attacking him with aggression and trying to seduce him with beautiful girls. That is a peak point, or moment of bardo experience. The point is that once we have achieved some higher state, a so-called higher state or more profound state of something, the negative aspect, or the mara aspect, is also going to be there—equally, exactly the same. And they both become more subtle. The subtleties of awakeness are exactly the same as the subtleties of sleepiness or confusion. Such subtleties continue all the time, side by side. Therefore, samsara and nirvana are like two sides of a coin. They occur together in one situation, simultaneously.

Such bardo experiences happen all the time with us. We don't have to have a peak experience or a dramatic experience—in ordinary everyday situations as well, we are not quite certain whether we are learning something or whether we are missing something. There is that particular point of doubt. If you are more paranoid, you will think you are missing something; if you are more confident, you will think you are learning something. But there is also the awareness of the learning and missing qualities occurring simultaneously in experiences all the time. This experience is very common and very obvious. In many cases, we don't have to ask any more questions: what is real, what is not real; what is safe, what is not safe. But when we are just about to approach safety, we are not quite certain whether it is really true safety or not. There is some faint suspicion of danger; at the same time we feel tremendous safety. The more we feel tremendous safety, the more we feel danger. That double-take takes place all the time. It is a kind of supposing, or looking back again. That is the basic experiential factor connected with bardo.

STUDENT: What's a good attitude to take to that ambiguity?

TRUNGPA RINPOCHE: You see, at that point you can't control the situation—you are the situation. So it depends on the technique or practice that you have already gained experience in. It really depends on that. You can't correct or change course at all. In fact, the idea of a change of course doesn't occur at that particular moment because you are so much into it: you are the situation rather than the situation being something external.

STUDENT: Is there any difference between the feeling of confusion and the feeling of confidence?

TRUNGPA RINPOCHE: It is the same thing. The same experience happens at exactly the same level. Fundamentally, at an experiential level, our perception is extremely fantastic and possesses all sorts of attributes. It is really fantastic to discover that perception has such a wide range, as well as a narrow range and a penetrating range. It has the capability of seeing a hundred things at the same time. That is why things are referred to as wisdom and things are referred to as confusion.

That's a very important point. It is really the key point when we talk about madness and about sanity. It is extremely important. Everybody should know that that is *one* point, rather than that you belong to either of those groups. You don't have to belong in order to become mad or in order to become wise or liberated. You don't have to associate yourself with either the good or the bad, but you become the one. And that one possesses both good and bad simultaneously. That's a very important point in terms of experience. It is extremely necessary to know that.

S: Whenever that happens, I feel there's something wrong. Doubt always occurs—always, always, always.

TR: Yes. It occurs always.

S: So there's no point expecting it to diminish?

TR: No. You don't have to make the distinction as to whether you belong to that group or to this group, but you see the situation as it is—that's the important point. You can't change that particular situation at all. You can only divert it through some kind of chain reaction process: you can impose your experience prior to that by becoming familiar with sanity or, equally, by becoming familiar with madness or insanity. Either way is safe and instructive, and either of them could be said to be insight. And then one-pointedness switches you into the awake or enlightened state automatically.

S: Is that awake state free of doubt or uncertainty?

TR: Yes, of course. The reason it is free of doubt is that there's so much reinforcement from what you have already worked with before that experience. You are quite familiar with what you've gone through. But I would like to say something else on this particular point. That is, when we talk about self-awareness, self-consciousness, self-observing—often that self-observing awareness is negative. When you try to work on self-observing or self-awareness in a self-consciousness way, then the reason you're being self-aware is that you are purely trying to ward off danger. It is sort of a conservative attitude.

In the general philosophy of conservatism, you don't think about what could go right, or what is the best thing for you to do; often the inspiration of conservatism starts with what could go wrong with you, what's a bad thing to do. Because of that, you give guidance to other people in a conservative way, saying "I am trying to talk to you in terms of safe and sound, so that what you're doing is not a mistake." The first statement comes from a negative view: " . . . so that what you are doing is not a mistake." That approach to the fundamental basic subtlety of self-awareness is not looking at the positive and healthy aspect of that state of mind, but constantly aggravating the negative "What could go wrong?" state of mind. That could pile up in the process of the path. And it's quite likely that when such a person is in the peak state of mind of both sanity and insanity happening simultaneously, then the immediate first flicker of mind will reflect back naturally to what's bad, that sense of paranoia. Then you could flip back into madness. It sounds quite dangerous.

STUDENT: Do you have to be a warrior?

TRUNGPA RINPOCHE: Well, I think the point is that you are willing to see the creative aspect rather than the negative aspect. The whole process is one of going along rather than looking back at each step.

STUDENT: Is this doubt a result of an impending sense that the peak experience is going to deteriorate and return to a less profound state of consciousness, or is it a result of a sense that perhaps the peak experience won't end, and you won't return?

TRUNGPA RINPOCHE: I don't think you will return. Once you've had it, you've had it. That doesn't mean to say there will be only one peak experience. There will be a succession of peak experiences—which happens with us anyway, all the time. I'm not talking purely theoretically. In our own experience of everyday life, flashes happen all the time, peak experiences. Doubt is not being able to match yourself with a prescribed goal. Whenever there is doubt, you also have an ideal concept of the absence of doubt, which is the goal.

STUDENT: Is this particular experience between sanity and insanity ever resolved by what's known as surrendering or openness to the guru?

TRUNGPA RINPOCHE: I would say both yes and no. You see, at that very moment nobody can save you. At the same time, at that very moment, things could be inspired—somebody could push you overboard. Both situations are possible. But fundamentally nobody can save you. You have to make your own commitment to the situation, that's for sure.

S: Then there's no surrendering.

TR: Surrendering happens early on. If you surrender, that

means you are associating yourself with positive experiences and you are not trying to hold back and be careful and conservative, as I have been saying. Surrendering to the guru is a very positive thing; therefore, it proceeds with inspiration rather than by holding back and checking the danger. You see, the idea of the term *surrender* is that once you surrender—that's the whole thing! You don't surrender because of something. Surrendering to the guru is quite different from an insurance policy. In the case of an insurance policy, you write down a list of all sorts of dangers, up to the point of the will of God or "acts of God."

STUDENT: You talked about the nirvanic and the samsaric worlds as being coexistent. Autobiographically speaking, I am very much aware that in certain chemical states the reality of the world of physics is revealed to me, the world of wave patterns and whirling molecules and whatnot. It seems to me this world, which modern physics has revealed to us, very often is equated with the nirvanic state, where you as an ego, as a separate item, cannot exist. Do you see the nirvanic state as I described it?

TRUNGPA RINPOCHE: The state of nirvana or freedom cannot be described in any way. If you are trying to describe it, then you are involved with wishful thinking of some kind more than natural reality—because immediately when you begin to describe it, you are separating the experience from the experiencer. Nirvana is something quite different from that.

S: But people still say they have seen nirvana, so they must have been aware of something.

TR: Yes, definitely.

S: Then the split remains. As you come out of nirvana, there is a moment where your senses react to the high state you've been in and say, "I come from nirvana."

TR: Once you've gotten into it, you are in it already—you can't come out of it.

STUDENT: Is there only one bardo experience associated with each world, or is it possible to have any of the bardo experiences in any of the worlds?

TRUNGPA RINPOCHE: I think so, yes. Yesterday we discussed the bardo experience associated with the world of the gods, and today we have been discussing the bardo connected with the world of the asuras, or jealous gods. Each bardo experience is connected with a particular sphere, so to speak, or world.

S: Then there's a one-to-one correspondence between bardos and worlds?

TR: Yes, but these corresponding experiences happen irregularly within one's own experience, all the time. You may begin with hell and continue with the world of human beings. From the world of human beings you could go back to the world of the *pretas,* the hungry ghosts, and so on. This could happen continuously. The whole point I'm trying to make is that bardo experience is a peak experience where you are not quite certain whether you have completely gone mad or you are just about to receive something. That particular peak point is the bardo experience. And the bardo experience cannot be resolved unless there is training. Without life-long training in the practice of meditation and in accordance with the practice of meditation, putting the skillful actions of a bodhisattva into practice, you cannot have a complete bardo experience.

STUDENT: Rinpoche, what is madness?

TRUNGPA RINPOCHE: That's a good question. At the experiential level, madness begins with some kind of confusion between the experience of reality and the experience of the perceiver of reality, a conflict between the two. Then, further on, one tends to go on with that confusion and try to discover some ultimate answer to pinpoint what is reality and what is the perceiver of the reality. You try and you struggle more and more—up to the point where you cannot discover the answer unless you give up the idea of the existence of both the experiencer *and* the experience.

At that level, you are so overwhelmed by such experiences that you make up all sorts of ways of convincing yourself. You either try to rationalize that there is such a thing as a self, that things outside are dangerous or seductive, and that "me" is the rightful person to experience that. Or, on the other hand, you begin to feel that you are out of control. Then you become ultimately mad.

You are so confused as to what is the experiencer and what is the experience. The whole thing is completely amalgamated into the one or the many. It is confusion between the one and the many. You don't have the earth-grounding process of seeing "that" as opposed to "this" anymore at all, because the whole thing is so overwhelming. You are completely sucked into it. You have all sorts of experiences of being claustrophobic, because the whole situation around you is so overwhelming. You experience paranoia because such overwhelming experience could try to suffocate you, destroy you, destroy the experiencer. And at the same time you would like to act as though nothing happened. You begin to play the game of deaf and dumb, but you pretend you actually never heard of it. Hundreds of millions of tactics begin to develop because of this overwhelming suddenness, this overwhelming crowdedness.

S: Is it possible to achieve enlightenment without becoming mad?

TR: We are mad anyway, in different degrees. We may not become completely mad unless we are maniacs—religious maniacs or political maniacs, whatever—unless we lose control of the situation. We have a sort of medium madness going on all the time, with the possibility of absolute madness. You see, that is samsara—madness. And that which is not madness is called enlightenment. Because such an idea as madness exists, therefore automatically there is that which is not madness, which is enlightenment. So once you begin to talk about enlightenment, or freedom, that means you are speaking in terms of madness.

STUDENT: Rinpoche, it seems that one thing you were saying is that when you approach this peak experience of the bardo, if you're not prepared for it, it's too sudden and you go mad.

TRUNGPA RINPOCHE: That seems to be the point, yes. That's the whole idea of why we mention bardo at all, because it is connected with the teachings, with the path.

STUDENT: Could you describe the bardo in the asura world again? I don't have any feeling for that at all.

TRUNGPA RINPOCHE: It is trying to give birth and at the same time trying to dwell on it. Suddenly, at the peak experience, you try to force things—you try to push your situation because you are about to reach some experience. That experience is pushed by a certain effort, extreme effort, and you would like to retain that particular effort.

S: You mean like a woman trying to give birth and keep the baby at the same time?

TR: Exactly. Yes. It is so action-conscious.

S: Is it a sense of having too much energy?

TR: Too much energy, yes, because the ground for this particular bardo of birth and dwelling is the realm of the asuras. The whole environment of the jealous god realm is very much action-conscious, all the time rushing. But you get more than that action at the asura level, you get a peak experience: you have to push yourself into some particular peak experience, and you would like to hold on to that, grasp it.

STUDENT: If you see somebody going crazy, is there anything you can do, or should you just leave them alone? They might be destroying themselves or trying to destroy others.

TRUNGPA RINPOCHE: You can do a great deal. But to start with, it is better not to do anything at all. It is better not to try to use any system or psychological school or concept—Freudian, Jungian, Buddhist, Christian, or whatever. You see, one problem is that when we come across somebody who is absolutely mad, our immediate response is to try to do something with them, rather than trying to understand the basic ground. So you have to allow yourself space and not allow the situation to be completely controlled by them. You should allow space and not associate with any category of philosophical or psychological school.

You should not analyze at all—that's the last thing you would like to do. That's the source of what's been wrong in the past. Without trying to fit things into pigeonholes of that category or this category, but with an open mind, you can relate with the situation of the moment—the person, the background of the person, as well as *your* own state of mind, whether that situation is your imagination or whether it actually exists independent of your imagination.

From that level, once you get a clear perception of the situation, then you can proceed to relate with the person. You can do a great deal, because generally madness is the ultimate concept of frustration, and frustration needs to work, or communicate, with some kind of external situation. Even though the person who is in a state of madness appears to be completely, absolutely incommunicative, absolutely going wild—at the same time, the wildness depends on the external situation, or the internal situation of mind being sparked up by the external situation. So nothing could be said to be completely impersonal. In other words, the point is not to relate with that person as an impersonal thing, but as something still living and continuing. In that way you will be able to relate with the person and go along with the situation.

Another important point is not to be either too compassionate and gentle or too aggressive. You should be aware of the "idiot compassion" aspect of being too kind, and at the same time, you should be aware of laying your trip on the other person. It is an individual matter and you should work along with it. These little details can't be generalized; they depend on the individual situation. But you can do great deal to help. There is a moment when you should let the person be what they are, and there also will be a moment when you shouldn't let them be what they are. That is individual inspiration, how you relate with that person. It also depends on how much space you allowed at the beginning, that you didn't rush in immediately.

S: I saw somebody who wanted to stick their hand in a fire to prove that they could withstand pain, and it was a thing for me to watch their hand swell up like a marshmallow. Then I had to say, "No, you can't do that."

TR: Well, you use your basic common sense. Actually, there is a particular mentality involved when you are dealing with people like that: the whole thing is regarded as a game. You analyze the person's every activity and appreciate its symbolic quality, and you let them do what they like. But completely letting the person do what they like is somehow too self-indulgent. One should use some common sense in the process, definitely. In other words, one should not expect any miracles. If a person says he can't feel heat and his hand is invincible, that person is trying to imagine himself as more than he is. Quite possibly he would like to become what he imagines he should be rather than what he is, and one should realize that situation. The earth-grounding quality is very important.

STUDENT: How can you respond when a maniac attacks you?

TRUNGPA RINPOCHE: You can stop it, generally speaking. But you have to deal with it individually, whether the person is attacking in order to get some reaction from you or because he would like to release himself. It depends on the situation.

S: Sometimes they attack without knowing why they attack,

because they are in a crisis. In this case, you can't say you respond according to what the person wants, because you don't know. Even the person doesn't know what he wants.

T R : It seems that often you have some knowledge of the person as the person is, in any case, unless it's somebody you just met that very moment on the street. If the person is a friend, then there will be some idea of that person's state of mind—not necessarily just that person as insane, but his aspects of sanity as well and his particular way of handling himself in terms of sanity.

S : No, but this is a case where my friend has to go to the hospital. She's completely out of herself—she can awake in the middle of the night and do anything, and if she doesn't go to the hospital she might kill herself.

T R : Quite unlikely.

S : How can you deal with that?

T R : You can deal with the given situation. If you are her friend, then you must have some understanding of her—not necessarily from the technical point of view of a psychiatrist, but in terms of being able to deal with her particular aspects and go along with them. You *can* deal with it, of course. It is exactly an aspect of the normality of the person—so you go along with *that*.

S : But then sometimes you have to use violence.

T R : Sure, you can. That also depends on the situation. I don't mean to say that you have to be completely gentle all the time— that's another weak point, trying to be too kind. In fact, a person needs reminders, shaking back—violence, in this case. So violence can be a reminder of sanity—presuming, of course, that you who are going to work with her are yourself sane. One has to use a sane kind of violence, not insane violence.

STUDENT : What happens if you're the one who's really feeling crazy, if you're the person who feels out of control?

TRUNGPA RINPOCHE: You don't purely have to live in your dream world, dealing with your imagination and your neurosis by yourself. You have something else to relate with—the actual physical world outside. And if you are going too far, your physical world will act as a reminder to you. That's a very important point: the only way to deal with yourself is through your relationship with the actual physical world outside. Therefore, the body is very important in this case, in human life.

S: Sometimes you begin seeing things in the physical world that aren't there, hallucinations.

TR: That means that you are not seeing the physical world as it is, completely. One should take a second look.

STUDENT: What is openness?

TRUNGPA RINPOCHE: Openness is without paranoia, I suppose, to begin with. You don't have to put up barriers or a boundary to your territory: in your territory, others are welcome as well. That doesn't mean that a person has to be absolutely polite, diplomatic, just acting. It is a genuine welcoming. Your territory is not defended territory but it's open territory—anyone can walk into it. By doing that, automatically the other person will be able to walk into it without putting out any territory of his own.

STUDENT: Is bardo experience possible in the awakened state?

TRUNGPA RINPOCHE: In the awakened state there will be the experience of the essence of the bardo, which is the constant act of compassion. A continual loosening process, either in terms of the other person or yourself, is taking place all the time.

STUDENT: Could you speak further on the difference between surrender to the guru and a life insurance policy?

TRUNGPA RINPOCHE: An insurance policy automatically talks of what could go wrong and how you can guard against it. An insurance policy often talks about being a guardian, in other words, sort of exorcising the danger. In the case of surrendering to the guru, the emphasis is not so much on the danger aspect, but that the danger could be transmuted into creative relationships. Everything that comes up in the pattern is a continual creative process. Both negative and positive could be used as stepping stones on the path, which the guru could point out to you as long as you don't try to hide from the guru. That's the ultimate meaning of surrendering, surrendering all aspects of yourself to the guru. And then you learn from that.

STUDENT: It seems to me that there is a boundary between the generosity of openness and self-defense. Sometimes you can't be generous without harming either yourself or both yourself and the other person.

TRUNGPA RINPOCHE: You see, the general idea is that if you open yourself to what the given situation is, then you see its completely naked quality. You don't have to put up a defensive mechanism anymore, because you see through it and you know exactly what to do. You just deal with things, rather than defending yourself.

S: But then the feeling might be that you have to refuse somebody.

TR: Sure, yes. Openness doesn't necessarily mean that you have to make yourself available to the other person all the time. Openness is knowing the situation—if it's healthy and helpful to the other person to involve yourself with them, or if it is more healthy not to involve yourself, if showing this kind of commitment is not healthy for the other person. It works both ways. Openness doesn't mean you have to take everything in at all; you have a right to reject or accept—but when you reject you don't close *yourself,* you reject the situation.

S: But maybe the other person doesn't want to reject the situation.

TR: Whether you accept or reject it depends on whether it's a healthy situation for the other person or not; it's not purely what they want. Openness doesn't mean that you are doing purely what the other person wants. Their wantingness may not be particularly accurate. They may have all sorts of ulterior motives and neurotic aspects to their desire, and often it's not recommended to encourage that. So you just work along with what's valuable there.

5

The Bardo of Illusory Body

We have been talking about bardo at a very personal, as well as a more general, experiential level. The third bardo, the illusory body bardo, is extremely experiential and particularly personal. The illusory body bardo, or body of illusion, starts from the river of passion and desire of the human realm. Such passion is very intimate. Everything is experienced purely at the naked flesh level—as though our clothing, masks, and skin had been peeled off. And this very personal, sensitive, and touchy aspect continues with our state of being all the time. We react to situations emotionally, and these emotions are so sharp and penetrating that we can't bear to see them.

It is very sharp. But at the same time, because of that experience of sharpness and because the intimacy of desire and emotions is so intense; automatically, of course, we put on the natural devices of masks, skin, and clothing. That is the problem. The minute we begin to put on masks or clothing, we have second thoughts. After all, we *do* like to experience these passions and emotions in their naked quality—but at the same time, it seems to be more manageable, pleasurable, to put some masks or clothing over them. There's that kind of ambiguity. In other words, we are not quite certain where we are at. On the one hand, we want to indulge, to dive into this experience completely. On the other hand, it is too embarrassing, even to ourselves, to do that. Having some kind of mask is good, from that point of view. That kind of uncertainty is an ongoing problem in life.

In talking about the human realm, in connection with the bardo of illusory body, a lot of problems and conflicts come from preconceptions and expectations. We have expectations of achievement, expectations of fulfillment. We remember that driving force, the energetic and speedy experience of the world of the asuras, the jealous gods. There's the nostalgic quality of wishing to go back to that level, where everything happened so efficiently. But in the case of the human realm, nothing happens very efficiently. We would like to imagine something before we get into it, and then we would like to create situations out of our imagination. We push that imaginary home, that imaginary convenience or luxury. We try to re-create them, to produce them physically as actual situations of now. The problem is that we are not able to achieve that, which brings us frustration.

Another factor involved with the human realm is choice. Choice is based on irritation. Without irritation there wouldn't be any choice but a choice between one particular category and another. In the human realm, for instance, there is a choice between the personal experience of analyzing oneself, or intellectualizing oneself, and the personal experience of instinct. Depending on a person's situation, one will automatically tend to pick one of those two. We may feel uncertain unless there's an explanation or analysis. Or else, in a situation based on instinct, analyzing it causes the experience to become uninspiring. Analysis doesn't allow any room for inspiration; one would like to have a pure state of passion.

These seem to be problems that run right through the human realm, that we all face. But then how do we work with them? How do we see a glimpse of transcending them in terms of bardo experience? When we talk of illusory body, it is obviously illusory, not the physical tangible body. It is a mind/body situation always.

This illusory body is based on a very healthy attitude: these confusions and polarities are being worked with at a realistic level in which we are willing to face the illusory aspect, the mirage quality, that hallucinatory quality.

So the human realm and its bardo experience has a hallucinatory quality, or illusory body. This illusory body is precisely the transparent nature of experiences: that we see, yet we don't see. We see something, yet at the same time we are not quite certain whether we are seeing the background or the scenery itself. Uncertain hallucination, ultimate hallucination. And that ultimate hallucination acts as a bardo experience. It is the choice between real and unreal—is this illusory body illusion itself, or is it pure imagination? One begins to question whether the illusion or mirage exists or not. And a person again begins to be involved with this threshold between the transparency of the figure and the solidity of its background. One begins to have a very confused attitude about this. It is exactly the same thing as we were talking about yesterday and the day before—the uncertainty as to truth and falsity. You are not quite certain whether you are actually getting somewhere or whether you are being fooled by something.

That uncertainty always happens, of course. We could use the analogy of our being here together: we are not quite certain why we are here; we are not quite certain why I am talking or why others are listening—but at the same time, it happens that way. It may have happened in the magical sense or the accidental sense, but it did happen, we can't deny that. It is quite certain, as far as we are concerned, that we are not going to wake up and find ourselves in our parents' house with breakfast ready for us—that's not going to happen. We are here. You may not know why you are here, what the hell you are doing practicing Buddhist meditation and listening to a Tibetan freak. But it is happening nevertheless.

That peak point of not being certain why, but things just happening, is the bardo experience of the human realm. Again, it carries the same sense of possibilities: I'm not quite certain why I am here, but if I pass that level of uncertainty, maybe after all there is something—or maybe after all there isn't something. It is the very threshold of not knowing who's fooling whom—but at the same time, something is fooling something. That foolishness is the illusory quality, of course, not knowing. There's nothing tangible at all. It is completely loose, irritatingly loose. I mean, it is worth getting aggressive about it. It is like trying to pin up a poster, to paste it on the wall—but somehow the wall doesn't exist and the poster doesn't exist. It shifts all the time; you can't fix it.

Realize this foolishness of who's fooling whom, which is the illusory body, the bardo experience of the human realm. It is desire which drove us into this particular experience, and which is the background of the human realm. In other words, we find ourselves here because the river of human consciousness, human passion, drove us here. And so we find ourselves here. But at the same time, having found ourselves here and then not knowing what we are doing is the peak experience of the bardo of illusory body, which is very important to realize.

The illusory body is made out of both yes and no; it is both negative and positive. You are not quite certain where it is, how it is—it is ambiguous, uncertain. At the same time, there is a general feeling or perception of the transparent quality of the body or, you could say, realizing the foolishness of us. It is like the analogy of us being here together and fooling each other: that uncertainty or vagueness, not knowing exactly whether you are going or coming, is the illusory aspect. But I wouldn't say this is confusion in the pejorative sense. It is seeing the abstract quality of nature as it is—*maya,* the dance of illusion.

The actual practice in everyday life is just to acknowledge that transparent uncertain quality as it is. There's no point in trying to stay back or run away from it—in fact you can't; you are in it. And you can't force its development either; it has its own pattern. The only way to work or deal with this bardo experience of the human realm is just to proceed along. Depending on your previous training and meditation experience—or your training in aggression and passion—you just go along. It's the karmic pattern: you got onto this particular train, and the train is going to go on and on and on. There's no point in panicking. You just have to accept it and face it and go along with it. All the bardo concepts that have evolved have that unchangeable quality, that natural powerful quality. Once you are in that state, you can't change it. The only way you can deal with it is to see its background quality.

STUDENT: I've heard you use the term *mind/body* before, and I'm still struggling to grasp this. Is it comparable to the concept of shunyata?

TRUNGPA RINPOCHE: In a sense it is comparable to the idea of shunyata, but the whole idea of mind/body is that every perception has its solidity as well as its loose quality. In other words, you can't fight it or destroy it, and you can't embrace it or cuddle it. It's a loose pattern of perception. Our version of body.

STUDENT: What do you mean by background quality or background?

TRUNGPA RINPOCHE: It seems that once you have gotten into something, the idea of undoing it is very much based on the idea of panic. So the idea is just to accept, ultimate acceptance of the whole situation. At the same time, asking questions doesn't help. The possibility is that once you begin to ask questions— "Why is this so?," for example, or "Why are we here?"—we are just here and questioning doesn't clarify it at all. In fact, it confuses you more, unless you are actually willing to accept that you are treading on this particular area, you are eating this food, you are sleeping under this particular roof—it is so. It's the unchangeable quality of situations.

There is the possibility that people might think: "I'm not going to accept it; I'm going to change it." But there again, you are involved with another experience—you are *in* here, and you can only change *from* here to something else. So you're still governed by the situation where you are, and your changing can only take place by relating with that place and accepting it. It's a question of seeing the whole background as it is and accepting it.

In other words, in human life, if you feel that you have made a mistake, you don't try to undo the past or the present, but you just accept where you are at and work from there. Tremendous openness as to where you are is necessary. This applies to the practice of meditation, for instance. A person should learn to meditate on the spot, in the given moment, rather than thinking, "I'm going to give up my job. When I reach pension age, I'm going to retire and receive a pension, and I'm going to build my house in Hawaii or the middle of India, or maybe the Gobi Desert, and *then* I'm going to enjoy myself. I'll live a life of solitude and then I'll really meditate." Things never happen that way.

STUDENT: Is physical pain an instance of this particular bardo?

TRUNGPA RINPOCHE: Using the analogy of mind/body, usually physical pain is translated by the mind; mental pain has been translated into physical pain. So often there's not really such a thing as actual physical pain per se; it's mind pain, mental pain.

STUDENT: If somebody is meditating and having a lot of confused distorted thoughts, would you consider it good meditation to regard everything as really not there, solid but kind of floaty?

TRUNGPA RINPOCHE: Well, if you are clinging or trying to solidify thoughts, then the basic idea of meditation is lost completely, because you fail to see the illusory quality of thoughts. But you see, fundamentally, in terms of meditation, such ideas as good meditation and bad meditation are a child's game. They don't exist. Meditation is just so. Once you try to put it into categories then you are already lost. Meditation becomes a giant thought process in itself. But if a person is able to open completely to the situation of meditation, then anything which happens within that realm is usually transparent or translucent anyway.

STUDENT: If you feel close to a bardo experience, then there's really nothing you can do except try not to clothe it or put projections on it?

TRUNGPA RINPOCHE: Just go along and don't panic. Just go along.

STUDENT: When you're in the awakened state of mind and there's no identification of the ego with the mind, is the mind still there? Do thoughts come? Are the mind processes still there?

TRUNGPA RINPOCHE: That depends on the level of confidence in yourself. At the beginning, mind is very much there. Meditation is a mental game to start with, but at a certain stage you begin to accept and you begin to relax more and go along with the pattern of practice. Then there is less mind and more space. (I am talking in terms of the grasping quality of mind, in this case, rather than consciousness or intelligence.)

S: So the proper attitude to meditation is that you just sit down and there you are, and everything sort of goes through?

TR: Exactly, yes. Just sitting there. Absolutely doing nothing.

STUDENT: If the mind is as important as the body—if you are here and your mind is in New York, for instance—then how can you be sure where you are?

TRUNGPA RINPOCHE: In exactly the same way that you are here, because your attitude to things is still here. Whether the temperature is hot or cold, your mind attitude of being here still continues. But the imaginary quality of memories goes along as well.

S: But at a given moment you can be somewhere else.

TR: You could be, yes but you are still here as well. You see, mind has such an expansive range: all kinds of memories, including childhood memories or memories of several thousands of years ago, as well as presently being here.

STUDENT: Are you not tending to solidify our thoughts by answering our questions?

TRUNGPA RINPOCHE: I think so, yes. We have to speak the language of confusion—that is what has been happening. But once you begin to go along with it, then it is possible that the language of confusion, the language of samsara, begins to be seen as absolute truth.

S: Then we wouldn't be here?

TR: Then you wouldn't be here. Our method is very primitive; that's the only way, it seems.

STUDENT: Are we living in a bardo state now, and if we are, is this part of the illusory mind that you're talking about?

TRUNGPA RINPOCHE: Definitely.

S: Where does the awakened state of mind relate to this?

TR: Within illusion. If we are able to understand the illusory quality as it is, then that is a glimpse of the awake state as well, at the same time. In other words, we are operating on the illusory body level along with some seed of wakefulness, otherwise we wouldn't be discussing the subject at all. The intelligence to talk about this subject, work on this subject, meditate with it, is the awakened state of mind.

STUDENT: How do you put together the illusory state and the structure of Buddhist thought—which lays all sorts of trips, on me anyway, about higher states and goals and the aim of relieving all suffering and so forth. It seems to me that there is a rigidity, or something concrete there. Yet all the practices that lead you there are so illusory, as you say. How could I come to terms with what I consider to be a complete dichotomy?

TRUNGPA RINPOCHE: I suppose the only way to relate with that, or to understand it, is purely by not trying to categorize it. That's where the acceptance comes from. The methods or techniques put out are dualistic ones, illusory ones; but at the same time, the inspiration for these techniques is the inspiration of awake. So the way to work with it is not to put things into pigeonholes anymore at all—a noncaring quality as to whether it's illusion or not.

S: They coexist, then.

TR: That is so, yes. But we are not trying to put them into categories.

STUDENT: Is this like saying that when you meditate, after a while the thoughts are still there, that they'll always be there?

TRUNGPA RINPOCHE: Exactly, yes.

S: But they won't be there?

TR: Exactly, yes. That's a good one.

STUDENT: Rinpoche, the buddhas are often called "conquerors," or *jina*. What is it that they conquer?

TRUNGPA RINPOCHE: They conquer the limitless range of self-deceptions. It has been said that they destroy the seven great mountains of conceptualization. This comes up in the *madhyamika* philosophy of Nagarjuna. In a dialogue called *Vajra Spark*, the vajra spark destroys nine gigantic mountain ranges, which are a succession of mountain ranges one after another, each protecting the previous mountains—it's the succession of self-deceptions.

STUDENT: During meditation, if at one point you're seeing the solidity of thought and at another point you see the space in between them and the looseness, and you're not doing anything, isn't there still that witnessing quality?

TRUNGPA RINPOCHE: There is that witnessing quality, yes.

S: Should one try not to be a witness?

TR: You don't try to do anything, you just accept and go along with it. That's the whole point, you see. Then, at a certain stage, you begin to realize that any techniques or frameworks that you put things into are also foolish things. So you drop them. But until you actually see that foolish quality, you just go along with being a fool.

STUDENT: With the bardo of illusory body, for the first time I get a sense of its being pejorative—with the other two bardos I didn't get that sense. Why is that?

TRUNGPA RINPOCHE: You see, the whole point is that we are trying to speak the language of samsara. In speaking of the inspiration opposite to all these bardo experiences, we are speaking purely in terms of duality. Therefore it is not an absolute answer in any case. In this sense, even mentioning freedom at all, teaching at all, dharma at all, is a pejorative thing, fundamentally. It is not an absolute thing, because we are talking about it. We are panicking in some sense by talking of the teachings.

STUDENT: What is the difference between samsara and bardo?

TRUNGPA RINPOCHE: They seem to be the same. *Samsara* is a general term which means a sort of whirlpool, a continual circle of confusion. One confusion sows the seed of another confusion, so you go round and round and round. Bardo is the same kind of experience. But at the same time, there is the possibility of stepping out of the confusion of samsara, as well as getting some understanding of the bardo experience and transcending it. It is the same thing. Bardo experience could continue all the time: these peak experiences of illusory body, jealousy, and the eternity of the god realm could continue to come up. Then you go back to the confused level—and you repeat that again and again *and* again.

STUDENT: It seems to me that as long as all these things are happening, there's a need for meditation.

TRUNGPA RINPOCHE: Yes. Bardo experience is very important to know about. For one thing, nothing is regarded as some unexpected revelation coming up. A general tendency in meditation is that people come to these particular highlights of experience; and not knowing about these highlights of experience, they regard them as revelation. Having understood bardo experience, or *knowing* bardo experience, removes this trip of a sudden glimpse of enlightenment, which causes a lot of people to tend to freak out. They have a satori experience, and since then their life has been changed. And they try to hold on to it—which is the most dangerous, lethal aspect of all. Having understood bardo experience, then such a sudden glimpse could be associated with a particular state of mind, whether you belong to the hell realm or hungry ghost realm, whatever it may be. So nothing is regarded as extraordinary; it's just one of the patterns.

STUDENT: Is bardo a breakthrough?

TRUNGPA RINPOCHE: Yes and no. It depends. Bardo experience could be a breakthrough, but at the same time it is not a big deal. It is not ultimate freedom, necessarily. There's something funny about people saying that their lives have been completely changed; for instance, that since the first time they took acid or had some kind of experience, their lives have been completely transformed and changed. That brings up the idea that they want to discontinue what they are. They don't like what they were, but they like what they are now. Bardo understanding brings them into the very earth-grounding quality that nothing is changed before bardo experience, and nothing is changed after bardo experience—the experience is simply gone through. That is a very important point. Bardo experiences are not transformations of your life; they are continuity. And that continuity takes the shape both of highlights and of ordinary situations as well.

S: Bardo could be a very impressive peak experience or it could also be just a regular little wave?

TR: Yes. But either way, nothing is regarded as a complete change. That is very important. The continuity of the process of what you are cannot be escaped. You can't regard achieving something as abandoning your bad self and latching onto the good one.

STUDENT: Is the level of intensity at all revelant?

TRUNGPA RINPOCHE: If you are involved with confusion or with hope and fear more intensively, then that kind of bardo experience comes up; whereas if you are involved with the practice of awake, with meditation practice and other attempts to see reality or the awakened state of mind—then that kind of peak experience develops with the same intensity. So bardo is just a building-up of energy—it could be either negative energy or positive energy. The intensity is the same. It really depends on how involved you are with your pattern of life before you have the experience of bardo.

S: So intensity is not really relevant?

TR: No, intensity is not relevant.

STUDENT: You mentioned the word *freedom* several times. Would you define it for us?

TRUNGPA RINPOCHE: Freedom is the possibility of being generous. You can afford to open yourself and walk on the path easily—without defending yourself or watching yourself or being self-conscious all the time. It is the absence of ego, the absence of self-consciousness. That is ultimate freedom. The absence of self-consciousness brings generosity. You don't have to watch for dangers or be careful that you are going too far or too slow. It is the confidence which is freedom, rather than breaking free from chains of imprisonment, exactly. Developing confidence and breaking out of psychological, internal imprisonment brings freedom naturally. In other words, it is generosity.

S: You would have to have both self-discipline and detachment in order for that freedom not to turn into simple self-indulgence. Is that not true?

TR: If you begin to indulge in self, then you also have to keep that self-indulgence safe, which automatically becomes self-conscious—it ceases to be freedom, anyway.

STUDENT: You've spoken several times about space. I remember your saying that people wanted to fill up space with material objects, filling rooms with chairs and things. I was wondering if you also fill up empty space with thoughts—say, conversation? I'm sort of afraid of empty space, and I notice that when I'm in empty space I begin to talk.

TRUNGPA RINPOCHE: Well, space is everywhere, isn't it? If you have any kind of activity going on, that activity must have some space in order to move about. So space is anywhere, everywhere, all the time. That space, or openness for that matter, is the room in which creative process could develop. For creative process to be possible, you have to have space. For instance, you can't grow a plant without room—the more room you have, that much more could the plant develop.

STUDENT: Rinpoche, in meditation, if one is plunged into colors and diagrams and images—not thinking, but just in it—would that be hallucination, illusion, or reality?

TRUNGPA RINPOCHE: What do you think?

S: I was just there. I don't know. There weren't any thoughts.

TR: I would say, it is the reality of illusion.

S: Where does hallucination come into it, then?

TR: That *is* hallucination. But there's nothing wrong with that. It is so. It is hallucination and it is real and it is vision—as far as it goes. I mean, that much we could look into. There's no really fixed, ultimate, one-hundred-percent or two-hundred-percent answer to reality. Reality depends on each situation.

S : Where does that fit into the bardo experience?

T R : Well, there *is* a possibility of building peak experience in meditation practice. If you begin to see some particular big experience or breakthrough, that is bardo experience. But bardo experience does not necessarily take place in meditation only. It takes place in everyday life as well, when you think you have a big breakthrough. For instance, if you have a big argument with somebody, which could be regarded as your peak experience, there will be the element of bardo in it. It could be called a bardo experience. So bardo experience doesn't have to be only a meditation experience; it could happen in everyday life.

6

The Bardo of Dreams

The animal realm, or the confusion of being utterly involved with self-consciousness, seems to be next destination. There's a certain point that we should be clear about—the very word *confusion*. Usually when we talk of confusion, it is just simply not being able to make up your mind, such as whether you should belong to that or to this. But in the case of fundamental confusion, you are proud of your confusion. You feel you have something to hold on to, and you do not want to give in or to yield. You are extremely proud of your confusion, extremely self-righteous about it, and you would even fight for it. Your could present the validity of your confusion, and you could also present your pride in that confusion as a valid thing, an absolute thing.

This type of confusion happens on a larger scale a great deal, as well. In particular, if there is a notion of validating confusion, that means there is also a tendency to overpower others. So power over others is one of the other factors involved in the animal realm. You are aggressively sure of what you are, and because of that you would like to influence other people and draw them into your empire, your territory. That is the meaning of power over others. Such power could happen politically or spiritually. It could happen spiritually in the romantic idea of the guru, or teacher, as a powerful person who can act on that power, who can relate to people and overpower them. Politically, it is that as a leader, you have fixed patterns of ideas as to what the society or the social pattern should be, and you put forth your ideas and your doctrines. Fundamentally, this approach is more a matter of confusion than of pride or egohood. It is confusion because one is not quite certain what one is; but the very fact of that uncertainty provides an extra boost to push forward. The basic twist of ego is that such uncertainty doesn't become humble, but instead becomes proud. If you don't see the situation as it is—it doesn't matter whether you know what to do or not—you just push through and present a show of force. And accidentally something happens—something clicks. Then you take over.

That tendency to overpower through confusion is the dominant characteristic of the animal realm. It is like attacking a tiger. The more you attack a tiger, that much more does the tiger become egocentric and aggressive, because the tiger is not quite certain whether you are going to kill him or he is going to kill you. He's not quite certain, but he's taking advantage of that confusion, that ignorance. There is no reason a wounded tiger would be more aggressive than an ordinary tiger, a fresh young tiger; or, for that matter, there is no reason old tigers would become more aggressive than young ones. They may know that they don't have sharp teeth or sharp claws anymore and that this act of aggression could become suicidal—but they still do it. That kind of crying and laughing at the same time, that pride, is the confusion of the animal realm. You are not quite certain whether a particular person is crying because of his or her humiliation, or whether this person is laughing because of his or her sinister opportunities.

That mixture of crying and laughing is confusion's quality—absolutely the whole thing is confused. And that confusion seems to be the peak experience of bardo in the animal realm—the dream bardo. A lot of people may expect that in the dream bardo we might discuss how to play games with our dreams—how to levitate and do astral traveling, visit our friends, visit unknown worlds, survey all this unknown territory. But if you look at the dream world as it is, there's no room for astral travel. It is the hard truth, the obvious truth, that dreaming—although very creative—is based on the uncertainty between day experience and night experience. You actually are not quite certain whether you are sleeping or not. As soon as you realize that you are asleep, that you are dreaming and having a terrifying dream experience—it immediately dissipates and you begin to awake. The nightmare begins to wake you up.

The dream bardo is the confusion of not knowing what you are—whether you are a gentle person or an aggressive person. You are not making an absolute reconciliation, but you are just trying to do something. Dreams very much reflect the day experience into the sleep experience. Metaphorically, we could talk of dreams not only as sleep experiences alone, but in terms of the dreamlike quality of the daylight experience, in which we are uncertain what is real and what is unreal. In other words, the dream bardo is a way of seeing yourself in that particular uncertainty. Whether you are absolutely weak or absolutely powerful, absolutely aggressive or absolutely peaceful—between those experiences there is a dreamlike quality, a hallucinatory quality. I wouldn't say exactly hallucinatory, but there is a quality of ultimate confusion, absolute vagueness. I'm sure a lot of us have experienced that. In a drug experience, for instance, you are not quite certain whether you are completely able to see the subtleties of things as they are—there is a sharpness to the color and the overall experience, but on the other hand, it has an imaginary and confused quality as well. You are not quite certain whether you are going crazy or whether you are actually seeing something. That kind of ambiguity is also a particular source of dream bardo.

Dream bardo also has to do with the confusion involved in making decisions. Often, a lot of us try to make decisions: "Should I be doing that or should I be doing this? Should I commit myself into this or shouldn't I commit myself into this?" There is uncertainty, ambiguity, confusion. That confusion of making a decision between two options involves a certain living experience of the two polarities: "Should I give up my job or should I stick to my job? If I give up my job, I will be good and free and I will no longer be bound to that particular commitment. On the other hand, if I give up my job, then I won't have any source of insurance. I'll be purely living a life of chance, trying to find some means of survival." For that matter, there are all sorts of decisions. "Should I involve myself with this particular religious organization and attain enlightenment, or should I slow myself down and just try to relive what I've been trying to do in the past?" All sorts of decisions come up, and those kinds of decisions come up because of confusion—obviously. Fundamentally, confusion is based on not knowing the actual situation, not being able to see the meeting point of the two—"Should I or shouldn't I?" I wouldn't exactly say the answer lies between them, but the actual experience lies between them. Experience lies between "should" and "shouldn't."

That no-man's-land quality of bardo is the answer, in some ways; it is the way of breaking through. Further on, once you are able to see that particular precision of the in-between experience, that no-man's-land experience, you may begin to see that "you should" and "you shouldn't" have been childish. You can either do that or do this, but there is no *permanent* experience, no permanent security, involved. You begin to see that some kind of basic core of continuity is taking place, rather than trying to change from one black to another white. So confusion and tension, in this case, are extremely useful and helpful. Without that, there would be no pattern of seeing the situation, or learning process, at all. In other words, confusion and uncertainty are like the letters or initials for each step that you have to go through. That is the bardo experience of the dream world. That dream bardo that you go through, you walk through, is an extremely important and very personal experience.

STUDENT: If you make a decision, it is going to bring you tension because you don't know how it is going to work out, whether it's going to be good or bad. Do you just go along and continue to accept it?

TRUNGPA RINPOCHE: You see, ultimately decisions don't come out in terms of yes and no, black and white. The ultimate answer, so to speak, would say you're right but at the same time you are wrong.

S: So that brings up the tension?

TR: That *releases* tension, the ultimate tension. If you are involved with something, and if you reject or accept it absolutely, one hundred percent, then the tension is going to remain all the time. There is no way of solving the problem of tension by making black-and-white decisions, in other words. The only way of transcending that tension is through the acceptance of all aspects.

S: That's in the future someplace. Immediately, you can't have this lack of tension—you have to wait for the situation to clear itself.

TR: Exactly, yes. Nothing is going to be a magical sedative. But strangely enough, once you begin to accept that, then half of the problem has been solved.

STUDENT: You seem to stress that the tension coming out of indecision is more detrimental than the disaster which may arise from making the wrong decision. For instance, in your book *Born in Tibet,* you had to decide which of three passes to go through.[5] I would have been in absolute stitches, because there would really be no way to judge. Then you made the decision as to which way to go, and you did the right thing. In that moment, do you also accept that it may *not* be the right thing?

TRUNGPA RINPOCHE: That sounds good. Yes, exactly. I suppose you could boil all this down to saying that as long as there is no expectation of magic, then everything is in its proper order.

I wouldn't say everything is perfect; I would say everything is in its absolute order. You see, once you begin to ward off something, thinking that you are going to be the perfect decision-maker, then, like a lot of politicians we know, it works in the opposite way, because you are exposing yourself to criticism, to negative, unhealthy situations, and to chaos.

S: How about in relation to meditation, where you said you accept the possibility that you won't get anywhere at all—or you might, who knows; I don't know. It seems like I've sat and sat and sat and all I have gotten is a sore ass.

TR: Yes? That is the essence of what we have been talking about all the time, in fact. It seems that you might go crazy or you might attain something.

S: I don't worry about going crazy. It just seems dull. A lot of people sit around in these discussion groups and everybody says, "Oh, I had this great experience. I met this lama and all of a sudden I was . . . it took me three weeks to get back down to earth." But I just see people and they say hello and I say hello. And I ask you a question and you say, "Mm-hmm."

TR: You see, the point is that you can't have a one-hundred-percent absolute waiting period at all. Whenever there is any kind of process going on, there are always ups and downs—little flickers of doubts and little flickers of understanding. This goes on and on and on. Maybe we don't need dramatic flashes of bardo experience, but detailed bardo experiences are equally good. And these little details, which we generally ignore, or little problems that come up, are the only way. It could start from the absolutely insignificant level—the very fact of your relationship to your ass is in itself very interesting.

STUDENT: Rinpoche, what is the root meaning of these three words: *magic, miraculous,* and *miracle?*

TRUNGPA RINPOCHE: Well, I suppose you could look that up in a dictionary.

S: No, not from the dictionary.

TR: The Oxford dictionary? It's generally pretty clever in giving definitions. But I think the fundamental idea of miracle, or magic, is having something that you don't believe in, in order to prove your belief. That is, your belief is challenged by its opposite. If you expect the world to be this way, downside up, and if you suddenly see it upside down, that's a miracle. There are numerous acts of magic and miracles that we have heard of and that we know about, such as water changing into fire and all sorts of little details like that. But somehow they also bring a kind of faith or trust which is based purely on mystery. You don't bother to understand anything, but you are willing to submit to that mystery. For instance, you are not interested in studying how an aircraft works mechanically, but you are still willing to fly. It is that kind of laziness: such and such a thing works, but I just want to get service; I don't want to go into the details of how it works. That seems to be the most damaging attitude of all: that we expect things to work purely because we want them to, rather than because they are.

Fundamental miracles usually only occur at the situational level. For instance, there is the miracle of our being here together. Such an incident takes place that I came all the way from Tibet, and generally every individual here has their own story about how they happen by accident to be here. That type of miracle works continuously, all the time. It happens. You can't change it. You can't divert the pattern of that miracle into another one, because the miracle has already happened.

STUDENT: You said that the acceptance of the situation solved half of the problem of making a decision. I wonder if the other half—actually having to go ahead and decide—grows out of the acceptance.

TRUNGPA RINPOCHE: Well, the acceptance is faith and gentleness; therefore, it could be said to be compassion. Once you see the situation as it is, then you just involve yourself in it and it takes you along. In fact, you can tell what the end is going to be. That is developing egoless common sense. Egoless common sense is not based on "because-of-anything," but it is based on "it-will-be-so." You could project your future quite accurately or take the right path quite accurately if you had that general egoless common sense. With such precision and clarity, as well as egolessness, you are not dwelling on hope or fear. Then things take place naturally.

S: Can things take place completely passively in that way? I read a passage in the scriptures comparing wisdom and skillful means, and it said that to abide in wisdom without skillful means would be a one-sided nirvana at best. I want to know if there's an active side to the picture.

TR: Of course, the physical situation of committing yourself and taking actual symbolic gestures, so to speak, is itself an earth-grounding quality.

S: Can that active side be described? Is it moving like a cow? Is it leaping? Is it being like a warrior?

TR: Yes, definitely. It is a warrior type of experience. I mean chance, of course, all the time taking chances. You have to be brave.

S: Does a warrior go back and forth? Does he or she sometimes just sit and watch? That image of warrior doesn't seem to go along with the attitude of passive acceptance necessary for seeing situations.

TR: Acceptance doesn't mean not committing yourself, just dwelling on the idea of such and such. It is accepting and then putting yourself into that situation of acceptance. That also allows space. You don't rush into something completely because you had a flash—you take a portion and then you eat it and digest it and then you eat the next portion.

STUDENT: What should one's attitude be toward possible mistakes?

TRUNGPA RINPOCHE: It's no good trying to look at it philosophically and trying to comfort yourself. But it is apparent that mistakes also have a point to them. As far as the warrior's steps go, there is no defeat at all, there are no mistakes at all. Both positive and negative are the path, the general pattern. Any negative experience which occurs is an invitation or vanguard of positive experiences, as well. It just happens that way.

STUDENT: In any experience, how much of that experience would you say we have control over in terms of will? Give me, if you can, a percentage there.

TRUNGPA RINPOCHE: That's a rather dangerous point. When we talk about will, it is purely based on ego's terms of benefit, or whether ego is willing to leap out and sacrifice itself. But there is some kind of faith, rather than will, which is seeing things as they are. Then you are not afraid of acting. It is an intuitive way of living and relating with situations. That kind of faith or determination, in fact, dominates the whole process. It's the most important point of all. It is the fuel to drive yourself.

STUDENT: What does being brave mean?

TRUNGPA RINPOCHE: Not looking back.

STUDENT: How can you tell when you're just being greedy? You may be pushing and you don't want to give up because you think you are attaining something. But you are being greedy and you're going too fast. At the same time, you are afraid you may be going crazy—so you try to knock yourself down. You may drink some alcohol or something like that. So you alternate between being greedy and pushing on and being afraid and trying to turn off.

TRUNGPA RINPOCHE: Turning off seems to be dangerous. If you are driving a hundred and six miles an hour on the highway and suddenly you realize you are going too fast—if you turn off your car, that's a cop-out.

STUDENT: I like to think not in terms of decision but in terms of direction. Is there such a thing as recognizing a direction? For example, that you are here and that we are here is a direction—we happen to be converging at one point. Is there such a thing as recognizing your own direction?

TRUNGPA RINPOCHE: Of course you have to have a close relationship with the direction. In this case, when we talk about direction it is just the direction itself, without being self-conscious about it. Once you are able to realize that particular direction, the path is the goal and the goal is the path—and travel is also the path, as well as the traveler. All things are one. Once you are able to see that, to have that kind of relationship, then it happens as a natural process.

STUDENT: The way you use the word *warrior,* the way Don Juan uses the word *warrior,* and the way we've been relating to warriors altogether, is in terms of fighting. For instance, saying that "a warrior is brave" means not to look back, and to step out toward those things which are coming to meet you, also has a sense of fighting—as opposed to the more passive way of being open to see. Don Juan seems to say that to be a warrior is a lesser way than the way of the seer, because the man who sees puts things in relationship to seeing.

TRUNGPA RINPOCHE: Yes, that seems to be absolutely fitting. The warrior is a practitioner like the bodhisattvas; the seer is a man of wisdom like the buddhas, who see the situation as it is but don't have to enter into manipulative actions of any kind at all. In the case of the warrior, there's still duality. Even though it may not be the duality of awareness of oneself as ego, there is still the duality of action and the object of action. That's where bravery comes in—not to hesitate because you see action as it is; not to interpret in terms of concepts, but try to work with action itself and go along and along. But somehow that doesn't mean struggle. Absolute warriors, ideal warriors, don't struggle. They just proceed along because they know their work, they know their abilities. They don't question it. Their actual inspiration comes from the situation as it is. If the situation becomes more and more overwhelming and powerful, that much more energy goes along with it. It's like judo: you use the situation as your power rather than trying to fight with it.

STUDENT: A lot of times I think, "Well, why do it?" A situation comes up and I'm inspired to act, but then I get a flash that says, "Well, what if I leave it alone, don't do it?"

TRUNGPA RINPOCHE: The point is that the situation is there anyway and you do something. That's a natural process. You don't do anything *for* something. That would be like questioning the nature of fire as burning and the nature of water as wet. But you do it because of the situation. You don't have to do something *for* anything at all; you just happen to do it. It's a natural process, an absolutely spontaneous process. That's the difference between the ordinary puritanical practice of discipline as opposed to the bodhisattva's practice of discipline. The bodhisattva is working along with situations as things happen. You don't force things or work because you want to achieve something. It is like the natural growth of plants. If there's enough rain and sunshine, the plants will grow; if there isn't enough rain or sunshine, the plants won't grow. It's as natural a process as that.

S: But why do it? A plant can't turn away from the sun, but it seems as if some part of me can turn away from an action.

TR: It would be like telling a plant to go from one area to another area and reestablish itself because it's a better situation. This wouldn't happen to a plant.

S: We really have no choice in this—the situation takes over.

TR: I wouldn't say the situation takes you over, but you are working with the situation. And in this case, if you are completely open and completely one with it, then having a choice or not having a choice is irrelevant. It doesn't apply anymore.

S: You don't make a choice?

TR: I would say you don't don't make a choice, or you do make a choice.

S: Why not just make random choices in that case, and then live with whatever random choice you make?

TR: Why choice at all, if it happens to be random? I mean, why choice anyway?

S: Well, we always think we have a choice, but we very often don't realize that we don't.

TR: That's what we *think,* but we haven't actually experienced it. We haven't seen the other side of the coin at all.

STUDENT: If you're meditating and it's becoming very painful and very hard to continue, would being a warrior mean keeping on with a course of action that's very difficult and painful?

TRUNGPA RINPOCHE: Well, you see, you don't evaluate the situation. You don't regard a situation as good or bad, but you just go along with the situation. So endurance doesn't come into the picture. When we talk about endurance, it is related with our physical sensibilities, our individual feedback—"If I hit somebody, would my fist hurt?"—that kind of relationship. But in this case, it doesn't happen in that way.

STUDENT: If you are experiencing extreme tension, frustration, and difficulty, would that be a clue that you're on the wrong path? Would you consequently change it, or should you persist in what you are doing?

TRUNGPA RINPOCHE: You could continue what you are doing and you wouldn't ask questions. But that doesn't mean you have to be completely instinctive, like an animal. That's another idea, which could be misleading.

S: That brings will back in again. There is a force in us that we define as will.

TR: There is, there is. You're *willing* to let yourself be in that situation intelligently. You expose yourself to that situation and that situation then plays back. It happens, so it is both wisdom and compassion, wisdom, and action all together.

S: So *will* becomes *willingness?*

TR: The generosity of openness, yes.

STUDENT: When you're a warrior, don't you tend to forget that other people are warriors too? Isn't there a danger of getting lost in your own actions and feeling superior?

TRUNGPA RINPOCHE: I don't think these complications would occur if you were a complete warrior. A warrior doesn't just mean being blunt, but being wise or intelligent as well. You would appreciate others. Because you've opened yourself completely and you have the intelligence and precision of seeing the situation as it is, if another warrior comes along the path, you would acknowledge them—as well as enemies who come along the path, possibly very devious enemies.

S: Then isn't there the trap of always looking for justification for what you are doing?

TR: You don't look for justification. If you look for justification, that means you are not communicating properly, because you have to refer back. For a moment you have to close yourself inwardly, and then you expose again. Such an alternation of that and this doesn't happen in the case of the warrior. Instead, it's an ongoing process; you do not have to refer back and work out a strategy anymore. The strategy happens through the situation as it is. The situation speaks for you.

STUDENT: When you have some obstacle or weakness in your nature that you recognize, should you take that as part of the situation?

TRUNGPA RINPOCHE: Yes, exactly. That is the situation.

S: And whatever judgment you have about a situation is the situation also?

TR: I wouldn't say judgment. Whatever situation happens presents itself to you—beyond judgment.

S: Are thoughts included?

TR: Perceptions of situations are. Yes, definitely. But this has nothing to do with judgment.

STUDENT: I'm not understanding the power aspect. What's the relationship between the blind quality of forging ahead and the power of the warrior? They seem to be related, but I can't put them together.

TRUNGPA RINPOCHE: Do you mean, what is the relationship between the blind quality and the warrior quality? Naturally, whenever there is a tendency to refer back to oneself, that is the power aspect of building something up because you would like to overpower others. In order to overpower others, you have to develop strong qualities in yourself, and that completely undermines the actual situation happening there. Power knows no logic; power just operates. If anything gets in its way or challenges it, the natural instinct is just to smash it rather than to try to develop a relationship with it. It has a sort of blind quality and is a pure ongoing process based on some central theme or characteristic. So it is very much referred back to *me:* "If that happens, then what happens to *me*? And therefore, how should I act for *my* benefit alone?"

It's like the two ideas of compassion we discussed earlier. One is that *you* would like to see somebody happy; the other is that you help somebody because *they* need you, which is a different idea altogether. The first type of compassion is based on overpowering, undermining the colorful and beautiful aspect of situations, and trying to mold them into your shape, your pattern; whereas the other is just purely relating with the situation as it is and working along with it, which is the warrior quality. The warrior has to make every move of his or her practice of fighting in accordance with that without failing. If he reflects back on himself for one moment, one flash of a second; if he reflects back on his territory, his ego, his survival, then he's going to get killed, because he wasn't quick enough to relate purely with things as they are.

S: If we act only in response to people's needs—if we wait to be asked—will we still have plenty to do?

TR: You wouldn't wait to be asked. You don't have to put yourself in such a formal situation.

S: No, but sometimes we act because the situation obviously requires help, and sometimes we act because we project a need onto the situation.

TR: Yes, I see what you mean.

S: So if we eliminate that one side of our behavior based on projection, will we still have enough to do?

TR: You begin to realize what you have been missing. Situations are there always.

STUDENT: It seems to me it is very difficult to help. I would very much like to help people and I have plenty of opportunities, but it is not an easy thing. One has to be pretty advanced. It seems to me that in order to have compassion one has to be passionate as well, otherwise you are always working through your ego and you are half dead and half alive.

TRUNGPA RINPOCHE: You see, getting tired of helping, feeling that it's too monotonous, happens because you want to get feedback in terms of ego.

S: No, I want to help people, but my helping people is blocked.

TR: Well, one should continuously do it, continuously put oneself in the situation of helping. And generally, that doesn't mean that once you try to help somebody that's going to be the whole experience at all. It takes practice. And practice means making mistakes as well as learning something out of those mistakes. So it needs continual persistent action going on all the time. It doesn't mean that one or two times is going to be the perfect situation at all, by any means. The whole thing is very manual. You learn by mistakes; you learn also by the skillful means you've been practicing. There will be occasional shocking experiences of yourself, and there will be occasional surprising experiences of yourself, that you've undermined yourself so much. So helping another person is also knowing oneself in this case, trusting oneself.

STUDENT: Could you discuss our relationship to our body? Is it important to be concerned with diet or yogic practices or breathing exercises?

TRUNGPA RINPOCHE: In connection with what?

S: In connection with learning to see what is.

TR: Well, body doesn't have to be a special thing. The whole world is your body. There's a tendency to view the body as your private possession. And because of that you tend to forget the rest of the world and the greater orbit of experience involved with that. If a person is able to relate with the world, he is also able to relate with the body. And if a person is able to relate with the body thoroughly, then that person also would learn how to open to the world. It's sort of an arbitrary thing: fundamentally, relationship to body is relationship to *things,* objects, that aspect of solidity which continues everywhere in the world, constantly.

S: So trying to purify your body doesn't affect consciousness?

TR: There again, it depends on your attitude. If you are working on the body, purifying the body in order to purify the mind, then it could become self-deception, because you are working purely from one direction. In order to purify mind, you could work directly with mind rather than working with the body. And if that is the case, needless to say, why don't we just work directly rather than using a middle man, if that is the object?

S: If you're purifying the mind, does the body just kind of follow along with it?

TR: Well, that's the next question.

S: Is it only *your* mind that you have to purify?

TR: One mind, did you say? Well, it's difficult to say one mind or many minds; it's like talking about one space and many spaces. But you see, [Trungpa Rinpoche lights a cigarette] the point in looking at the relationship of body and mind is to discover how much of the body is the true body and how much of the body is an imaginary body. And if we involve ourselves with such complications, we have to involve ourselves with a whole theology, which may take thirteen or fourteen years to try to work out.

STUDENT: Rinpoche, what is resistance and what is its relationship to wisdom? It seems that when I'm just being passive, resistance dissipates into no resistance.

TRUNGPA RINPOCHE: Usually any kind of resistance is a reminder either that you're going too far or you are not going far enough. It is a sort of natural force which works in that way. And when you realize that, you no longer have to view resistance as a problem or an obstacle or as something that you have to destroy or overcome before you discover the truth.

S: Is that an act of wisdom?

TR: That is an act of wisdom, yes.

STUDENT: Rinpoche, could you talk about active and passive? It seems that there's a need to be passive, simply to attend, and at the same time it seems like there's also a need for action.

TRUNGPA RINPOCHE: They don't occur as contradictions as such. It's a natural situation. In actual fact, there's no such thing really as absolute passivity or absolute activity. Active is, I suppose you could say, penetrating involvement; and passive is the space or atmosphere around where you are involving yourself. So they go together. You have to have both of them or neither of them. It seems that the speed of action cannot survive without something to relate to the action. In other words, you can't play music without silence; silence is part of the music as well.

7

The Bardo of Existence

Hunger and thirst and trying to find an alternative to them is the realm where we are today, the hungry ghost realm. (It is interesting that the subject we are working on and studying together always has relevance to each day's change of temperament and mood. That seems to be quite a curious coincidence.) Hunger and thirst also could be said to be waiting, or expectation. There is a constant demand for something, constantly being busy at something, constantly wanting to learn, constantly wanting to know, wanting to "get it." So one subject connected with the hungry ghost realm is the disease of the learners, or the hangup of learners. There is so much ambition and hunger to learn something, to know something, which is connected with expectations as well. And that in itself, that ambition to learn, is the obstacle to learning.

You might ask, "Shouldn't we have ambition? Shouldn't we be conscientious and drive ourselves to knowledge? Shouldn't we work hard on our homework? Shouldn't we read hundreds of books? Shouldn't we become successful? Shouldn't we not only be good students, but become famous teachers?" There is that kind of chain reaction of building up status, building up your collection of knowledge, which may be necessary if you only want to *learn,* and if you know that learning is purely a technical thing with no reference to *knowing* at all. You can learn without knowing, and you could become a teacher by being learned—but it is not possible to become wise by becoming a good student. Through this ambition that we put out, in this hunger for knowledge, every word is questioned, sucked in by our pure desire, by our magnetizing state of mind, in order to gain something.

There is a difference between that kind of hunger and grasping, and actual communication with the subject that you're going to learn, making an actual relationship with the subject. It is like the difference between reading the menu and deciding to eat. If you have a clear idea what kind of food you want to eat, you don't have to read the menu—you immediately order it. But in fact we seem to spend so much time just reading the menu. There are all sorts of temptations of possible dishes: "Shall we order this or that? That sounds good as well. I never tasted this, but it sounds foreign; it sounds good, exotic. Shall we have a drink before we order? Shall we have wine with the meal? What shall we do?" Such a scene is created around just purely reading the menu. "And before we read the menu, should we have something special, so we are inspired to read the menu? Appetizers? Cookies and nuts?"

Also, of course, the secret criteria that we use in ordering the food, reading the menu, are very embarrassing ones which we don't want to share with anybody. They are purely restricted to you, particularly if you have invited guests. You don't talk about how much it costs; you just talk about what would be a nice thing to eat. You are tasteful in public, with your friends, but in actual fact you are thinking about how much it's going to cost. If you are a very efficient person, you will work out the total price, depending on how many people are going to eat. A whole culture is based around the eating and drinking process, a whole independent culture, another kind of civilization, almost. As far as your experience in that particular restaurant is concerned, the whole world is eating there. It's another world. Everybody's complaining;

everybody's ordering; everybody's eating; everybody's drinking; everybody's paying; and more people are coming, more and more. Everybody's being served. It is the world of the *hungry* ghosts.

If we simplify, we eat because we are hungry and we drink because we are thirsty. But somehow, that primeval motive is not relevant anymore. We don't eat because we are hungry; we eat because we want the taste, or because we want to go out. The whole idea of going to a restaurant to eat is because it is different, a change from home cooking, a way of relaxing in many cases. We choose from one highlight to another highlight—constantly changing, all the time.

According to the scriptures there are several types of craziness or levels of hallucination involved in the realm of the hungry ghosts. In the first stage, you dream of food, how delicious it will be to have it. For instance, you may have an irresistible driving force to have chocolate ice cream. You have this whole image of chocolate ice cream in your mind. In fact, you reach the meditative state of chocolate ice cream. You see it in your vision, your hallucination. The whole world becomes that shape.

Seeing the world as a gigantic chocolate ice cream waiting for you, you go toward it. But when you get near it, the chocolate ice cream begins to become just a pile of rocks, or a dry tree. That's a second kind of hallucination.

A third type of hallucination begins with having a certain idea of food in your mind, a hallucinatory or visionary quality of food. You have in your mind a strong driving force to work for it and eat it, and that driving force goes on and on. In the distance you see food being served and you go there—but suddenly the hostess and the waitresses and waiters become the guardians of the food. Instead of serving you, they have swords, armor, and sticks to ward you off. But the food is still visible in the middle of that whole scene. That's a third type of hallucination of the hungry ghost realm.

And then there is the fourth type. You see the food and you

have a tremendous desire to eat. Your desire to eat becomes very active and aggressive, so you have to fight with those guardians and knock them out. Then you rush to the food, you pick it up and eat it. But the minute you swallow it, it turns into flames in your stomach and begins to burn you.

These are all analogies of the different degrees of hunger. That grasping quality of the hungry ghost realm could take different shapes. It could take the shape of some kind of communication with the food or the object of desire—but that could be distorted, once you see it as it is. Or that grasping could be seen as a succession of situations you have to go through, like the person who eats and then finds that the food becomes flames in the stomach. These particular types of hunger and thirst give a general feeling of the hungry ghost realm.

But there's something more than that. In terms of bardo experience, the particular type of bardo experience associated with the hungry ghost realm is called *sipa* bardo, the bardo of existence, creation, or becoming. You actually manufacture a completely new experience, another type of experience. And the particular experience of sipa bardo, the bardo of existence, is the threshold between grasping with hunger and the experience of letting go—not quite letting go, but the experience of giving up—in other words, giving up hope. Giving up hope doesn't mean just naively declining, or giving up hope purely out of frustration, that you can't bear it anymore. The absence of hope in this case is based on being able to see the humorous situation of the moment, developing a heightened sense of humor. You see that your striving and grasping is too serious and too concentrated. A person can't have a sense of humor, generally, unless he or she is extremely serious. At the height of seriousness, you burst into laughter. It's too funny to be serious, because there is a tendency to see the contrast of it. In other words, humor cannot exist without contrast, without two situations playing. And you are seeing the humorous quality of that.

So what is lacking in the hungry ghost realm is humor. It is a deadly honest search, seriously searching, seriously grasping. This could apply to seriously searching spiritually or materialistically, anything: seriously making money, seriously meditating with such a solemn face. It could be said to be like perching, as though you were a chicken just about to give birth to an egg. In my personal experience, you see this with babies. When you begin to see a serious face on a baby, you have to make sure that there is a diaper. When we want something, usually we perch very seriously. It is completely humorless. You want to give birth to something: you're trying to pass through, or manufacture something. Then you grasp it, possess it, eat it, chew it, swallow it.

The world of the hungry ghosts, or pretas, is based on the seriousness of wanting to grasp something, and it is heightened by the bardo experience to the point where you are not actually hungry anymore. You see, that's the difference between the bardo experience and the ordinary hungry ghost experience. In the ordinary hungry ghost experience, you are hungry; in the bardo experience of the absolute intensity of hunger, you are not hungry anymore. Because the vision of whatever you want to have is so much in your mind, you reach a certain kind of obsession. In fact, you are so overwhelmed by the desire of wanting something that you forget you are hungry, that you're starving. You become more concerned with the presence of what you want; you begin to become one with the presence of the thing you want. That's where the seriousness begins to be involved; that's where the perching begins to develop.

At that point it is possible to develop a sense of humor and be able to see that you are actually perching. And you begin to see the ironic aspect of it. Then there's no hunger and no hallucination or desire. That is beyond the bardo experience, when you get through it. But when you are in it, the seriousness still continuously goes on. That's the hungry ghost experience, or the bardo of existence. So fundamentally this realm is based on the relationship between the self-conscious ego, myself, and me. That ego wants to be; it wants to have certain particular things as "my idea;" it wants to be fulfilled. The frustration comes from the danger of its not being able to be fulfilled completely and properly.

STUDENT: When Gautama Buddha sat beneath the bodhi tree and he was being tempted by the maras, he vowed to attain enlightenment even if his bones crumbled and turned into dust. In that situation, would he be in the hungry ghost realm? It seems like a sort of hopeless seriousness.

TRUNGPA RINPOCHE: Exactly, yes. You see, once you reach the higher spiritual levels of enlightenment, the higher your state, the more advanced your state of development, the more temptations there are. Therefore the temptations also become very sophisticated as you become more sophisticated. This goes on and on. That is exactly the point of the hosts of mara beginning to attack the Buddha. I would say that point is the most advanced level of the hungry ghost realm, in a sense, in terms of our own personal experiences. That is why the maras have to come and why the temptations of mara are necessary. They are exactly what is needed in order to provide contrast between awake and confusion.

STUDENT: Rinpoche, you said the danger is in being unsatisfied. What did you mean by that?

TRUNGPA RINPOCHE: Well, I suppose it is the possibility of continuing in a state of confusion and not being able to make a relationship with present experience. The danger in this case is the possibility of being extremely self-creative, as opposed to self-destructive, meaning the destruction of ego. Instead you could become extremely self-creative, learning how to play the game of ego and how to develop all sorts of luxurious ways of feeding and comforting ego—an ego-fattening process.

STUDENT: Would you say something about how the energy ends up in this hunger where you are looking at the menu and looking at the waitresses and looking at how much it's going to cost and whether your friend has ordered something better than you? All of this is enough to put a person in bed for a couple of hours because he's run out of energy. How is it that you do not use up all your energy when you're with your friends in that way?

TRUNGPA RINPOCHE: There again it's a completely humorless situation. Everything is regarded as an extreme case.

S: It doesn't seem very funny to be worrying about all these various things.

TR: It would be funny if you realized what was happening.

STUDENT: You said that the hosts of mara are necessary in order to provide contrast. Is that because the hosts of mara bring confusion to its peak?

TRUNGPA RINPOCHE: Exactly, yes. Very sophisticated confusion, purely matching the possible awake state that you're going to attain. It's equal. Yes.

S: So one should not really have to strive to develop that completely, but just accept it and not try to call it awake.

TR: Once you accept it, it becomes the force of compassion. In the story of the Buddha, each arrow shot at him turned into a flower. There wouldn't be flowers unless the maras shot arrows. So the whole thing becomes a creative process, a rain of flowers. Each act of aggression becomes loving-kindness, compassion.

S: That's the thing. When you get into confusion, it becomes overcrowding sometimes, and the temptation then is to move away from the confusion.

TR: Yes, that's the general temptation. But then what happens is that the temptation follows you all the way. When you try to run away, the faster you try to run, the faster the temptation comes to you all the time—unless you decide not to run. You're providing more feedback to the temptation when you decide to try to get away, unless you are willing to make a relationship with it.

STUDENT: Could you say something about how this relates to the pain of sitting in meditation? There seems to be a possibility of accepting the pain, having it be just simply part of what is. But most of the time it's a teeth-gritting type of thing where you think, "When are they going to ring the damn bell?," hoping that something might drop and another might appear.

TRUNGPA RINPOCHE: Again, it's the same thing. There is a certain tendency to translate all mental pain and discomfort into physical discomfort. In sitting meditation, for instance, you imagine that getting up and walking away is the way to solve the pain—the psychological pain which has been translated into physical pain. That is a kind of confusion. If a person is able to relate with the irritation and the pain of sitting, he or she sees that it is nothing more than purely looking for another change, away from the psychological level. In that sense, of course, pain becomes irrelevant.

S: I was a bit lost on that. That state of gritting—what can let go of that in the right way?:

TR: If you are able to see that you are perching, then the whole tension that has built up becomes different; and in fact, it won't be there anymore. It needs humor, a sense of humor, all the time. You see, a sense of humor is associated with the living, a lively situation. Without a sense of humor there is the solemnness associated with death, a dead body. It's completely rigid, cold, serious, and honest—but you can't move. That's the true distinction.

STUDENT: Jesus said about the lilies of the field, "Be not anxious, saying what shall we eat, what shall we drink? Consider the lilies of the field: they toil not, neither do they spin. But I say unto you that Solomon in all his glory was not as attired as these." Could you comment on this?

TRUNGPA RINPOCHE: It seems self-evident, self-explanatory. It's the same as the Zen saying, "When I eat, I eat; when I sleep, I sleep."

STUDENT: When you talked about the temptations of mara, you said that as we go along they become more and more subtle. Could you relate the meditative absorption in the world of the gods to those kinds of temptations? What's the difference between the meditative absorption in the god world and temptation?

TRUNGPA RINPOCHE: That's a good one. You see, the interesting point is that in the complete meditative absorption of the world of the gods, there wouldn't be temptation because nobody wants or demands your attention. You are paying full attention all the time to ego. So the maras are satisfied. They don't have to try to shake you back, bring you back to samsara—you are already in samsara and you are grooving on it. It seems as if temptation can only occur if you are trying to get away from centralized ego.

S: When you are in a blissful state, you are also perching?

TR: Yes. You are perching. Perching is the self-consciousness of not knowing how to relate with situations and so trying to work out some strategy. That moment of contemplating strategy is perching, so to speak.

S: Are you a hungry ghost?

TR: Yes, a hungry ghost as well. That is quite so, because you want to get more and more feedback continuously, all the time.

S: So there is not a situation when you are just in the world of the devas, the world of the gods, because when you are in the world of the gods you are also a hungry ghost?

TR: That's right, yes. But it's less dramatic, because when you are in the world of the gods, the whole situation is more relaxed and self-satisfactory.

S: Yes, but you somehow unconsciously want to remain in it, or if you fall down to the world of the asuras, you want to go back to it. So you are a hungry ghost.

TR: Yes. You see, you could say that all six realms have a hungry ghost quality of one kind or another, because all six worlds consist of grasping and hanging on. That quality is always there. But when we talk about the hungry ghost realm as an independent thing, it's more obvious, more vivid.

STUDENT: In Buddha's temptation, could you explain his saying, "Go away!"—in a sense rejecting the beautiful girls and the food offered him and the monsters? Is there a place in our meditation for saying, "Go away"?

TRUNGPA RINPOCHE: No, I don't think so, because you are not at that stage.

STUDENT: Are all the bardo states ego?

TRUNGPA RINPOCHE: The bardo states *are* ego. Definitely, yes.

S: All of them?

TR: All of them. They are the heightened qualities of the different types of ego and the possibility of getting off ego. That's where bardo starts—the peak experience in which there is the possibility of losing the grip of ego and the possibility of being swallowed up in it. There is that kind of confusion between freedom and escape, freedom and imprisonment.

S: So in each bardo state, there's a possibility of escape?

TR: I think so, yes. The Buddha described that in the scriptures by an analogy. The bodhisattva's actions are as if you are about to step out of a room. At the point when one leg is outside the door and one leg is inside the door, the bodhisattva wonders whether he or she should step back or proceed. That's an analogy for bardo.

STUDENT: Could you get hung up on the bardo state? Instead of passing through the bardo experience, could you get hung up and just stay there, like in the realm of the hungry ghosts?

TRUNGPA RINPOCHE: Yes, you can. You can. That's a very interesting point. In that case it is the level of madness, you are hung up on it. Exactly.

S: So what do you do then?

TR: There's nothing that you can do, in terms of changing the situation of the moment. The only way to relate is by trying to relate with the actual experience of pain and pleasure as an earthy, earthy situation. That's the only way of getting out of madness. Madness is extreme spacing; it is without solidity in relationship to earth.

STUDENT: Did I understand you to say that when you are in the world of the gods, you have your ego?

TRUNGPA RINPOCHE: Yes.

S: Oh, that's very disappointing.

TR: I know.

S: Then one should not attempt to meditate more. If one is more and more in the state of meditation, then one should try not to be, because then one is a hungry ghost.

TR: Exactly. That's it exactly, precisely.

STUDENT: Is that so? One should try *not* to be in a state of meditation?

TR: Exactly. You see, that's the point of meditation in action— that at a certain level the meditative state becomes too static, and then the important point is the bodhisattva's action.

S: But the meditative state is an action; it's quite literally an action. Should you try to act without being in a meditative state because even in action you want to be in a meditative state, and so it is still hungry ghost?

T R : Yes. The point of action in this case does not mean you have to try to maintain a meditative state and act simultaneously, as though you were trying to manage two at the same time. But action is that you truly act, you act properly. The idea of saying, "When I eat, I eat; when I sleep, I sleep," is acting properly, thoroughly, and completely. That is stepping out of dwelling on something. You see, meditation in the pejorative sense is dwelling on something. Action demands attention. You go along with that particular paying attention to situations and working skillfully with situations without reference back to yourself—how you should act, how you shouldn't act. You just act.

STUDENT: How does patience come into all this?

TRUNGPA RINPOCHE: Patience is not expecting an immediate answer if you experience pain—not trying to change pain into pleasure. It is the willingness to submit yourself to the situation, to wait. In other words, you are willing to see properly and clearly. When we are completely wrapped up in situations without patience, we become blind.

STUDENT: You said in the beginning that consciousness is the last development of the ego. If eventually we wish to give up our ego, does that mean that we will lose our consciousness?

TRUNGPA RINPOCHE: Consciousness in this case means something quite different from the ordinary sense of consciousness as being aware of what's going on. In terms of the development of ego, consciousness is centralized consciousness—always relating backward and forward. It's not consciousness of what's going on, but consciousness as to whether you are maintaining your ego or not. This kind of consciousness is quite different from simply being aware. In fact, you can't gain complete consciousness until you step out of ego. Then consciousness begins to become the play or the dance, *lalita,* where you actually dance with the rhythm of situations. That sort of transcendental consciousness is quite different from the one-track-mind consciousness of ego.

STUDENT: Why is your ego involved in the world of the gods?

TRUNGPA RINPOCHE: Because the world of the gods is a sophisticated state of ego, where you experience pleasure all the time. And once you experience pleasure, then you want to retain your pleasure. You always want to refer back to yourself. That is ego.

STUDENT: Could "resting" have anything to do with true meditation, as opposed to the pejorative kind? Being at rest?

TRUNGPA RINPOCHE: It depends on whether you are just resting, being in a state of rest, or whether you are resting *for* something.

S: No, no. Being in a state of rest as opposed to doing something. In other words, you said that the pejorative kind of meditation was dwelling on something. I'm saying, could the opposite kind—true meditation—be just being at rest?

TR: It could be, yes. I mean, there again, rest without any relativities—just being is rest.

STUDENT: Is sitting meditation action, in terms of breathing and the heart beating and sitting—or is it mental? You said the other day to forget the body and deal directly with mind, but then you said that it had to be meditation in action. So I wonder, what is the principal expression of action in sitting meditation?

TRUNGPA RINPOCHE: It is a general comprehension of the relationship with earth, rather than regarding the earth as separate from you, as though it were your opponent—which involves the body. The earth is not regarded as an opponent or an extra thing, but is part of the earthy quality of mind, which is quite different.

S: Is the doorway to that through mind, or is it through the body? Or is it through some other way, like paying attention to one's thoughts?

TR: I would say both—body and thoughts.

STUDENT: How do you step out of ego?

TRUNGPA RINPOCHE: I suppose, you could say, by developing a friendly relationship with ego.

S: Then it becomes more inflated, like a balloon.

TR: You mean ego itself, if you are trying to like it, trying to love it? No, ego wouldn't like that. Ego would like to be the boss all the time.

STUDENT: In the realm of the gods, if there is wisdom and the joy of being, I take it that you say that this relates back to pleasure and to ego taking its pleasure. But isn't there a joy of being that transcends the pleasure-pain principle?

TRUNGPA RINPOCHE: There may be, but at the same time, as you experience it, there is a watcher happening. That's the problem.

S: In other words, the gods experience the experience and the experiencer.

TR: The experience and the experiencer, yes. You may be experiencing some transcendental experience of going beyond something; but at the same time, there is an experiencer who takes note of that.

S: And this is the great temptation with the realm of the gods?

TR: Yes, exactly, because then you are getting something. You are getting more and more feedback, more food to sustain yourself—until you realize that there's nothing to transcend at all.

S: But isn't there a joy that's a simple expression of the earth's own energy? Just simple energy, a kind of lightness?

TR: Definitely, yes. But that's a simple one, isn't it? Therefore it is more difficult.

STUDENT: How is it possible not to ask a hungry ghost question?

TRUNGPA RINPOCHE: You can't. Once you begin to try to do that, then that in itself is a hungry ghost act. There's no end to it.

STUDENT: I read somewhere that when Mara came to Buddha, Buddha recognized her as being a part of himself, and he was compassionate because he already had loving-kindness. And I was very impressed with this, because this might be a very good way of dealing with one's ego, or oneself. He recognized that she was only a part of him.

TRUNGPA RINPOCHE: Yes. In fact, Milarepa's song about his experience of the temptation of the maras is like that. When he tried to use mantras as spells to exorcise them, nothing worked. But the moment he realized they were his own projections, they vanished.

STUDENT: When you get to the point where you feel that you can't laugh, even though you know intellectually the absurdity of where you're at and you see that you're perching—is there anything you can do to go a step further, so you could break through that?

TRUNGPA RINPOCHE: It seems that that moment is a very sensitive moment, in which you don't have to try to do anything at all. You just have to be patient and go a little bit further—but not watch yourself experiencing that. Just go a step further. Then you begin to develop a sense of humor about it, that the whole thing is a game, however serious. You see, the whole thing that we have been talking about—*how* to conduct ourselves, *how* to do things, *how* to get out, all this—once you begin to regard any method or practice as a sedative, or a way of getting out, then it doesn't work anymore, it's another way of self-deception. In other words, if you regard the skillful means or methods as ways of escaping, as medicine, then nothing works. It's as simple as that.

STUDENT: Is the bodhisattva path an expression of a hungry ghost?

TRUNGPA RINPOCHE: Definitely not.

S: From what you were saying, it seems to have some of that character. Is taking the bodhisattva vow the expression of a hungry ghost?

TR: I don't think so, but again, there are different types of bodhisattvas. You could be an evangelical bodhisattva or you could be just a bodhisattva bodhisattva. Taking the bodhisattva vow is just a commitment—going further. In fact, you are deliberately taking a vow not to refer to yourself at all—that *I* am going to be taking a vow, that *I* am going to become a bodhisattva. I am just a simple, insignificant person; what is more important are all sentient beings, they are more important than I am.

S: Is there some way in meditation to avoid watching the processes that go on in your mind?

TR: That's exactly why techniques are important in meditation. You have been given certain techniques, and you can go along with them without watching—because whenever there's a watcher involved, that means you are intellectualizing your meditation, you're not actually feeling it. Techniques make you feel it. For instance, the technique of following the breath makes you feel the breath completely. So you go along completely with the technique, whether the technique is for sitting meditation or for walking meditation, or whatever it may be. That is automatically a way of stepping out of the watcher; whereas, if you're trying to suppress the watcher, then that in itself becomes another watcher, and it goes on and on and on. So instead of approaching the watcher from the front door, we are approaching it from the back door: that's the technique of meditation.

STUDENT: Rinpoche, if one were looking at what we are doing, going through life, as a jigsaw puzzle, a strange puzzle, how would you relate the pieces in the puzzle to, say, freedom or so-called mystical experiences?

TRUNGPA RINPOCHE: You see, there again it's a question of approaching it from the back door or approaching it from the front door. All the pieces of the puzzle are not the answer; it's the ground where your jigsaw puzzle is situated.

S: You mean they're all the same?

TR: All the same, yes. But at the same time, the ground makes it possible to have a jigsaw puzzle displayed.

STUDENT: In the realm of the gods, does everybody that you see appear to you to be a god, and you yourself feel like a god?

TRUNGPA RINPOCHE: I think so, yes. It's the same thing with hatred, for instance. If you hate yourself, you hate everybody, and you hallucinate that everybody is aggravating your hatred. The same thing applies the other way around. As long as you centralize your attention inwardly, to a personal involvement with ego, that puts out similar kinds of radiation continuously.

S: So the best you can do is to try somehow to realize that you're in a given state. It's like you get so caught up in it that if you can somehow realize that that's what you're doing, or somehow realize that you're seeing everybody in a certain way, then you have a chance to get a bigger picture.

TR: Well, yes. It's a question of seeing things as they are, rather than your version. If you have jaundice, you see every white as yellow. That's the analogy which has been used.

S: So no matter what color of sunglasses you are wearing, you're always tinting things one way or another.

TR: Yes.

STUDENT: If I may use the word *high* for a moment—whether it be mildly drug-induced or just suddenly feeling like you're a god, you know, and you look around at your friends and you feel a definite change of consciousness and you feel like you're in a royal court and you're all gods and goddesses inhabiting the planet—is that sort of a bardo experience?

TRUNGPA RINPOCHE: Well, I would say that's the realm of the gods experience—the ground where bardo is developing.

STUDENT: You said that the hungry ghost world was the disease of the learner. My questions are from that framework—to learn. If that's the framework, you said that the food given to the hungry ghost turns to fire in his stomach. Sometimes I get that same sensation from your answers—often. And other times I get the opposite feeling—of encouragement, or the suggestion to do it this way or such and such. But both questions seem to be motivated from that learning point of view.

TRUNGPA RINPOCHE: That's the interesting point. It is like the idea of transmission, which takes place not only by the power of the teacher but also through the openness of the student. The meeting of the two minds takes place simultaneously, and then transmission takes place on the spot. So I would say that in the same way what happens generally is that we try to cover ourselves up—all the time. But there are occasional gaps where we forget ourselves, we forget to cover up. Likewise, in this case there will be gaps of open mind which transcend the hungry ghost level. That's the whole point. Otherwise it would seem that whatever you do is hungry ghost, there would be no way out at all—but that is not so.

All the experiences of bardo and of the different types of realms are patches of experiences—not completely covered whole situations. That is why there are possibilities of sudden experiences like satori. Sudden experiences of intelligence, or buddha nature, come through on and off. One doesn't have to achieve complete perfection trying to bring up that experience all the time, necessarily; but the occasion to acknowledge yourself as a hungry ghost and the occasion to acknowledge yourself as transcending the hungry ghosts take place alternatingly, all the time.

STUDENT: The desire of ego to be fulfilled—how does one liberate those desires of fulfillment that ego presents? Is it by fulfilling them and actually experiencing the fulfillment? Will that satisfy it? Does one have to see that and liberate it by going through the experience?

TRUNGPA RINPOCHE: It seems that trying to fulfill is another escape—equally the same as trying to suppress. Generally there is a conflict between you and your experiences, your desires. It is a kind of game between ego and its extensions. Sometimes ego tries to overpower the projections, and sometimes the projections try to overpower ego—that kind of battle goes on all the time. So the point is to see that battle as it is, rather than fulfill the desires or suppress them.

STUDENT: Is the hunger for enlightenment related to this other hunger that you're talking about?

TRUNGPA RINPOCHE: Definitely.

S: Then you have to stop wanting to be enlightened, is that the idea? Because if you're hungry for enlightenment, if you want it, it would seem as though you'd have to quit thinking about it or something.

TRUNGPA RINPOCHE: Well, you see, the point is the same as in the bodhisattva path, in which you transcend the desire for the attainment of enlightenment and continuously work along the path. In that case, the path is the goal and the goal is the path. Then enlightenment becomes almost a by-product rather than a deliberate aim.

S: You have to give up thinking about enlightenment and just do it?

TR: In terms of ambitions, yes.

S: But don't we understand Buddha to have been a bodhisattva already before he sat down under the bodhi tree? Isn't that the way he's usually understood?

TR: Yes, exactly.

S: But you said that his vow when he sat down was an expression of the highest level of a hungry ghost. If he was a bodhisattva, how could he also be an expression of a hungry ghost?

TR: Well, it happens continuously. That's why he's a bodhisattva; that's why he's not yet Buddha. It has been said that once a bodhisattva reaches the tenth stage of the path, which is next to the enlightenment state, his view of apparent phenomena, or his projections, is like vision by full moonlight. He sees things relatively precisely and clearly, but not as clearly as by sunlight. That's why he is a bodhisattva; he has some more to go.

STUDENT: Would you give an example of being friendly to your ego?

TRUNGPA RINPOCHE: It is a kind of communication and understanding of the mechanism of ego and not trying to suppress it or condemn it, but using ego as a stepping stone, as a ladder. All the concepts and ideas of path and vehicles that we discussed are partly the formation of ego. In fact, the very idea of enlightenment exists because of ego—because there is contrast. Without ego there wouldn't be the very notion of enlightenment at all.

STUDENT: Could you say something about being fully awakened and the bardo levels? For instance, the bodhisattva is still treading through the six levels, but when he becomes fully awakened in buddhahood, does he still work through these levels in his bodhisattva role?

TRUNGPA RINPOCHE: I don't think so, for the very fact that there is no role. I mean, a buddha begins to realize that he has no role to play anymore, but to be.

S: But then would he still be a bodhisattva?

TR: He would be a compassionate person, in terms of a bodhisattva, but he would transcend changing into different levels because in that state, knowledge begins to become a part of him rather than being absolutely learned, in which case knowledge and oneself are still separate things.

STUDENT: Is awakening in one of the realms good for all of them?

TRUNGPA RINPOCHE: Any kind of awake is just awake—in any realm.

STUDENT: I think you helped me see again today how a lot of the way I think about enlightenment has to do with my ego. Ego thinks it's so special, that it deserves something special—this word *enlightenment* sounds like it's right up ego's alley. I watch how my ego seems repulsed by the idea that it could be something ordinary. I get very confused at that point, the way ego looks upon enlightenment. Right here, it's very ordinary and simple—and then somehow it's very revolting and repelling. It's like I don't want to be like the other people here or the ordinary people out in the street. Ego seems to take that attitude.

TR: Yes, that's quite an interesting point. The awake state is the ordinary of the ordinary—an absolutely insignificant thing, completely insignificant. It's nothing, actually. And if you see it that way, then with all the expectations it built up, ego is really going to suffer and be irritated.

S: But even the path sometimes inflates the ego.

TR: Yes, sure it does. Therefore your relationship to the path should also be an ordinary one.

S: But even with the ordinary, the ego is still there, choosing something or other.

TR: Yes, that's always the danger: if we place more emphasis on being extraordinary or on being ordinary, it's almost saying the same thing in terms of ego.

S: Then it seems that you can't get away from it in any way.

TR: That's the whole point. Give in and stop trying to do anything at all. It is a kind of judo play: you don't push ego but ego is pushing you, which becomes ego throwing itself away by itself.

STUDENT: Rinpoche, is there any difference between enlightenment and freedom, or are they one and the same?

TRUNGPA RINPOCHE: In the ultimate sense, they are the same.

STUDENT: In regard to seeing through one's projections, I get the feeling sometimes that you can't see anything at all, that all you can see is your projections. Does that have something to do with just shutting up?

TRUNGPA RINPOCHE: I don't think so. It's the opposite.

S: I don't mean shutting up; I mean shutting up talking.

TR: No, no. Even metaphorically it is not closing. It is the opposite—really connecting, communication.

8

The Bardo of Death

This talk began with a long period of silence during which Trungpa Rinpoche was hidden from the audience by a large folding mirror. From behind the mirror he shouted, "Hell!" This was followed by a loud and long burst of laughter from the audience, after which the mirror was removed, and the talk continued.

Hell. The experience of hell comes from deliberate, basic aggression. That aggression is the opposite of patience. Patience usually means being extremely kind and cool. But here patience seems to have a different meaning than just keeping your cool. In this case, it is not only keeping your cool, but it is seeing the situation in its fullest extent. Such patience could be said to be active, extremely active and energetic. It is not necessarily a lot of waiting—waiting for things to happen, waiting to see. Instead, patience is having a proper relationship or exchange with the situation as it is. And you are part of that situation. It is not that you are working on some strategy as to how to work with it.

The basic aggression of hell comes from your wanting to destroy your projection. It is natural aggression: you want to destroy the mirror. As projection works as it is, in a very efficient and accurate way, it becomes too embarrassing. You don't want to go along with it. Instead of seeing the naked truth, you want to destroy the mirror—to the extent of not only destroying the projection, or the mirror, but also the perceiver of that mirror. The perceiver is also extremely painful, so there is the suicidal mentality of wanting to destroy the perceiver of the mirror as well as the mirror itself. There is constant struggle, destruction, going on.

The bardo connected with the experience of hell, the bardo of death, has to do with the claustrophobia of pain and pleasure, the sudden peak of anger in which you do not know whether you are actually trying to destroy something or whether you are trying to achieve something by destroying. It is this ambiguous quality of destruction and creation. Naturally, of course, destruction is in itself creation. But somehow there's a conflict. You have created destruction, therefore it is creation. In other words, one is not quite certain—because of the energy, because of the speed that you go through—whether you are actually going or coming. The moment you think you are going, you discover that you are coming. That extreme speed of running, rushing, becomes confusing, which is the particular peak experience of the bardo of death.

Death could be said to be birth at the same time, from this point of view. The moment something ends, the next birth takes place naturally. So death is the re-creating of birth. It is the same idea as reincarnation, the rebirth process. There is also the realization of death as being constant death. Things cannot exist or develop without momentum. Change is taking place always, constantly. That is why the teachings place tremendous importance on the realization of impermanence. Impermanence becomes extremely important at this particular point of aggression. Aggression is trying to freeze the space, still trying to sterilize the space. But when you begin to see the impermanence, you cannot solidify space anymore. That then is the peak experience of transcending aggression.

As we discussed yesterday in regard to hunger, if you are fully involved with the bardo experience of one of the six realms, you also experience your neighboring territory. This also applies to aggression, or the hell realm, which is next to the hungry ghost realm. So another aspect of aggression, or hell experience, could also be self-pity, completely closing in, self-condemnation. You condemn yourself because there is nothing attractive in you at all, nothing beautiful. You would basically like to destroy yourself or escape from yourself.

That kind of self-condemning quality in oneself could be said to be very positive in a way. You are just about to discover the opposite of that; you are just about to see the alternatives. Because of the possibility of alternatives, you ask questions based on being other than what you are, other than where you're at, which is a very healthy situation. In that sense, condemnation could be said to be inspiration—as long as the person can proceed further with that condemnation, to a further experience of himself. The condemner, or the person who condemns, and that which is the object of condemnation are different. As long as one is able to get knowledge of the subject, that particular condemner is removed. In other words, the watcher is removed.

When that instinct—that ego-centered notion of trying to achieve perfection, trying to achieve a perfect good thing—is removed, the whole process changes. One's whole attitude changes once you remove that. Yet the condemnation in itself remains as an independent situation. And that particular independent situation, or condemning quality, contains light and space and questions and doubts and confusions. That such confusion and doubt and questions managed to be born brings the possibilities of the dawn breaking through. In the tantric analysis of this, it is said that the dawn of Vajrasattva is breaking through. That is to say, the dawn of indestructible continuity is just about to show through. Talking about aggression from this point of view becomes a creative thing. The whole pattern of aggression, of the hell realm, becomes very positive, something that we could work on.

STUDENT: Can you talk about the creative aspects of paranoia?

TRUNGPA RINPOCHE: That is also exactly the same situation. If it is, so to speak, straight paranoia, then it is very positive. That kind of paranoia makes you see something, it makes you look into another territory, another area, whereas if it is diluted paranoia, which is to say manipulated paranoia, then you don't want to take off your paranoia at all. You would like to retain your paranoia as a cover, as a mask. All sorts of pretenses begin to be involved with that.

S: Can you explain that manipulated paranoia a little bit more?

TR: That kind of paranoia becomes comforting in some way because you could hide behind it. It keeps you company. Otherwise you feel alone, that nobody is with you, working with you. Paranoia is your only way of exercising action. Because of that, paranoia transforms into acting. Because of paranoia, you are inspired to do certain things. Then you begin to act as though you were not there at all, as though somebody else were taking you over or some other situation were taking you over. There is always a confused situation around you, and you try to immediately get into it and blow that situation up and make it into a shield. We generally become extremely clever at doing that. There's always something or other that we can catch at the last moment and make into a shield. That kind of paranoia is diluted paranoia as opposed to innocent paranoia. It could also be called "the basic twist of ego," because that particular paranoia teaches us how to play ego's game of deaf and dumb.

STUDENT: You said that self-condemnation or self-pity may be a positive action. Now, it is my experience from observing a lot of people that self-pity and self-condemnation decay into hate and withdrawal. I very rarely have seen people being able to get themselves out of this box. Yet you feel, from what I hear, that there seems to be a self-energizing element to it which forces people into self-examination, asking questions. I find this extremely rare, from what I have observed. I have wondered what was lacking in their lives, those who touched rock bottom more or less, flirted with suicide. I see very little evidence that something arises out of the ashes of self-destruction.

TRUNGPA RINPOCHE: Well, the intelligence of self-condemnation has an extremely keen eye, keen sight. It sees every move and every mistake that you make. It is very precise and very clear. And this seems to come from the ego's inspiration of wanting to protect oneself. But somehow, strangely enough, it doesn't work like that: it works on a wider scale, beyond the ego level, as well. Even up to the extreme level of discriminating awareness wisdom, there is this element. You see, the point is that intelligence is a neutral thing. A certain part of the intelligence is employed by ego, and a certain part of the intelligence is independent intelligence. Whenever you see a situation or see yourself beginning to play a game of any kind, then that intelligence becomes panoramic intelligence. It begins to see the situation as it is. So condemning could be said to be another way of shaking you up, or breaking you from the extreme belief of what you would like to be to what you are, in terms of ego. So it becomes a natural creative process as it is.

S: I think if I went deeper into it, though, once you are aware of all the things that go on, then the gulf seems that much deeper and the possibilities seem that much poorer.

TR: That is because you are looking from the point of view of the watcher. You are watching your condemnation, and you are manipulating it, you are commenting on it. That is why it becomes clumsy.

S: Without some energizing act to transcend this watching, you get fascinated by the self-condemnation. You wallow in self-pity. As I said before, I find it very rare that somebody boosts himself out of it. It does not seem to be self-energizing but proof of decay in so many cases.

T R : That is exactly the point that I'm trying to get at. Even if it is a self-congratulatory situation of pride, that pride and self-congratulation also do not have the inspiration of extending into limitlessness at all. From this point of view, self-congratulation and self-condemnation are exactly the same situation, because in both cases watcher is involved. Whenever there is no watcher involved, you are looking into the wide and wholly open ground of every situation, open space. You get an extreme aerial view of everything completely. That is why the analogy of the transformation of the negative into the positive, is very poor. In fact, it is a one-sided analogy.

S : You said that transforming the positive into the negative, or the negative into the positive, is a one-sided analogy. What's a better analogy?

T R : Well, obviously, it is to remove the watcher. Remove the criteria, the limited criteria. Once you have removed limited criteria, discriminating wisdom is automatically there. I wouldn't exactly call that a transformation in terms of changing one thing to another, bad into good. It is a kind of natural awakeness in which the negative *is* positive. The awakened state of negative is positive in its own raw and rugged quality.

S : What about transforming itself? Transforming anger into accomplishment, for instance?

T R : A whole range of transformations takes place all the time, of course. I would say the condemnation itself vanishes, but the intelligence and critical vision of the condemnation still remains. That is the ground on which positive things build.

STUDENT : You said that the reason why you have a kind of a revelation, instead of the luxurious self-condemnation you might have had, is that you see yourself suddenly from an entirely different angle, and it's a big shock. You feel very terrible at the moment, but a very strange thing happens: afterward there is a great relief.

TRUNGPA RINPOCHE: Yes. That sounds right. You see, that whole idea is like the four noble truths. The first truth, the truth of suffering, is condemning samsara, how bad, how terrible it is, how painful it is. Out of that condemnation, the second truth is looking into the origin of pain, how it develops. From that the goal, the inspiration of the goal, develops, which is the third noble truth. And from there, the inspiration of the path develops as the fourth truth. So the whole thing works in that way.

STUDENT: Can the watcher have a positive function, at least in the beginning stages of meditation?

TRUNGPA RINPOCHE: At the beginning of the beginning, maybe. If the watcher is being used purely as an observer, then it is positive in a sense. But if the watcher is being used as a guardian, then it begins to become a different thing, because once you have a guard, the guard must know whom to allow, whom not to allow. Those kinds of criteria begin to develop.

S: So it would be in the sense of a fair witness that it could be positive.

TR: Just a witness, yes, pure witness. But that is dangerous to talk about or to recommend. Generally we have a tendency to overindulge in the watcher, which has possibilities of becoming a guardian.

S: So when you have a flash of anger, it might be good just to plunge right into it rather than observe it, I mean to really become that feeling.

TR: Exactly. That doesn't mean either that you should murder somebody or that you should suppress your anger. Just see the natural anger quality as it is, the abstract quality of anger, like the abstract quality of condemning yourself.

S: Do you see that by observing the feeling or by becoming one with the feeling?

TR: Becoming one with the feeling. It seems to be quite safe to say that every practice connected with the path is a practice associated with nonduality, becoming one with something or other.

STUDENT: If a person is not aware of himself, then is he at one with himself—a person who is unaware of his or her anger, unaware of the things that he or she is going to do?

TRUNGPA RINPOCHE: I don't think so. There is a tremendous difference between being unaware of what is happening and identifying with what is happening. Being identified with what is happening is awake and precise, there is tremendous clarity in it; whereas when you don't know what is happening, there is tremendous confusion.

STUDENT: It seems as if suicide would be a kind of ultimate egohood.

TRUNGPA RINPOCHE: That is what you are trying to do when you realize that you can't release yourself—so you destroy yourself purely in order to save face.

S: It seems that if ego actually can destroy you physically, it really must be something.

TR: Well, you see, ego cannot really destroy you at all. Suicide is another way of expanding ego's existence, proving ego's existence, because destroying the body doesn't mean destroying ego. So it's saving face.

STUDENT: Are there negative emotions other than aggression in the realm of hell, such as fear or terror?

TRUNGPA RINPOCHE: That's all part of it. Fear and terror are part of the aggression, which is an absolutely highly developed state of mind of duality. Fear, for instance, is the absolute ultimate confusion of the relationship between you and your projections. That's why you get frightened.

STUDENT: What's the difference between the color red of violent anger and the red of Amitabha Buddha?

TRUNGPA RINPOCHE: Amitabha is like fire. The red of Amitabha has the quality of radiance extending to the point where there's no limit at all. That's why *Amitabha* means "limitless light." In terms of anger, red has an ovenlike quality. It's not like flames in the ordinary sense. It doesn't throw heat outward, but it throws heat inward, so we get baked in.

S: Does the oppressive quality, that feeling of being squeezed until there's no room, vanish if you stop watching?

TR: It seems that the watcher has this mentality of internalizing everything. Do you mean that?

S: It is like squeezing on yourself somehow, pushing against yourself or into yourself.

TR: That is the watcher. Yes.

STUDENT: What did you mean by saying that you should become one with the impulse?

TRUNGPA RINPOCHE: This is not introverted oneness but extroverted oneness, in the sense of going along with the speed of radiation, the pattern of radiation.

STUDENT: Is there a clean, egoless anger?

TRUNGPA RINPOCHE: That sounds like compassion.

STUDENT: Could you discuss the use of sexual energy for spiritual development?

TRUNGPA RINPOCHE: There is often a certain moral judgment which comes up in regard to this particular subject. If you look at it from a very rational point of view, then anger is the ultimate rejection, repelling; and putting anger into practice is destroying, killing. Desire, or passion, is magnetizing, grasping; and the ultimate expression of that is sexual experience. So from a rational point of view, we could say that if you recommend sexual experience as part of the spiritual path, then murdering somebody is also part of the spiritual path. Both apply, it seems.

But this is not quite so from the point of view of the true nature of the emotions. From this perspective, aggression is destroying; it is ultimately rejection, which is an uncompassionate act. But desire, or passion, is a compassionate act. At least it is accepting something, although it may have all sorts of neuroses involved with it. So that is the fundamental principle: compassion, love, and passion are all associated. And of course, sexual experience could be seen from that point of view to be an act of communication beyond words. On the other hand, it could also be said to be an act of communication based on not knowing how to speak in terms of words—which is confusion. It very much depends on the individuals. But at least there's hope in terms of sexual experience, as opposed to destroying other people.

STUDENT: Have you heard the American expression "love-hate relationship"?

TRUNGPA RINPOCHE: Very much so.

S: Well, apparently there are cases when somebody loves somebody very much and either he or she thinks it's not good or it's not socially acceptable or something—and this love can turn right away into hate, wanting to destroy. It might initially have been very truly a sincere sort of love, but then it turns into hatred and destruction.

TR: That is exactly the neurotic quality of love or desire, which contains aggression within itself. One aspect of that is a kind of ultimate frustration, that you can't express communication. And because you can't communicate, you decide you would rather destroy it. That kind of ultimate frustration.

S: Can you turn all of that into compassion, all those aggressive feelings, perhaps, or desires?

TR: It is not a question of whether you can do it or not, but seeing that situations would happen that way—which needs the tremendous generosity of stepping out of centralized ego and its demands. It seems possible.

STUDENT: Is crying over somebody that you love and can't see, can't be with, a part of this aggression that you are talking about? If you love somebody and you miss them, and you begin to cry, is that aggression?

TRUNGPA RINPOCHE: It depends. But there is that desperate quality: you are desperate and hungry. That quality of desperation is a form of aggression.

S: Is that a part of confusion, too?

TR: It could be said.

S: So what do you do to not have this anymore? You want to stop it, you don't want it to go on, you are in pain and suffering—but what do you do to stop it?

TR: You don't stop the process, you can't do it. That would be like trying to stop a bullet going on its way: once it is fired, you can't stop the result or fruition of it; you can prevent it only by not firing the bullet. In other words, we are trying to see the creator of all of this, which is the self-indulgency of ego, and to work with that.

S: When I get rid of my ego, will that make a difference?

TR: You don't get rid of your ego at all.

S: But if I don't get rid of my ego I can't be enlightened, is that right?

TR: It's not as simple as that. Without ego you cannot attain enlightenment, so you have to make friends with ego.

STUDENT: How about aggression which is not directed, non-directed aggression? I mean something like extra energy which is not directed to a situation or to a person or to yourself, but is just there.

TRUNGPA RINPOCHE: You can't have an ultimate nondirected hatred.

S: But there is a kind of aggression which is not hatred, it is just a kind of exuberance.

TR: Yes, I know what you mean.

S: It's inside and you have to get it out, but it's not hatred.

TR: Yes. It's like a lamp giving out light: the light is not directed to one particular spot, but at the same time there is a lamp and there is a burning flame, and without the flame there wouldn't be light. So it's a question of dealing with the flame. But any kind of aggression or speed, whether it is directed at a particular situation or whether it is abstract, is the same thing: it could develop into anger or hatred. You see, basically aggression is not allowing things to go on as they are but trying to force the issue, like growing vegetables with chemicals.

STUDENT: Rinpoche, could you give me sort of a structural approach to fear and explain where the intervals or gaps could be seen? For me, fear seems to be the root of almost everything. All of the things we're talking about seem to come from some sort of a fear syndrome. I've been confused, I haven't followed, it's muddled. The only thing I've gotten out of this was that fear seems to be the feeder to all of this, and if I could see the structure clearly and where the gaps were, then maybe I could connect to all the other branches of the whole tree.

TRUNGPA RINPOCHE: It is the intensity of the threat, that possible threat to the survival of the ego: the structure and natural patterns of fear start there. But we don't actually see the threatening quality ourselves; we only perceive the overwhelming quality of that threat, which is the fear coming back to us, bouncing back on us. It is like an echo: you don't know how loud you shouted, but you get overwhelmed by the echo coming back on you. The intensity of the echo is the result of your voice.

S: So the outward manifestation of the experience is the gap to look at, then?

TR: Yes, exactly.

S: If you can catch that as it's happening, you can almost be *with* that thing, right?

TR: Exactly.

S: Aha!

TR: That's a good one.

STUDENT: Could you talk about how the projection process works, I mean the whole mirror idea? Who's watching whom?

TRUNGPA RINPOCHE: That's a good question. To put it very simply, you watch the mirror, and your reflection of yourself watches you back.

S: So then there's no one watching you but yourself?

TR: Precisely.

S: We're back to the watcher again.

TR: Yes.

STUDENT: Bardo experience would seem to be something that you go along with and let happen. It seems as if the watcher is something to get out of.

TRUNGPA RINPOCHE: The watcher is the self-consciousness. All six bardo experiences are connected with the watcher, with the peak experience of watching yourself and the possibility of losing your grip, the watcher's grip—which is freedom, the awake state. That ambiguity as to whether you will be able to maintain your watchfulness or whether you are going to lose your watchfulness builds into a peak experience.

STUDENT: How is it possible to make friends with the ego without going astray through indulgence in ego trips?

TRUNGPA RINPOCHE: Generally ego is not aware of itself. But in this case you begin to be aware of ego as it is: you don't try to destroy it, or to exorcise it, but you see it as a step. Each crisis of ego is a step toward understanding, to the awake state. In other words, there are two aspects: ego purely continuing on its own, as it would like to play its game; and ego being seen in its true nature, in which case the game of ego becomes ironical. At the same time, you don't try to reject it. The game in itself becomes a step, a path.

S: What do you do? You want to get rid of your ego, but you don't reject it. I don't understand.

TR: You don't want to get rid of ego. That's the whole point. You don't try to get rid of ego at all—but you don't try to maintain ego either.

S: Is that where a sense of humor comes in?

TR: Yes.

STUDENT: How do you deal constructively with aggression directed against your own person from another person?

TRUNPA RINPOCHE: I suppose it's a question of not providing a target, an expected target. When another person begins to hit you, he automatically expects you'll be there to be hit. If you are not there to be hit, then he is waving his fist in the air, and there's the possibility that he might fall back. It's judo.

S: So much aggression is of a spiritual cruelty type, and not providing a target is very difficult under these conditions. Somehow your own space is being invaded by the aggressor. You have to occupy a space, and so your theory doesn't really solve it because you're still there.

TR: Well, if they begin to invade you, you could welcome them. By welcoming them, you are invading *their* territory.

STUDENT: If I were to ask the question, "Who am I?," would an appropriate answer—I mean a realistic type of answer—be, "I am that which goes with the situation as it presents itself"?

TRUNGPA RINPOCHE: If you ask, "Who am I?"—if you don't regard it as a question but as a statement, then that question *is* the answer.

STUDENT: I'm still trying to clarify something about this question of the observer, because I think that where the confusion arises in me is the value I place on it. In other words, if I'm really going with the situation as it presents itself, maybe there is an observer there and maybe there isn't, but it's as if the whole value I place on it is absent.

TRUNGPA RINPOCHE: Well, you see, the whole point is that as soon as you try to get something out of something, there is the possibility that because you want, you may not get anything in return. For instance, if you want to learn, if you want to know, there's something poverty-stricken about that, it is a sort of hunger, ultimately. And the more you demand, the less you're going to get. But if one has the attitude of richness, if you ask questions not out of poverty but out of richness—with that mentality, the question just happens as a statement rather than as a question. Then the answer happens as a natural process.

STUDENT: Is there a constructive aspect to aggression?

TRUNGPA RINPOCHE: Definitely, it is the energy. It is like the techniques we use in meditation. All sorts of different techniques and all sorts of inspirations that we use could be said to be aggression, but aggression without an owner. It is not domesticated aggression; it's wild aggression, independent aggression. It floats in the air as electricity—tremendous, powerful, active, and penetrating—which is beautiful.

STUDENT: Somebody asked a question about how to transmute sexual energy and you didn't answer the question.

TRUNGPA RINPOCHE: I suppose it's a question of how you view the actual sexual energy. It may be seen as a kind of communication, an act of generosity without any demand. But once you begin to make demands, you are solidifying the space of communication. In that case, the other person is not able to communicate with you at all; whereas if there is openness, exchange takes place freely as it is, in the open sense of generosity. That is what is called the dance.

S: But what if you can't express it, if it's not possible for social reasons or for other reasons?

TR: Well, you learn from that, I suppose. You can't change the whole situation because you want it. There's no magic in this sense. If you are thirsty in the middle of the desert, you can't just miraculously create water. That is impossible. The only thing to do is to work with it and learn from it—and in the future, next time, probably you will have a very profound idea of what thirst is. It has a tremendous impact on you.

STUDENT: I get from all this that you should be rich and not hungry. But I'm rich and hungry at the same time. How am I going to jump over the hurdle of feeling rich and hungry at the same time? How will I be able to jump over and just be rich and forget about my hunger?

TRUNGPA RINPOCHE: You don't forget your hunger, your poverty, when you're rich; otherwise there would be no richness at all, there would be no criterion for richness anymore. Rich is in comparison to poor.

S: I don't understand.

TR: If you are rich, how rich you are is dependent on how poor you are not, isn't it? So you work along with that.

STUDENT: Is there a relationship between passion and compassion? What is the relationship?

TRUNGPA RINPOCHE: The relationship is this: compassion contains wisdom and intelligence and is awake, beyond neurosis; passion contains neurosis, sleep, and dullness. It is exactly the same thing we've been talking about in terms of the transmutation of sexual energy.

S: What if they are both there at the same time?

TR: Then it's like the bardo experience of reaching the peak point in which you are uncertain whether you are bound by passion or whether you are about to awake into compassion. And the only thing to do is to communicate with those experiences. You do not particularly try to off-balance passion into compassion or compassion into passion, but if you are properly communicative and able to perceive the situation as it is, then neither compassion nor passion exists. It is free, open space.

S: Then you are awake?

TR: When we talk about there being two things at the same time, we are talking about polarities. And if you don't have any criteria for or against anymore, then that is ultimate awake or, you could say, ultimate compassion.

STUDENT: In this talk of sexual energy, how does the state of orgasm relate to sleep or awake, passion or compassion?

TRUNGPA RINPOCHE: It depends on the background. It could be both—it's the same as any kind of physical contact, which could either be ultimate possessiveness coming through or ultimate openness, which is awakening.

S: Well, there is a difference right there between passion and compassion: one desires possession and the other just gives of itself and is satisfied in the act.

TR: If you see them as independent things, there is a difference, whereas, if you see them as polarities, there isn't.

STUDENT: Can aggression be used as skillful means, the way Marpa did with Milarepa?

TRUNGPA RINPOCHE: That happens all the time, sure. That kind of aggression is very accurate aggression. For instance, with Marpa's aggression, he never missed an opportunity or a chance. It is very accurate, very efficient. Such aggression contains wisdom, as compassion contains wisdom. It is awake aggression, always applicable.

STUDENT: It sounds as if passion is something bad, something to be avoided, and that we should be compassionate. There seem to be *shoulds*.

TRUNGPA RINPOCHE: On the other hand, unskillful compassion could be said to be passion as well. It is a different way of using words.

STUDENT: What about refraining from passion or anger or any of the emotions? Does that lead to a greater awake state, or is that just another trick of ego and of the watcher?

TRUNGPA RINPOCHE: Well, I wouldn't call it a trick. You see, *refraining* is a very vague term. It is a question of whether you refrain from the actual act or whether you fundamentally work with it. Refraining is suppression—but putting something into practice could also be suppression, or an escape. The ultimate meaning of refraining is not sowing any seeds.

9

The Lonely Journey

Since this particular session is going to be the last one, I think we should try to develop further perspective, or view, as to what we have discussed and its application to everyday life. Of course, everyone must go through different phases of so-called normality and so-called abnormality, such as tension, depression, happiness, and spirituality. All these phases that we go through constantly seem to be what we have been talking about in this seminar. Unless we are able to apply this to everyday life, there is no point to it. Often, before we begin to apply it to anything, certain reminders come up to show us whether we are going too fast or going too slow. I'm not talking in terms of divine power or psychic phenomena of any kind, but the kitchen sink level—conflicts of the bedroom and conflicts of the sink. Such situations are always present, but on the other hand we are left completely alone—without help, without a sympathizer, without a comforter.

It is important to see that this journey is a lonely journey. We are alone, completely alone, by ourselves. Nobody is really, fundamentally, going to comfort us at all. For that matter, nobody is really going to show us the path. There are a lot of big deals. People make a big deal about transmission or sudden enlightenment—but even that is interdependent. Transmission is a meeting of two minds: you come halfway, the teacher comes halfway, and you meet. It is very much dependent on personal effort. So any kind of savior notion is not going to function one hundred percent at all. Transmission has to be interdependent because we are trying to relate with something. As soon as we decide to relate with anything, there has to be judgment, relative criteria: how we are going to relate, how open we are, how much ground we are allowing to relate to the space. That is always apparent, it always happens that way.

In the same way, as we relate more, external situations come to us. We begin to learn; we begin to receive the instructions of the situation as it is. But we can't re-create such situations at all. Situations come up and vanish of their own accord, and we have to work along with them by not grasping, by not being fascinated by them. That doesn't mean that we have to be frigid, or rigid for that matter, and fail to communicate with situations. It seems that the whole thing is extremely simple. Therefore, it is too complicated to get into it by using the language of the mind of complications, the logic of that and this, this and that, "On the other hand, let's look at it that way," and so on. The reason we are suffering is that we are so involved with strategy or planning rather than actually putting this into practice as it is.

This whole series of situations, the six types of bardo experience, is present all the time. There is the domestic problem of the hungry ghosts, in terms of comfort, luxury, hunger, and thirst. There is the competitive problem of the jealous gods, the asura level. There is the spiritual problem of the world of the gods. There is the problem of communication and relationship, which is the world of hell, or naraka. There is the problem of not opening, or the animal realm. There is the problem of being sucked into situations and grasping, which is the human realm. These realms are not other lands, not situations *outside.* They are within us: we have domestic problems, emotional problems, spiritual problems, relationship problems. All of these are very apparent; they are right here. And each of these problems has its exit or highlight. In each there is the possibility of completely flipping out or of stepping out of the confusion. Each situation presents its highlight of this and that.

Once we go further and get more and more into the situation as it is, then we wonder whether we are going too far or going too slow. But at the same time, we are in this particular vehicle without any reverse, not even a lower gear. We are traveling in top gear, at top speed—with no brakes either. It is an ongoing process. In the movie *Space Odyssey,* there is that same kind of analogy: you are going on and on and on; once you begin to destroy the computer's brainwork, you are involved in an ongoing process, an infinite journey into space. It's quite an interesting analogy.

This seminar seems to be based on seeing the situation of sanity and insanity. It has to do not only with working with ourselves but working with other people. In the present situation, some people are actually flipping out and some give the pretense of flipping out. That makes it possible to look into this topic. Strangely enough, the situation gave the talks, the situation held discussions, rather than there being deliberately guided talks in terms of myself or yourselves. It seems that talks just happen, as the mutual effort of the audience and the speaker. However we would like to regard it, it is a mutual effort, the act of the meeting of two minds.

There was a question a few days ago about alcohol. That is a very interesting subject. It seems that such a question has different perspectives or views. There is the conventional attitude—that of the nonsmoker, nondrinker, good citizen, good Christian, good Buddhist, good Hindu, good Jew. But there is another aspect as well, not associated with such conventional attitudes, but with the human situation, which also includes the experience of grass, hashish, LSD, mescaline, and all the rest of it. It seems that the whole question is based on sanity, and on the many possible ways of providing temptations leading us to insanity. That seems to be the central question or theme. It is very much based on the user—but at the same time there is a big conflict, as we know, between a dream world and the actual world, the so-to-speak actual world. The dream world is associated with hallucinations, pictures, and visions—but it is still intoxication. At the same time, in the earthly world, or the physical world, there is so much sudden pain and sudden pleasure, making too big a deal about reality. Here too there is the question of intoxication. Alcohol intoxication, or intoxication by yeast, is closer to the earth; but at the same time, as far as one's personal experience is concerned, it should be worked with very carefully. Such a high on earth could lead to being high on space, or it could just remain high on earth—that's the criterion.

That same criterion could apply also to the situation as a whole: what we've been talking about and doing in this particular seminar, and in general what I'm trying to do in this country. In fact, I think everybody here without exception is involved in a very dangerous game. Everybody here is involved in a very dangerous game because we are working on the karmic pattern of America. We are trying not only to fight it, but we are trying to infiltrate it. That is quite dangerous. The magical powers of materialism and spirituality are waging war, so to speak, all the time. From the beginning of such a setup, it has worked out that way. Spirituality is against worldliness and worldliness is against spirituality. So we are facing tremendous danger. Every individual who takes part in this seminar is subject to an attack from materialism, because we are working on the infiltration of the materialistic world. According to history, a lot of people who attempted to become teachers or outstanding students were struck by such power, such energy—either through a direct physical attack or through a psychological attack. That has been happening. So it is very dangerous—to the extent that we should not be involved. If you insist on being involved in it, working with it, then you should be brave enough to work with it and go along with the infiltration.

That brings up the next subject, which is the practice of meditation. Meditation is the technique of infiltration, or the transmutation of negative hostile forces into positive creative situations. That is what we are doing. In other words, what I am trying to say is that involvement of this type is not going to be easy by any means. It is going to be extremely difficult. For one thing, it is a lonely journey. For another thing, it is a lonely journey with bridges, ladders, cliffs, and waves. It includes turbulent rivers that we have to cross, shaky bridges that we have to walk on, slippery steps that we have to tread on amongst hailstorms, rains, snowstorms, and powerful winds. Constant patience is needed as well: we are going to cross an inexhaustible stretch of desert without water. All of this is very frightening. And you cannot blame that situation on anyone: you can't blame it on the teacher who led you to it, and you can't blame it on yourself, that you started on it. Blaming doesn't help. Going along on the path is the only way to do it.

At the same time, some energy and encouragement continue on the path as well—it's not as black as that by any means. The first inspiration is that you decide to step in or involve yourself in such a path, which is based on our communication and our connection. Take the example of our local situation, for instance. If you are involved with the work of Suzuki Roshi in California, and if you also decide to become involved with the work which is happening here with me, such a situation contains tremendous power, reinforcement, and energy behind it. It is not only that the teachers themselves are particularly forceful teachers or powerful as individuals, because they are human beings. But the energy behind that inspiration comes from a lineage of two thousand five hundred years of effort, energy, and spiritual power. Nobody in that lineage just took advantage of that power, but they received inspiration from it, and everybody worked, practiced, and achieved. And their inspiration has been handed down generation by generation. As the scriptures would say, it is like good gold, which is put on the fire and beaten, hammered, twisted, refined, until it comes out as pure gold—living pure gold. Or it is like hot baked bread. The knowledge of baking bread has been handed down generation by generation, so present-day bakers who belong to that particular lineage can still provide hot, living, tasty bread straight from the oven and feed you. Such a living quality of inspiration continues. It is that which keeps us continuing on the path, going through the deserts, going through the storms, bridges, ladders, and so on.

The whole thing is really based on whether we are going to acknowledge it in terms of our relationship to ourselves. Nobody particularly has to belong to a syndicate, or to a spiritual scene, just for the sake of belonging. It is the relationship of ourself to ourself which seems to be important. And the inspiration of belonging to ourself, working with ourself, relating with ourself, has different facets, which are the six types of world—the world of the gods, the world of hell, the world of the hungry ghosts, human beings, animals, and jealous gods. Making friends with ourselves is not very easy. It is a very profound thing. At the same time, we could do it, we could make it. Nevertheless, making a long story too short, involvement with ourselves means making an honest relationship with ourselves, looking into ourselves as what we are and realizing that external comfort will be temporary, that our comforters may not be there all the time. There is the possibility of us being alone. Therefore there is more reason to work and go along with the practices that are involved.

And usually what happens—and also what happened to me, "on my way to the theater"—is that I established a relationship with my guru, Jamgön Kongtrül Rinpoche, and learned from him, spent some time with him. There were also certain times when I couldn't see him and I couldn't talk to him. Later I would be able to talk to him again and relate my experiences to him. When I saw him for the last time, I felt I really made communication, with real commitment and understanding of his teachings. I was very pleased about it. I regarded that as the beginning of our relationship. But then I had to go back without him. I had achieved tremendous insight, understanding, as to what he was and what he had to say and I was dying to relate that to him, just to tell him. That would be so beautiful. It would be such a beautiful moment to relate to him that at last I had heard him, I had understood him. I was waiting for the occasion to do that— and it never took place; nothing happened. Jamgön Kongtrül was captured by the Communist Chinese and he died in jail. I never met him or saw him again.

A similar situation happened in terms of Gampopa and Milarepa. Milarepa told Gampopa that he should practice certain meditations and relate with his experience—and he did it, he achieved it. But it happened that he forgot the particular date he was supposed to come and see Milarepa, which was the fifteenth day of the first month of the year, according to the Tibetan calendar. He was about fifteen days late. He suddenly remembered on the twenty-fifth day that he must go and see Milarepa on the fifteenth, so he decided to set out. He rushed, but halfway there some travelers came to him with the message that Milarepa was dead. He had sent a piece of his robe and a message for Gampopa. So Gampopa was never able to relate that last experience to Milarepa.

Situations like that take place all the time. They are a kind of encouragement, showing us that we are able to work with ourselves and that we will achieve the goal—but we will not receive the congratulations of the guru anymore. Again you are alone: you are a lonely student or you are a lonely teacher. You are continuously becoming alone again. With such independence, relating with spiritual scenes or other such situations is not so important. But relating with ourselves is very important and more necessary. There is a really living quality in that.

I'm not saying these things because I want to raise your paranoia, but as in the historical cases or evolutionary cases that took place, nobody is going to congratulate you, that finally you are buddha. And in fact, your enthronement ceremony will never take place. If it did take place, it would be dangerous, the wrong time—it would not be real anymore. So the lonely journey is important. And particularly, many of you who took part in this seminar and experienced our individual relationship are going to go back to your own places and try to practice by yourselves and work hard on all this, trying to relate with the different realms of the world. But at the same time, no teacher or situation should be providing comfort to anybody. I suppose that is the point we are getting at. In other words, nobody is going to be initiated as a fully enlightened person decorated by the guru. It is just about to happen, you think you are just about to get a decoration—but it doesn't take place; it never happens. So any external reliance does not work. It is the individual, personal intuition, working on oneself, which is important.

STUDENT: Rinpoche, the path that you're talking about is not very complex. It is very simple, just the way it is right now, without any trips. Isn't that it?

TRUNGPA RINPOCHE: Yes, I think it is simple and immediate. We are talking about not only what we should do when we finish our meeting here, but what we should be doing right now—let alone when we retire and buy a house and land somewhere and *then* meditate. It happens right now.

STUDENT: You have said that in tantra there is a colorful aspect, beyond shunyata. Do you mean real colors, physical colors, vision, eyesight? Sometimes you don't see at all; you look but you just don't see. At other times you can see every little thing.

TRUNGPA RINPOCHE: Generally, we are preoccupied all the time. When that wall of preoccupation is removed, for the first time we begin to appreciate colors: visual situations, which could become the inspiration for symbolism, as well as psychological and emotional colors. But that doesn't mean you are going to see beehive mandalas, or that your bright carpet is going to turn into *herukas*.

STUDENT: Could you speak more clearly about infiltration and other tactics?

TRUNGPA RINPOCHE: I think it involves a certain kind of acceptance at the beginning, so that you could enter into a situation. Having entered into a situation, then you could work with the heart of that situation. I don't see using any other tactic apart from infiltration. The other tactic would have to be an attack, an external attack or invasion—which is like trying to throw out the whole wall by force. In that case, there is the possibility that you might get hurt; whereas if you decide to work brick by brick, you will never get hurt, but you will be able to destroy the whole wall. Infiltration begins by working on the sensitive areas which are not guarded by the meshwork of materialistic forces. It is like trying to infiltrate at the time when the changing of the guards is taking place: at that point you have a chance to go in. It is trying to see the gaps, the unguarded situations where you can infiltrate through.

S: So it is not only a matter of demolition, as it were, but a transformation of the situation you find yourself in?

TR: Yes, yes, this is so. Another analogy has been used in Chinese philosophy, as well as by Mao Tse-tung. He said that if you are trying to invade a country, you don't attack the capital to start with. Instead, you first try to work your way into the countryside, make friends with the peasants, and occupy the rural areas. Then finally the capital becomes just a little island, an insignificant thing.

STUDENT: Isn't infiltration a dangerous idea? Doesn't it imply that we have the concept that we have something that's better than what is, so we're going to change it?

TRUNGPA RINPOCHE: That depends on your understanding. Take the example of the local situation. In order to teach meditation or nonviolence to America, first you have to become a complete American, you have to become a super-American. Then you'll be able to speak their language as well as what you're trying to say. So a certain giving is necessary as well as attacking or changing, because change cannot take place if you don't know what you're going to change. In that sense, I don't think it is going to be dangerous.

S: It just seems like it would be dangerous to develop into some kind of crusader.

TR: Of course. It would be dangerous in that case—if you became evangelistic, carried away, with a sword in one hand and a Bible in the other.

STUDENT: Isn't there a conflict in becoming American? On the one hand, as students of meditation we lean toward a kind of pure life. For instance, maybe we'll want to get up early in the morning, or maybe we'll want to eat a simple diet. On the other hand, Americans watch TV and they go window shopping and do other sorts of things. Isn't there a danger in leading the pure life, and isn't there also a danger in watching too much TV?

TRUNGPA RINPOCHE: Well, you see, that's precisely the point I'm trying to raise. I'm glad you raised that question. If you lead a complete American middle-class life—watch television, football, go into business—then you begin to see the foolishness of that; and if you live in a simple place and are trying to do the hippie trip, equally there is something lacking there as well. The point is to see both perspective views as they are and then to penetrate through it. At the same time, you don't get hurt by watching television, going to parties, and having polite conversation with people. That doesn't overwhelm you, because you already know what is happening; whereas generally you don't know what's happening, you just go along.

STUDENT: Would you say that practicing meditation would be like the bridge or ladder joining together the bottom and the top?

TRUNGPA RINPOCHE: Meditation practice is like getting into no-man's-land. It is the act of doing absolutely nothing, which provides the right perspective, or view, of the ultimate meditation experience. Because of such understanding, the postmeditation experience also becomes broader and more open, because you have that vision. It is working with duality in some sense, the two extremes. Both extremes are being seen as they are by going into it.

STUDENT: While you're still around, can I maybe buy you a beer?

TRUNGPA RINPOCHE: Go ahead.

STUDENT: Rinpoche, I really didn't understand what you said about alcohol, when you compared getting high off earth and getting high off space. Can you be clearer about that?

TRUNGPA RINPOCHE: There are actual deliberate differences between being high on drugs and high on alcohol. Being high on drugs is very much a dream world—that is why a lot of people find it difficult to reconcile themselves when they come out of it. You might get a hangover from alcohol, of course, but alcohol intoxication is being high on earth: people cry, people fight, such earthy situations happen. It is based directly on living. But what I'm trying to say is that any kind of extreme or any attempt at replacement or escape doesn't seem to be right.

S: So there could be danger in getting high on alcohol as well?

TR: Yes. It might lead to being high on space.

S: That's what I didn't follow before. How would being high on earth be any different from being high on space?

TR: Because all sorts of concepts begin to develop. Being high on earth could lead to being high on space at the same time— based on such conceptualizing. But that doesn't mean one should always be guarded and keeping a happy medium. Everybody says,

"Moderation in everything," which is a well-known phrase, jargon. But somehow that doesn't work either. It should be experiential, personal.

STUDENT: Rinpoche, how does the idea of its being a lonely journey relate to the possibility of going into it with your family, making the journey as more than one?

TRUNGPA RINPOCHE: There will be hundreds of people making the same journey. It doesn't have to be purely your family. Hundreds of people here in this gathering are making a similar journey. At the same time, the whole idea is that you cannot actually relate one hundred percent of your own experiences to anybody; you cannot relate everything to anybody completely. The ways we have of relating are words and situations, and words and situations are very inadequate, clumsy ways of communicating. Ultimately there's only one way—being alone. You might take your family and friends along into the same situations, but that doesn't mean you are sharing absolutely every moment of those situations with them. So in any case there is no alternative.

STUDENT: Do you have any comments on such activities as painting, writing, music, and theater—those kinds of things?

TRUNGPA RINPOCHE: They are the expression of man's inspiration, including landing on the moon—which is beautiful. It is the result of being brave enough to experiment, brave enough to go along with the truth of nature as it is, and accomplishing it. That's the dignity of man, or whatever jargon we'd like to use. It's beautiful. You see, the point is that once you begin to put these— painting, music, scientific experiments, whatever it may be—into practice, at the beginning it is deliberate effort but in the end you transcend deliberateness. Your work becomes a masterpiece. An accomplished artist wouldn't think of how his audience is going to be impressed, he just does it. It is the same thing with scientific experiments: a master scientist wouldn't hesitate; he or she is continuously going more and more into the depths of reality, of things as they are.

STUDENT: A moment ago when we were talking about infiltrating America, someone said, "I do this, but Americans watch TV," as though Americans were somebody else. I think if we have any ideas about doing something for America, we have to remember, like it or not, that America is us. In a sense we don't have to infiltrate America—we're already in it.

TRUNGPA RINPOCHE: That's true, yes. Infiltrating is already taking place and actually taking effect. Good for you.

S: Is that infiltration at the political or sociological level, or can it take place within each individual, infiltrating one's square side and one's hippie side—becoming friends with those and realizing the foolishness of both extremes?

TR: It works both ways. Usually the reason we are here is because we want to learn something. We ask questions all the time at the beginning. Then we begin to realize that infiltration is taking place already. That is a kind of acknowledgment, a confirmation that it has happened already, rather than that we have to work on a tactic of any kind.

Infiltration works inwardly as well as outwardly. It is the same analogy as how to stop the war. War is aggression, an act of aggression; so the only way to stop the war is not to make a nuisance of ourselves to ourselves. We start by dealing with the closest aggression that there is; that is the starting point of trying to stop the war. I know that most idealistic peace marchers and nonviolence groups, who are involved with actual problems, wouldn't agree with that—it would seem to be too timid and cowardly. Because of that, they begin to create another kind of war. In fact, people actually believe that if they start one kind of aggression in order to stop another aggression, that is absolutely justifiable aggression. But as far as aggression goes, there is no justifiable aggression at all. By fighting aggression with aggression, you're adding to the complications and confusions of both the country and the individuals.

STUDENT: In a previous talk you mentioned the concept of sane violence and insane violence. Is that sane violence related at all to the so-called aggressiveness of the peace marchers? What is the difference between sane violence and what the peace marchers are doing?

TRUNGPA RINPOCHE: It seems that what they are doing is insane violence, the confusion of violence. They are not able to learn judo; instead they take part in an ordinary fistfight game, based on not having enough understanding of the nature of violence. I mean, one obvious way of defeating somebody is to kick back. But then there is a continual chain reaction set up—which I would say is insane, because the whole thing is based on defeat and victory constantly. Actual sane violence transcends both defeat and victory at the same time. It is like the analogy of the Buddha being attacked by the maras: each spearhead or arrow thrown at him became a flower.

S: I think that for me the peace marches were one of the first steps I made in looking at my society. I suppose that has a lot to do with me being here now.

TR: It serves a purpose, of course. Anything you will do serves a purpose. If you commit suicide, that will make someone stop and think, but that doesn't necessarily mean that that is the way, the only way. What we are talking about is that we actually don't want to hurt others. Once you begin to do something, there is going to be a natural chain reaction: your love or hate is going to reach somebody else and they're going to be subject to that as well as you.

S: Do you think they actually hurt others then, the marchers?

TR: Well, they built up all sorts of animosity.

STUDENT: They seem to be very self-righteous.

TRUNGPA RINPOCHE: That's the whole point. You develop a philosophy of your own at the beginning, which may be good, based on Mahatma Gandhi's idea of nonviolence and so on. But then you have to hold on to that: you have regular prefabricated answers to every question, and you don't think for yourself at all. You just churn them out because it is already worked out, it is already planned. That's the problem with any kind of dogma: that prefabricated quality becomes lifeless, without any personality.

STUDENT: In talking about the path of the bodhisattva, you say you destroy what needs to be destroyed. What do you mean by this?

TRUNGPA RINPOCHE: That is the precise, clear vision of compassion that sees the situation clearly, obviously, as it is. Whenever you have to play the role of tough, you play it. Whenever you need to play the role of gentleness, you do it. You see, there is a tremendous difference between blind compassion and skillful compassion.

STUDENT: Why are you here rather than in a cave?

TRUNGPA RINPOCHE: This is a cave. In fact, twenty-four hours a day I work in a cave.

STUDENT: Will you speak about the family and its importance on the path?

TRUNGPA RINPOCHE: Well, each relationship is energy. The concept of *sangha,* for instance, means a group of people working together as brothers and sisters, working together as spiritual friends to one another. That is an important point. In order to be brothers and sisters, you have to be open to each other as well. Being open is not being dependent on others, which blocks *their* openness. In other words, the sangha does not create a situation of claustrophobia for each person in it. If somebody falls, you still stand independently; because you are not leaning on the other person, you don't fall. When one person falls it doesn't create a chain reaction of other people falling as well. So independence is equally important as being together, acting as an inspiration to one another.

S : Should you let people pick themselves up if they fall? It seems if you try to help, sometimes that can be a reflection of your own ego. I think that for myself, it is better for me to pick myself up. If somebody tries to help, unless it's done just right, it's wrong.

T R : The important point there is exactly parallel to what we were saying about the changing of the guards being a chance to infiltrate. Such things could also take place in reverse. If you try to help somebody, when you are leaning down to help, somebody could easily kick both of you equally. That doesn't mean that you shouldn't help others, that you just purely want to survive. You should be working with situations. But there is the danger of something else coming in and knocking both of you down. It's the notion of the blind leading the blind.

STUDENT : You use the words *hope* and *fear* in the same way, meaning that they both need to be transcended, as though hope is as much of an obstruction as fear. I was wondering how that fits in with your schemes for the community here. It seems to be a very hopeful thing. You use the word *inspiration,* but it seems to be the same thing.

TRUNGPA RINPOCHE : It seems to depend on your relationship to that concept. If inspiration is hope, then fear is not a part of it. But the inspiration I was trying to express contains both hope and fear—in other words, both destruction and creation. Destruction is as creative an inspiration as creation. Both are inspiration.

S : Does that mean you have to be willing to give up all plans of any type?

TR: I wouldn't give up plans, but I wouldn't relate plans with the future alone—I would relate plans with the present moment. The potential of the future is in the present moment rather than purely in the future. We work in the present—with the future potential of possibilities in the present. So it is relating with the present moment, as your relation with yourself and as your stepping stone.

STUDENT: Could you mention some positive aspects of ego that would allow us to make friends with it?

TRUNGPA RINPOCHE: That is what we have been saying, that inspiration includes both hope and fear. Any negative aspect of ego which presents itself then becomes material to work on. In that sense ego *is* the inspiration. Without ego, there wouldn't be realization at all, from our point of view.

STUDENT: I was thinking about what you said about your relationship with your teacher, and the story of Gampopa and Milarepa, and the fact that there's no gratification. And it seems as if I'm the one who wants to get enlightened—I mean me, Steve. Steve wants to get enlightened, but it also seems as if Steve is never going to get enlightened because he won't be there when he's enlightened; there's no gratification in being enlightened. So why do I want to get enlightened so bad?

TRUNGPA RINPOCHE: You see, that's the whole point—attaining enlightenment doesn't mean gratification, does it?

S: But what is it that makes us want to get enlightened? I mean, it seems everything I do is for gratification, and I want to get enlightened for no less reason—but there must be another reason.

TR: Sure. There is pain and pleasure, and you want to have a proper relationship with them.

S: I identify enlightenment with pleasure, I suppose, because I'm either looking for pleasure or looking for enlightenment.

TR: I think that's the problem, in fact. Enlightenment has nothing to do with pleasure—or pain, for that matter. It just *is*.

S: If we're really aware of what we are and accept it, then is that the same as enlightenment?

TR: Enlightenment is, as we said, an honest relationship with ourselves. That is why it is connected with the truth—*being* true rather than truth as something external you are relating to. Just being.

STUDENT: It seems ego is really clever. First we tell him we'll make friends with him, come along, help out—and at the last minute we throw him overboard. And he's really smart about it. He says, "Why should I be friends with you? You're trying to suck me into something. What's in it for me?" What's the tag line?

TRUNGPA RINPOCHE: Why not?

S: Just go along for the hell of it?

TR: Quite.

TWO

The Six States of Being

KARME-CHÖLING   1971

Pain and Pleasure

Generally the concept of bardo is misunderstood to be purely the gap between one's death and next birth. But in this case, the idea of bardo is being presented as it was by Padmasambhava. The whole concept is based on the continuity of the bardo experience. So although some scholars and people claim that the idea of bardo, or of *The Tibetan Book of the Dead* as a whole, is purely related with the details of the hangups and hallucinations connected with the colorful world after death and how to relate to it, what we are working on in this case is not necessarily connected with that purely colorful world and its hangups. Instead, it is connected with the continuity of the psychosomatic situation. As long as there is a physical body involved with life, that automatically brings pain or pleasure. Pain and pleasure could be interpreted as illness or sickness or problems or neuroses of all kinds. They have psychosomatic case histories constantly.

The word *bardo* means "in-between state." *Bar* means "between," "in between," the medium situation which exists between one extreme and the other extreme. *Do* could be explained as being an island, a remote island which exists out of nowhere, yet is surrounded by an ocean, or desert, or whatever. So *bardo* is that which is outstanding like an island in terms of your life situation, that which is in between experiences. You could have experiences of extreme pleasure and extreme pain. When the experience of pleasure is extreme, automatically that experience of pleasure becomes irritatingly pleasureful. *Bardo* is that irritating and heavy-handed quality of pleasure just about to bring pain, invite pain. It is that kind of uncertainty between two situations. For instance, hot and cold are uncertain: either it is too hot or too cold. If it is too hot, therefore it could be said to be too cold; but if it is too cold, therefore it is regarded as too hot. Such uncertainty and the psychophysical buildup associated with it brings an extreme case of uncertainty, and at that point, one begins to lose criteria of any kind.

The concept of bardo has six types. It seems to be quite worthwhile to relate these six bardos with the six realms of existence: the realm of the gods; the realm of jealous gods, or asuras; the realm of human beings; the realm of animals; the realm of hungry ghosts, or pretas; and the realm of hell. Those prescribed situations, or realms, seem to provide an extremely interesting way of looking at bardo. Each of these realms has some quality of extreme pleasure and extreme pain, and in between the two there is also a kind of extreme. But those extremes have entirely different textures in the various realms. For instance, there is the extreme hunger, rigidness, and stupidity of the animal realm; the extreme indulgence of the human realm; the extreme relativity of the jealous gods level. All kinds of realms take place, each with their bardo states. What we are going to discuss is largely the psychological state where there is pain as well as pleasure—physical pain, psychological pain, or spiritual pain; spiritual pleasure, psychological pleasure, or physical pleasure. All six realms are characterized by this continual process of striving, the continual process of trying to reach some kind of ultimate answer, to achieve permanent pleasure.

As far as this particular human society is concerned, the concept of bardo is extremely powerful and important to us. We have continual problems related with questions such as "What is sane and what is insane?" "What is the purpose of life?" Those are popular questions often asked of spiritual teachers when they are interviewed on the radio or television, or give personal interviews. Always, "What is the purpose of life?" What is the purpose of life?—what isn't the purpose of life, for that matter? These questions are not concerned with fixed answers as such, at all. But these questions could be answered in the psychophysical sense. What is not body? What is body? What is not mind? What is mind? What is emotion? What isn't emotion? How does emotion function? What is the texture of emotion that you can switch by being loving as well as by being aggressive? What makes these changes? How does the whole creation take place? Creation does not take place through the revelation of God, and creation does not take place purely by trying to change your living situation. If you are irritated by yourself or your particular situation—for instance, living with your parents—moving out of your parents' domain and renting your own apartment somewhere else does not solve the problem at all, because you carry yourself with you all the time, as the tortoise carries his shell. So the question has not been answered, the problem has not been solved. There is something more fundamental than that. Pain and pleasure are not as gullible as we would like to think. They are very subtle and deep-rooted in our life, and take place constantly.

The bardo experience tells you the details of the texture or the color or the temperature of godlike mentality or hell-like mentality, whatever it may be. It tells you in great detail about these basic situations or realms, about things as they are in terms of panoramic vision. It seems that a lot of people experienced this in the past and achieved the perfection of it. They understood those situations—so much so that the message has been handed down from generation to generation. People have experienced it. So it seems that what we are involved with in this particular seminar is the tremendous opportunity to discuss the texture and, you could almost say, the case history of emotions. It is an opportunity for a different way of living and relating to our human existence—the inhuman quality of human existence as well as the human quality of human existence.

Bardo experience is an extremely powerful way of solving the problem of extremes. At the same time, it is not presenting for or against, but trying to present both extremes simultaneously. That provides a way to the bardo experience of clear light. Such experiences as *chönyi* bardo, which is based on absorption into basic space, creating enormous, overpowering expansion—how does that relate with such bardos as sipa bardo, the bardo of existence, continually creating new situations? That whole process of the six bardos seems to be very much related with our own psychological portrait. Somebody in this audience—or everybody in this audience, shall we say—has animal qualities, as well as hungry ghost qualities, as well as realm of gods qualities, as well as human qualities. We are all part of this gigantic network, or amalgamation, of all colors, all textures, all temperatures, all emotions—we are part of the whole thing. That is why we exist as what we are, why we function as what we are. Otherwise, we could not function in terms of samsara. We have managed to maintain our confusion up to now very skillfully. Such an achievement! Why? Because we could become hell beings, because we could become realm of gods beings, because we could become part of the animal realm, because we could become hungry ghosts. We improvise constantly, very skillfully drawing out these possible alternatives.

That whole situation brings up the question of the survival of ego. In order to survive as a human being who is based on passion and aggression, in order to maintain those ideas of passion and aggression, we have to relate with all kinds of subsidiary ways of maintaining ourselves. We have all kinds of ways of doing that. We could present cold as completely frozen, icy cold, or just a chill. We could present cold which is just about to become hot, and then we could switch into hot: just chill off hot, warm, body temperature warm, irritatingly hot warm. We could present all kinds of textures, all kinds of beings with all kinds of living situations. We are being trained in some strange way, immediately from the time we are born and presented until we are grown up, up to the point we become the emperor of the world. We constantly operate all those realms, improvising that as opposed to this, this as opposed to that.

So the bardo experience is the description of a skillful artist who managed to paint such a balanced picture, or a skillful musician who managed to play such beautiful music—but that music belongs to somebody, that picture belongs to somebody. That always seems to be the problem. That is what is called ego. But we cannot just forget the whole thing and try to present a beautiful and blissful heavenly situation which answers all the problems or shows the great promise of liberation. Before we know what liberation or enlightenment is, we also have to know what is not liberation, what is not enlightenment. Studying bardo seems to create a stepping stone. That seems to be most important. We need to learn how to relate to our daily experience, how to relate with our own experiences rather than with doctrinal assumptions, philosophical views, scientific theories, or what have you. So bardo is a very practical way of looking at our life.

This particular talk seems to be more like an appetizer than the actual main course. But even the appetizer itself has the quality of the environment and of what meal is to come. So that also seems to be useful. If you just decide to have the appetizer, if you decide to walk out of the restaurant before you have the main course, that's possible. We could do so—or you could do so.

STUDENT: What do you mean by spiritual pleasure and pain?

TRUNGPA RINPOCHE: Spiritual pain is extremely powerful pain, because it transcends the ordinary pain of daily living; and spiritual pleasure is delightful, because it is regarded as transcendental pleasure, which supposedly transcends any human concerns. In either case, the whole idea is based on an inhuman attitude to spirituality, rather than the human aspect of spirituality.

S: Is it still concerned with ego?

TR: If it is concerned with pain and pleasure at all, it is always concerned with the ego, I'm afraid.

S: So it is more in the realm of what you are wont to call spiritual materialism, Rinpoche?

TR: Precisely, yes. As long as we talk in terms of greater achievement, or greater liberation, in terms of "me" achieving greater liberation, "me" experiencing greater pleasure, then the whole thing is related with that relative view, which doesn't liberate at all. Therefore, if anything is concerned with that and this, relative situations, it is regarded as spiritual materialism because it has something to hang on to. You automatically try to destroy the handle, but at the same time, you provide another handle out of the absence of that handle.

STUDENT: I don't understand the relation between bardo, or the concept of in-betweenness, and realm. When you say *chönyi bardo,* or the name of some other bardo, you're not referring to any of the realms, are you?

TRUNGPA RINPOCHE: Not necessarily, because you could say that all aspects of bardo have the same quality.

S: Do you mean that all the realms are aspects of bardo?

TR: They are all bardos, in between, because you are trapped in something. The whole idea of bondage or entrapment is that you are not there, not here. You are captivated somewhere; therefore it is bardo.

STUDENT: I had the opposite impression. I always had the impression that bardo referred to a gap.

TRUNGPA RINPOCHE: Yes, gap. When you are born in the realm of the gods, or when you are born in the animal realm, you manage to be born in a realm by misunderstanding the gap.

S: So is the bardo the time in between living in one realm and another, say between hell and the realm of animals?

TR: No, not necessarily. Bardo is the realms as they are. You want to achieve absolute pleasure. At the same time, you demand that absolute pleasure because you experience pain. As the pain gets worse and worse, the pleasure becomes more demanding. So finally, you are not quite certain whether you are experiencing pain or pleasure. Then you are born in the realm of the gods, because you are completely bewildered into pleasurehood, or whatever it's called, "godhood."

STUDENT: You mentioned a bardo between death and birth. Is there a bardo between birth and death also?

TRUNGPA RINPOCHE: Yes, it is called sipa bardo.

S: So we are always in between.

TR: You have been born and you are just about to die, or you have died and you are just about to be born. You are relating with birth—or death for that matter.

STUDENT: Is there a principle that creates the whole bardo experience and also the other experiences that we create?

TRUNGPA RINPOCHE: It comes from our living situation, life.

S: So it is continuous, right? From birth to death, during that cycle?

TR: I think so, yes.

S: Is that sort of like ego being handed down?

TR: Yes.

S: Is that a subconsciousness being handed down?

TR: Well, it is always a hidden wish or hidden fear which is the source of involving ourselves in continual bardo experiences.

STUDENT: Could you explain again what bardo is the gap between?

TRUNGPA RINPOCHE: A gap between two extremes.

S: Then the bardo experience is not an experience of extremes?

TR: In a sense it is continual experience, which also presents a meeting of the two extremes. Later we will be going into the details of the different realms, such as the realm of the gods, the realm of animals, and the realm of hell. We constantly go through these realms. We have some kind of trip going on all the time. These trips are brought about by the extreme meeting point of hope and fear. So we are constantly trapped in that product of our work, the product of our wish or desire.

STUDENT: Rinpoche, is the confusion between pain and pleasure that you're talking about different from what Milarepa discusses as the nondistinction of pain and pleasure? He talks about recognizing the identical nature of the two extremes, not distinguishing between pain and pleasure.

TRUNGPA RINPOCHE: That seems to be an intelligent effort; but in this case, it is completely mechanical: one is uncertain whether one is experiencing pain or pleasure, and one is swept away. Because you are uncertain about pain or pleasure, therefore you are pushed and thrust into new situations automatically. Otherwise, if you are on the side of pain or the side of pleasure as it is, you cannot get into the bardo state at all, because you are in a meditative state at that moment. You regard pain as pain, pleasure as pleasure. Whereas the way we get caught into the extreme of the bardo state is that we are not quite certain whether we are actually experiencing pain as pain or whether we are experienc ing pain as occupation, which means pleasure in some sense. So we are caught up in it. That is why we manage to hang on here, in this samsaric world. It is a very beautiful tactic somebody developed.

S: What attitude should one have toward pleasure?

TR: It doesn't matter what attitude you have, it is what it is. Pleasure is pleasure, pain is pain. It does not matter about attitude. Attitude doesn't play a part, particularly. Obviously you would have some intelligence in relating with your experiences. But that could hardly be called an attitude, in fact. It is just instinct.

S: Rinpoche, how is the idea of the meditative state being the complete experience of pain as pain and pleasure as pleasure related to the statement I've heard that pain and pleasure are the same thing?

TR: If you experience pain as pain in the fullest sense, then it is what it is—as much as pleasure could be. That is intelligent. You are not confused or uncertain as to what is pain and what is pleasure, but you are seeing things precisely, directly as they are. In that way, pain and pleasure are one in the realm of intelligence, realm of *prajna,* realm of knowledge.

S: Rinpoche, does the opposite hold true, when you experience pleasure fully?

TR: It is saying the same thing. True pleasure is true experience as much as true pain, for that matter. But that is not at all involved in a dream world; you are experiencing things really as they are.

STUDENT: Would someone who didn't have a neurotic state of mind still be experiencing these different realms?

TRUNGPA RINPOCHE: Yes, in terms of display. You cannot exist without a world of some kind to exist in. But that doesn't mean you are confused between the two worlds.

S: Between which two worlds?

TR: Pain and pleasure. For instance, you are not confused about the pain of the hungry ghost realm or the pleasure of the hungry ghost realm. You just see the hungry ghost realm as what your world is, precisely and clearly.

STUDENT: How do you see yourself in that? Do you separate yourself at all?

TRUNGPA RINPOCHE: You do not separate yourself from it. You begin to see that you are part of that world entirely, fully, thoroughly. That is why you begin to see it, because if you see yourself as separate from it, then you fail to see it—you are too self-concerned, too self-conscious.

STUDENT: The description of the neurotic state implies oscillation, whereas the description of pain as pain, pleasure as pleasure, indicates a fixed point. We also perceive through oscillation. Does that have any relation to all this?

TRUNGPA RINPOCHE: Relating with the world is the key point. Relating with the world could be said to be the idea of complete involvement, seeing pain as pain and pleasure as pleasure; whereas whenever there is distance between you and the world, whenever there is failure to connect, or absent-mindedness, then automatically confusion begins to crop up, because you have failed to relate with things as they are. That brings bewilderment and confusion. You begin to lose track of it—which brings the bardo experience. Then that bardo experience goes to the extreme—it becomes an absolutely extreme and rising crescendo of confusion, big pain and big pleasure. You go up and up and up, because you have lost track. It is as if you have lost your anchor and you are floating in the ocean endlessly, constantly, because you have lost contact, lost any real way of relating with things as they are.

S: If you can hold the point where you see things as they are, what then causes the shift from one world to the next? How do you go from, say, the realm of the hungry ghosts to the realm of humans? What causes that jump?

T R : You cannot live in one world constantly. Whether you are involved with an aggressive or a pleasurable situation in your living world, it seems that the situation demands a change, not that you make a change. It is like traveling from one place to another. The place invites you to adapt to your situation there, rather than you trying to adopt a new situation by force.

S T U D E N T : If you remain in the meditative state, do you eliminate the bardo experience?

T R U N G P A R I N P O C H E : Constantly. At the same time, you still have to relate with the living bardo potential from other people's points of view. So you can't reject it altogether. In other words, if you are in a meditative state constantly, you do not get into the bardo state as such, but you share the bardo experiences or environment of other people.

S T U D E N T : What state are *you* in?

T R U N G P A R I N P O C H E : Any state.

S : If you don't get into the bardo state as such, if you share other people's bardo state, what state are you in?

T R : You are in *their* state. If you are in America, you are in America. You share the American experience with Americans.

S T U D E N T : You said that when you begin searching for pleasure, pleasure and pain build up simultaneously, so you have this confusion. In what way does this happen? I'm not clear about that.

T R U N G P A R I N P O C H E : Well, partly the situation demands that process, and it is also partly the state of mind which brings it.

S : Why do you seek more and more pleasure? Is that innate? Do you just naturally seek more and more pleasure?

TR: You don't necessarily search for pleasure. If your whole world is based on pain, you just try to swim through that pain. Each stroke of your hand could be said to be directed toward pleasure, but you are not getting pleasure, you are just roaming about in that particular painful realm.

STUDENT: Oh, so the problem is that you're seeking to be something that you are not, rather than accepting at that moment exactly what you are.

TRUNGPA RINPOCHE: Yes. Supposing you were starved, following the mentality of the hungry ghost realm, just swimming in this tremendous hunger. There is a possibility of satisfying your hunger, but that doesn't seem to be your aim or object at all. Instead you are just maintaining your own hunger as it is. You try to roam about constantly and as much as possible. You may swim faster and faster, or you may try to give up on swimming and float about, but in either case you are in it already. You have managed to raise a kind of excitement onto the surface, because you regard the whole situation of being in such hunger and thirst as your occupation. You begin to develop the limitless quality of this ocean of hunger; it is constant, everywhere. If you begin to see mountains or land beyond your ocean, probably you won't like it. Although you want to be saved, at the same time there is some irritation about that because then you would have to adapt to a new situation. You would need to get out of the ocean and climb up on the land and deal with the natives. You don't like that at all. You would rather float. But at the same time, you don't really want to drown in it. You would rather just exist in it, float about.

S: Why does one seek to maintain one's state of being?

TR: Because that is the comfortable situation at the time.

S: Do you mean someone can be in pain and really have a good time?

TR: Yes. That is what is meant by pain and pleasure happening simultaneously: the security of the pain becomes pleasure.

STUDENT: Where is the motivation for compassion if everybody is having a good time? Why disturb them?

TRUNGPA RINPOCHE: Why disturb them? Because fundamentally that is not a healthy place to be. I mean, you do not belong to the water, you belong to the land. That is the whole problem: if you want to help someone, that also is going to cause them pain, tremendous pain. That is precisely what it is. You don't want to be too kind, to save them from pain. You have to take that pain for granted. It is like an operation: in order to remove the sickness, you have to cut them, you have to take things out, the illness or growth or whatever.

S: As far as their own pleasure-pain situation is concerned, they are already happy.

TR: They are not really happy. They are not really happy, but they have accepted their involvement as an occupation.

STUDENT: If you are not projecting any bardo and if you are with someone else who is likewise not projecting any particular bardo trip, is there any state which exists?

TRUNGPA RINPOCHE: I suppose you could say clear light.

S: That would be a true meeting of minds?

TR: Precisely, yes. That is where—what you call—transmission takes place.

S: What you call. [Laughter]

STUDENT: You mentioned how we just float around, say in the hungry ghost world. When meditation enters in, what changes in that floating around?

TRUNGPA RINPOCHE: What does meditation change, did you mean? At the beginning meditation could be regarded as an intrusion, as an extremely painful thing to do, because it takes you away from your habitual dwelling. All kinds of painful situations churn out because for the first time, you create another relative situation, other than your dwelling. Gradually you gain a new perspective, new ideas from the meditation experience, which show you another living situation other than your own. It is a way to broaden your mind. It seems to introduce another land that exists beyond your own realm. That is why we find sitting meditating practice very painful. Any kind of practice is quite painful, irritating.

STUDENT: Some Tibetan book that I was reading, I forget which one, said, "Meditate until you hate it."

TRUNGPA RINPOCHE: Well, you don't have to wait.

S: I don't have to meditate that long not to like it.

TR: In regard to meditation, if one begins to enjoy doing it, then there must be some kind of entertainment going on, which is quite fishy.

STUDENT: It seems to me if you become really aware of pleasure as pleasure and pain as pain, it doesn't necessarily get you out of the search for pleasure. If you really experience both the pleasure and the pain, doesn't that continually involve you in the search for pleasure, because it is preferable to pain?

TRUNGPA RINPOCHE: I don't think so. If you regard pleasure as an external entity which entertains you, you could perpetually swim in the pleasure because it is a foreign element, yet it is also intimate. Whereas if you begin to see pain as pain and pleasure as pleasure—as it is—then the whole game of intimacy, the relative situation or love affair, begins to wear out. Finally you begin to realize that it is your own creation. You automatically begin to see the transparent quality of the pain or the pleasure.

S: When you begin to see pain and pleasure for what they are, what determines when you panic?

T R : When you begin to lose the crew who entertain you. You begin to realize that the last of the entertainment crew is walking out of your sight—and you end up just by yourself.

STUDENT: Buddhism seems to put a great value on pain, and you said good meditation is painful. How come? What's wrong with good meditation being investigating the nature of pleasure? There seems to be a great value in negativity, which seems to be true—but why not a great value in positivity?

TRUNGPA RINPOCHE: I don't think it is particularly that a value is placed on pain at all. The basic idea is letting things go as they are. It is just open space, an entirely new dimension in your meditative state, letting whatever is there come through. If it is a pleasurable situation, you also let that come through. In a description of Milarepa meditating in a cave, he had a tremendously pleasurable experience of the joy of inner heat coming through. For several days he found that particular experience extremely pleasurable. But that worked through and was gone thoroughly. It sort of wore out. Next, continually irritating situations came through as well. So it is a question of opening your whole being and letting whatever comes through come through. This particular discussion of pleasure and pain in meditation seems to be based on counteracting the current simple-minded attitude toward meditation, which is that it is supposed to give you bliss or pleasure. From this point of view, meditation is not geared to giving you pleasure alone at all. It is possible that it might give you pleasure, but on the other hand it is also highly possible that it might be an extremely painful thing to do. So it is just letting things be.

S : What determines whether it is pleasurable?

T R : I suppose it depends on your criteria, it depends on you.

STUDENT: What's wrong on the path, despite the pleasurable or painful effect of meditation, with the kind of pleasure of feeling you are walking in the right direction?

TRUNGPA RINPOCHE: At the same time there is tremendous paranoia about that as well—if you are not walking on the path. Once you realize you are on the path, then you are also extremely aware of what is not on the path, which brings tremendous insecurity. So you cannot really rely on that.

STUDENT: It seems as though life is terribly irritating, and in seeking the path we're seeking that which we hope will prove better. That isn't necessarily borne out by subsequent experiences, and as the pressure builds up on either side, the oscillation, the path seems to be the only way out.

TRUNGPA RINPOCHE: I think so, yes. But because of that, therefore there are more terrifying nightmares that you might lose that ultimate hope as well. That is equally powerful. You see the path as *the* only cord that you can hang on to to save your life. Suppose this cord is fragile, breaks away—then you are doubtful. As long as there is any kind of maintenance going on, that always seems to be a hangup, a problem—until the bodhisattva idea of giving up attaining enlightenment, which is the biggest step. Then your lifestyle *becomes* enlightenment. You don't need any kind of reassurance any more at all. You just maintain what you are constantly.

S: Maintain what you are?

TR: Behave normally. Of course, this normality is quite special.

STUDENT: I got into a strange thing last week, while sitting—the realization that this striving for results had to give way. This recognition would appear, but somehow it didn't change the situation at all. There would be a moment or two of peace from the striving, but then it would always come back. I'm sort of riding on the coattails of this idea of yours of renouncing enlightenment and trying to be free of striving.

TRUNGPA RINPOCHE: What about it?

S: Is this an ever-present part of what goes on?

TR: Automatically, if you disown the path, then the path is you. If you stop making money, then you're rich enough not to make any more money. You are really ultimately rich, because you don't have to try and make money anymore at all. That is the real mentality of richness; whereas if you are trying to maintain and make money, that is still the mentality of poverty. You are still maintaining your mentality of being poor.

S: This striving has to give way.

TR: That's right, yes.

S: But it doesn't. So in what direction does freedom from this striving come?

TR: You begin to realize that the whole area has been covered already. The only thing that bothers you is the striving, which is a hangup. It is the one true, irritating obstacle on the path. Striving is the obstacle on the path—nothing else.

S: Is there any way you could use that striving?

TR: At this point, there doesn't seem to be. You could say that you could use striving as energy, patience, all kinds of ways. Of course you could say that. But at this point it seems to be too dangerous even to suggest the notion of striving transmuting into energy or patience. You really have to give up. You really have to cut the whole cord of ego out completely.

STUDENT: It has been said that meditation develops bold will and that the enlightened man acts directly; his whole being is involved in any act that he does. How does this differ from striving?

TRUNGPA RINPOCHE: That is a sort of inborn delight, inborn delightfulness. For instance, if you want to meet your friend whom you haven't seen for a long time, making a journey toward seeing this friend doesn't seem to be an effort at all. You just drift along in the direction of your friend. It just happens, because you delight in the situation. It has nothing to do with punishing yourself or pushing yourself. Likewise, because you have such conviction in the idea of the awakened state of mind—in seeing that, in working with people, and helping them compassionately—you just enjoy that occupation, you just do it. That is the most powerful will of all, rather than purely trying to fight with yourself all the time. Our being here together also could be said to be the same example. People didn't try to go out to a restaurant and eat or have a bath or relax in their bedrooms, but they decided to sit here on the floor and wait and listen. Nobody imposed that will on anybody. They just did it because they liked doing it. There may have been all kinds of obstacles in coming up to Vermont, for that matter, but they just decided to do it and they enjoy doing it. Therefore they are here, which could be said to be an example.

STUDENT: Isn't there something fishy about *not* enjoying meditation?

TRUNGPA RINPOCHE: It is not a question of enjoying the actual practice, which could be extremely horrible, but a step toward it is necessary. You have to do it anyway. You know that you are not going to enjoy it, but you still do it. You like the idea of it. There's something in it which is very hard to explain, very hard to describe intellectually, but something draws you toward it, a kind of instinct. It seems the whole basic idea is working on basic instinct, basic intelligence.

STUDENT: Would you mind giving a bit more on the striving trip, please? It is connected with the watcher, I can see that. The watcher is checking things out: "How about arriving where I would like to arrive?" I really can't see anything beyond that point. Obviously, if the watcher gives way, then the striving isn't there—and the watcher also isn't there. What then?

TRUNGPA RINPOCHE: Then you just happen.

S: Just like that.

TR: The situation just happens. It just happens.

S: Then why doesn't it just happen?

TR: Because the graveyard of the watcher is a very attractive place to be. You lost track of yourself for the last time. That is a very interesting place to be. Finally you have lost your hangups.

S: So there is an element of fascination?

TR: There is some kind of fascination which is not the watcher. It is a magnetic situation because the watcher is ultimate irritation, and you lost that on that particular spot. You come back to that spot constantly on and on and on. And finally, the killer is regarded as a friend.

S: I see that.

TR: I'm glad you do.

The Realm of the Gods

Each experience of psychological hangups or extremes has a pattern of its own, and that pattern could be seen in its distinctive character and qualities. In other words, in the human realm or the realm of gods, there are certain familiar desires and certain familiar longings, as well as in the realm of hell or the hungry ghost realm. There is a kind of fascination to maintain oneself constantly and not give up or give into any possible spaciousness in which dualistic clingings no longer apply. So there is a great deal of grasping and holding and there is a great deal of effort to maintain.

We are willing to stick to confusion as our occupation and make it a habitual pattern of everyday life. In fact, that seems to be one of the main occupations of ego, because confusion provides a tremendously stable ground to sink into. Confusion also provides a tremendous way of occupying oneself. That seems to be one of the reasons there is a continual fear of giving up or surrendering. Stepping into the open space of the meditative state of mind seems to be very irritating. Because we are quite uncertain how to handle that wakeful state, therefore we would rather run back to our own prison than be released from our prison cell. So confusion and suffering have become an occupation, often quite a secure or delightful situation.

In the case of the realm of gods, that confusion has taken on a more genteel and sophisticated shape. The fundamental characteristic of the realm of the gods is dwelling on spiritual ideas of some kind. You experience a form of meditative absorption which is largely based on the ego or on a spiritually materialistic approach. Spiritual materialism provides the framework of the occupation in this realm. Such meditative practice has to maintain itself by dwelling on something, that is to say, finding a particular topic of meditation. However profound, however high—seemingly profound, seemingly high—it may be, at the same time it has a solid body, rather than being transparent.

Such meditation practice is based, to begin with, on tremendous preparation, or one could call it self-development. Self-development meditation is acknowledging that you are going to practice meditation as a way of dwelling along with the ego. In order to find a place to dwell, not only are you creating the solidness of the place, but at the same time you are creating the self-consciousness of the dweller as well. There is tremendous self-consciousness. It is as if you are walking on slippery ground, icy ground: the ice in itself is not slippery, it is just icy; but immediately when you see ice, you associate it with being slippery. That is the self-consciousness: "If *I* walk on this ice, therefore *I* will be slippery, I will be falling down." So the ice has nothing to do with the slipperiness at all. Instead, it is that we are walking on this particular block of ice, and therefore it will be slippery to us. It is the same situation when we try to get hold of something in terms of meditative experience. It is not so much the experience itself, but it is that "I am going to experience this particular experience." Therefore it is automatically self-conscious: one is less conscious of the meditation and more conscious of the meditator. That is ego dwelling on itself.

One could apply all kinds of practices along this path, such as the self-absorption of limitless space, the self-absorption of limitless consciousness, and even the self-absorption of nondwelling and the self-absorption of complete emptiness. All kinds of states of mind, all kinds of states of meditation, could be experienced or manufactured by the self-conscious mind as definite things. Because of that, the meditation becomes mind-made, manufactured, prefabricated. Such meditation practices could include dwelling on a particular technique, such as the repetition of a mantra or a visualization. They are all connected with that dwelling process: you are not completely absorbed into the mantra, but *you* are doing the mantra; you are not completely absorbed into the visualization, but *you* are visualizing. The basic criterion is based on "me" and "I am doing this." So there is self-consciousness in the meditation practice, which leads to the realm of the gods.

By no means is this at all a frivolous effort. You *do* get extremely dramatic results out of these practices if you are completely into it, extremely dramatic results. We may experience bodily pleasures, absorption, physical bliss, and mental bliss. Because we try to get into ourselves with ourselves, it is an extremely crowded situation. We and our projections are put into one bag, and we try to push as hard as can. Having pushed, having forced it somewhat and tried to fit ourselves into one particular bag makes us dizzy, obviously. And quite possibly physical symptoms of all kinds occur in that kind of meditation of the realm of the gods.

In terms of our biological state of being, this may be referred to as hearing the sound of infinite universality. Obviously we do hear our own sound—but at that moment it is uncertain whether it is the universality of sound or whether it is the universality of ourself. It is based on the neurological setup of trying to hold on to one basic situation, one basic principle. So there is tremendous confusion between the ego type of sound-current yoga practice and the real transcendental type, although it is very hard to distinguish at that point. Sound-current vibrations could be heard as a neurological buzz in your head. For that matter, neurological visions could be provided from the extreme tension of being centralized into one thing. Trying to fit projections and projector into one square corner, one particular pigeonhole, automatically brings a kind of self-hypnosis. So in fact, neurological visions or neurological buzz could be heard or seen, perceived.

Likewise the experiences of limitless space and limitless consciousness could be seen as limitless because you are trying to lay a concept of limit on it—which is you, the moderator. Therefore you are seeing things as limitless because the moderator cannot reach beyond certain things. If the moderator decides to let go slightly, beyond its reach, it becomes limitless space or limitless consciousness or limitless emptiness, or whatever it may be. The result of that tremendously hard work and effort of dwelling on ego is that literally, psychologically and physically, we get high. We are completely intoxicated into that extreme way of pushing ourselves, demanding something from ourselves, and dwelling on ourselves. And that is the source of our living in the realm of the gods. So the realm of the gods is mostly the ego's version of spirituality, or spiritual materialism. That seems to be the starting point.

The other aspect of the realm of the gods is trying to dwell on any seduction that happens within our living situation. Health, pleasure, beauty, and all kinds of things are taken into consideration. Trying to dwell on any of those is dwelling in the realm of the gods. The difference between reaching the realm of the gods and just enjoying pleasure is that in the realm-of-the-gods experience, or the bardo experience in the realm of the gods, you have struggle, a fear of failure and a hope of gaining. You build up, up, up to a crescendo manufactured out of hope and fear. One moment you think you are going to make it, and the next moment you think you are going to fail. The alternation of those two extremes builds up tension and striving. Such a process of striving is more than just simple discipline, or even transcendental discipline, in the sense of the second paramita. Because these ups and downs occur in our state of being and because they mean too much to us, so much to us, we go up and up, down and down and down. So we have all kinds of ups and downs, all kinds of "This is going to be the end of me" or "This is going to be the starting point of my development or my achievement of ultimate pleasure."

That struggle takes place constantly, and finally, at the final stage, we begin to lose the point of hope and fear. Hope becomes more likely fear, and fear becomes more likely hope, because we have been struggling so much. We begin to lose track of what is hope really and what is really fear altogether. We begin to lose track of who's going and who's coming. We are speeding so much that we get into extreme chaos. We lose track of who is against us and who is for us. There is a sudden flash—in terms of ego-hood, bewilderment, confusion—a moment in which pain and pleasure become one completely. Suddenly the meditative state of dwelling on ego dawns on us. Such a breakthrough! Tremendous achievement!

Then the pleasure, or bliss, begins to saturate our system, psychologically, spiritually, or physically. We don't have to care anymore about hope or fear, because we have achieved something. And quite possibly we could believe that achievement to be the permanent achievement of enlightenment, or whatever you would like to call it, union with God. At that moment, everything we see seems to be beautiful, loving. Even the most grotesque situations of life seem to be heavenly. Anything that exists, even the unpleasant or aggressive situations in life, is seen as something extremely beautiful, because we have achieved oneness with ego.

In other words, ego has lost track of its intelligence. This is the absolute ultimate achievement of bewilderment, the depth of ignorance, the spirituality of ignorance. It is extremely powerful. I once read a quotation in a Communist Chinese magazine under a portrait of Mao Tse-tung, saying, "Mao Tse-tung's inspiration is a spiritual atom bomb." This is that kind of spiritual atom bomb. It is self-destructive as well as destructive in relating with the rest of life with compassion, communication. And it is also destructive to stepping out of the bondage of ego. The whole thing about this approach of the realm of the gods is that is is purely going inward and inward and churning out more and more cords or chains to bind yourself further. The more the practice goes on, that much more bondage are we going to create. According to the scriptures, it is like the analogy of a silkworm, which binds itself as it produces silk thread, and finally suffocates itself.

So we could say that the realm of the gods has two aspects: one is the spiritual aspect, which has a self-destructive, self-hypnotic quality; the other aspect is the extreme search for pleasure, mentally and physically. Because such striving goes on all the time, you begin to lose the point, you begin to become accustomed to struggle, and you begin to learn to moderate your determination. You begin to accept what is given to you, and you begin to become somewhat sensible. Because the achievement of pleasure is limitless, because there is no end to achieving something, you begin to strike a happy medium. You try to be moderate or sensible, and you try to dwell on temporary happiness, materialistically. Those are two types of god realm. Both are pleasure-oriented entirely in the sense of the maintenance of ego. But in both cases the very thing which places you in the realm of the gods is losing track of hope and fear. We could see it spiritually or we could see it in terms of worldly concerns. The achievement of happiness, as it is experienced in the realm of the gods, is based on that particular experience of losing track of who is searching and what is our aim and object and goal—but trying to make the best of it. That could be seen in terms of worldly concerns and social situations as well as spiritually.

At the beginning we are searching or looking for happiness. But then we begin to enjoy the practice toward happiness as well, at the same time. We try to relax into the practice toward happiness, on the way to achieving absolute physical pleasure or psychological comfort. At the same time, halfway to achieving such comfort and pleasure, we begin to give in and make the best of it. It is like an adventure also being used as a vacation or a holiday. You are on the way to your adventurous journey, your actual ultimate goal, but at the same time you use every step of every journey, regarding them also as a vacation, or holiday.

The realm of the gods, therefore, doesn't seem to be particularly painful, as far as its own actual situation is concerned. Instead, the most painful aspect of the realm of the gods is that when you think you have achieved something spiritually or worldly and you are trying to dwell on that, suddenly something shakes. Suddenly you realize that what you are trying to achieve is not going to last forever at all. For instance, at a certain stage, spiritual absorption in meditation becomes very shaky. You thought you were continuously going to enjoy this blissful state. But at some stage, that blissful state begins to become shaky and more irregular, ragged. The thought of maintenance begins to come into the mind. You try to push yourself back to this blissful state, but the karmic situation brings all kinds of irritations into it and at some stage you begin to completely lose faith in that blissful state. Suddenly there is the violence that you have been cheated. You realize that you cannot stay in the realm of the gods forever.

When the karmic situation shakes you up and begins to provide extraordinary situations that you have to relate to, then the whole process becomes disappointing. You either experience disappointment or anger toward the person who put you into such a journey. You begin to condemn yourself or the person who put you into that, and that sudden anger seems to turn you around. You end up angry, and your anger develops as hungry ghost—like anger, or the anger of the realm of hell, or the anger of human beings or jealous gods. You develop all kinds of anger or disappointment that you have been cheated, so you go back to one of the other five realms of the world. So you go on and on and on. At some stage, you might come up to the realm of the gods again, but then the same disappointment takes place and you go down again. The same thing comes up again and again. That is what is called samsara, which literally means continual circle, whirlpool, the ocean which spins round again and again. There is no end. That seems to be one of the qualities of bardo experience: you are in no-man's-land somehow, in terms of your daily experience as well as the experience after death, before the next birth.

STUDENT: If you are in between different realms, how long do you stay stuck in the transitional state between one realm and another?

TRUNGPA RINPOCHE: It depends on the force of your struggle, how violent it is. The more you are violent, the more you are forceful, the more you are speeding, that much more are you spinning around. In that way you get dizzy. So you introduce yourself into the bardo experience of the six realms of the world. It depends on your speed.

STUDENT: Rinpoche, do you have to experience all six realms of the world before there is a possibility of release?

TRUNGPA RINPOCHE: It is not a question of really being necessary by any means. The whole thing is useless, you could say—but it happens constantly.

S: Rinpoche, if we see our meditation moving toward that, should we go with it?

TR: You have to have confidence in yourself and your practice, and you have to have clear perception. Then you automatically learn how to work with yourself.

STUDENT: Would it be possible to go through the complete path of bardo experience and know the whole thing, and still not be able to stop it? Could one be aware of the process, and still not be able to stop it?

TRUNGPA RINPOCHE: I think that is possible. You would only be able to stop it or to slow it down at the point of the journey itself, the journey leading up to a crescendo. At the moment you are speculating between hope and fear, at that moment you could slow down. And that is what is usually happening with us. But once you are at the fruition of it, it is very hard to stop it. That would be like trying to redirect the course of an arrow when it is on its way already.

S: You're helpless?

TR: Yes, it is a helpless situation at that point. It has been said that even the Buddha cannot change or interfere with your karmic fruition, and that it is impossible to do anything once you are in any of these realms. These realms we are talking about are different psychological states of madness. The six realms of the world occur within the human situation when you have gotten yourself into such a heavy trip that you do not hear somebody trying to help you. You do not see anything at all; you become completely deaf and dumb. Those kinds of neurotic states of being that you manage to get yourself into in your living situation, in this life in particular, seem to be the subject that we are talking about, rather than the six realms of the world after death. The realm of the gods is also based on what we are in that daily living situation. So the six realms of the world could be said to be six types of psychotic states.

STUDENT: Rinpoche, when a bodhisattva takes a vow to renounce enlightenment, would he be in the realm of the gods at that point?

TRUNGPA RINPOCHE: If you are a bodhisattva, you are supposed to be out of those realms.

S: Then what are you renouncing, if you are out?

TR: You are renouncing attaining enlightenment.

S: What is the difference between being out of the six realms and enlightenment?

TR: Well, being out of the six realms of the world is an intermediate state. You could be in the situation of having come down from one realm and being just about to enter into another realm, which is still part of the samsaric circle. The bodhisattva could be in that state of no-man's-land as well, where you are not connected with any of the six realms or, for that matter, the idea of enlightenment. But the bodhisattva is directed toward enlightenment.

STUDENT: Could you clarify the idea of bardo?

TRUNGPA RINPOCHE: There are two definitions of bardo at this point. Bardo is in-between experience. And also when you are actually in the six realms of the world, you are in a bardo state. In particular, the sipa bardo is described as the bardo of existence, and you are in it. But in terms of bardo as intermediate state, you could say that it is a kind of relative bardo state. It is not quite a definitely fixed bardo state, as you experience in the six realms of the world.

S: So the difference is that in one you cannot prevent yourself from going into the others, like a psychotic change, and in the other you can.

TR: That's right. In the other, something can be done about it.

S: You said there were two situations. The helpless one is when it has come to the point where you cannot do anything about it.

TR: At that point, the karmic pattern just carries out.

S: At the other point, where there is hope, what do you do?

TR: You try to reduce your speed of jumping from one extreme to another.

S: How do you do that?

TR: Through all kinds of disciplines—like meditation, for instance.

S: But then we are just on the hope part of the hope and fear again.

TR: You have to reduce that as well. I mean, hope cannot be regarded as an achievement. If one regards hope in that way, it is also a hangup; then fear becomes a hangup as well.

STUDENT: Rinpoche, in the biography of Milarepa, it says that anyone who hears his name will be saved from the lower realms—magically.

TRUNGPA RINPOCHE: Well, it depends on whether you hear his name—I mean, if you *hear* it.

STUDENT: Rinpoche, how can you ever tell if you are slowing down and relaxing, or if you are just using that as something to achieve, as what you have to do to get out? If you are just doing it to achieve something, you are not really relaxing at all.

TRUNGPA RINPOCHE: If you are really relaxed in the fullest sense, you do not have to watch yourself relaxing, you just happen. Relaxation just happens. Because you are fully being there, you do not have to maintain your relaxation as such. You are just there, being there completely. That is what the idea of relaxation really means; whereas in the other case, you are trying to maintain yourself in something. If there is maintenance of your relaxation, then it seems to be hypocritical.

STUDENT: Rinpoche, it's very fascinating for us to listen to you describe the six states of bardo or six realms of being, but how do you, as an instructor or as a spiritual friend, think that it helps us to listen to these descriptions?

TRUNGPA RINPOCHE: I suppose that the whole idea of listening and learning is based on relating with ourselves constantly. I mean, it is quite possible that some people in this audience are not actually hearing the whole thing at all; they are just taking part in it very graciously. The words sort of pass through their minds, bypassing them. But in some situation of their life struggle, these words they heard come back again; sudden flashes begin to come to their mind. Suddenly such sentences, such ideas, begin to dawn in their mind—whenever it is needed. So it seems that whatever you have heard, whatever you have understood, becomes applicable all the time, rather than that you deliberately try to apply it. I mean, the six realms of the world and all the ideas about bardo in this case are rather speculative. Discussions on how to meditate or practical things like that seem to be more realistic. But nevertheless, these speculative ideas also suddenly come into our mind when needed, flashing into applicable situations.

S: So we don't necessarily have to do something on the basis of what we've heard, but the flash itself is helpful?

TR: Well, that seems to be the way. But at the same time, it is also good to understand the intellectual aspect of the teaching. That is obviously very important. We can't just abandon everything purely to practice and not study. So if anybody is seriously thinking of getting into the path and practicing, you have to know the scholarly or the intellectual aspect equally, as much as the practice, if possible, so that you may be able to help others.

STUDENT: Rinpoche, in *The Jewel Ornament of Liberation,* in the section on karma, Gampopa talks about wholesome states of mind. He mentions limitless space and limitless consciousness, and describes them as leading to those wholesome states of mind. Yet you seem to regard them as almost pathological, or at least useless. Is that the same thing? What does Gampopa mean by wholesome?

TRUNGPA RINPOCHE: I think he actually describes that in great detail in describing the six realms of the world. He describes the realm of the first jhana, second jhana, third jhana, and fourth jhana, and the realm of the formless gods and their experience of limitless space, their experience of the meditative state. These practices could be based on egolessness, which could be said to be wholesome, or on ego. The difference between wholesome and unwholesome is based on how you relate with your ego.

S: In other words, limitless space could be based on ego or nonego?

TR: Either could be possible, yes. These four jhana state practices are also regarded as the foundation, or common ground. In Tibetan, they are called *thünmong thekpa,* which means the vehicle or common ground where you develop mind training, to begin with, but with one condition—the absence of ego practice. In other words, you can meditate with ego or in an egoless way; it is your decision.

STUDENT: I always thought that even if I decide to meditate without ego, when I sit it seems to be a function of what happens.

TRUNGPA RINPOCHE: Well, it's not quite that simple. We can't say that it is a decision, as such, but it seems to be a continual process of successive situations. And largely, the whole idea is that if you have a competent teacher who is not on an ego trip at all— otherwise he wouldn't be competent—such an egoless spiritual friend could relate with your egolessness, because he or she is egoless himself. I think that is the basic point where the need for guidance begins to arise, definitely. You need an example. You need someone to inspire you, so that you can afford to step out of ego without doing too much damage to yourself. That kind of inspiration is most important. And that seems to be the starting point.

STUDENT: Ordinary everyday kinds of impulse, feeling, and thought are very much like the six realms of the world, but they are much less intense. All the time you are getting thoughts and reactions and feelings that, when you look at them, really are the six realms of the world. What is the difference?

TRUNGPA RINPOCHE: Because you have these potentials in you all the time, that is why you could get yourself into such states—if you work yourself up.

S: But once you get into them, when it becomes so intense, you are locked in your intensity.

TR: Yes. You are completely stuck then.

STUDENT: Aren't you always in one of those six realms?

TRUNGPA RINPOCHE: No, not necessarily. There could be a state of mind which is loose and filled with junctures all the time. That is the fertile ground where a person could hear the teaching. But once you are in those six realms of the world fully and thoroughly, you become deaf, so you cannot hear the teaching at all. You cannot direct it anywhere, you are just stuck there.

S: What do you mean by "filled with junctures"?

TR: Alternatives, possibilities of giving up or taking on. I mean possibilities of letting yourself be inspired or possibilities of letting yourself be seduced. These kinds of junctures happen constantly—with, of course, an element of the six realms of the world in it as well, but not fully being in them.

STUDENT: Rinpoche, in the *Tibetan Book of the Dead* seminar you mentioned that the human realm was the realm of possibilities, and that in the other realms you were more or less fixed. What is there psychologically about the human realm that gives it these possibilities to get out of samsara?

TRUNGPA RINPOCHE: In this case we are talking about all six realms as being fixed extremes, so the human realm is also a fixed extreme. But generally the experience of the six realms of the world could be felt only in the human realm, as we are doing. And those junctions also seem to be attributes of the human realm, in that sense. But then you could get into the human realm *of* the human realm, which is an extreme case. You could get stuck in it.

S: With those junctures, as soon as you choose one, don't you start to eliminate that point of juncture? In other words, we can only have possibilities when we're not moving. As soon as we move, we eliminate some of the possibilities.

TR: That is why you can step out of all those extreme cases.

S: By not moving?

TR: By realizing the possible inclination toward the next extreme case.

S: By not choosing it?

TR: You don't have to choose, but it comes to you. I mean, these six realms of world are just presented to you. The extreme search for sensual pleasure of the realm of the gods or the extreme anger of the realm of hell are just presented to you by a succession of coincidences, seemingly.

S: If you want to stay cool—

TR: You can't stay cool—unless you have some practice, like training your basic mind through the discipline of meditation. Otherwise, you cannot stay cool just because you do not want to take part in any of those. You can't do that at all. It's almost an involuntary thing. You have been programmed into the samsaric world because you are in it.

STUDENT: Rinpoche, you said that scriptural knowledge was necessary in order to help other people. But why is that so? Once you realize the truth, why can't you approach it directly and transmit it directly as opposed to going through the scriptures? Why do you have to use the scriptures?

TRUNGPA RINPOCHE: Well, you don't have to use them as though you've been programmed by the scriptures. But you can't help relating with such earthy ideas, the earthy statements that lineage people in the past have made and the practices they have gone through themselves. Their examples, the messages they left behind, are automatically applicable to your life, so you can't help imparting that to others. It just happens naturally. You don't have to become a preacher at all, but you just sail along through the ocean of dharma.

S: Why couldn't we just separate out or emphasize things like mindfulness or the technique of meditation, as opposed to talking about the scriptures?

T R : Well, if you are talking about mindfulness, I think you are talking about scriptures.

S : Not in the historical sense.

T R : I don't mean scriptures in the historical sense, but as actual descriptions of life. The experience of the six realms of the world that we have been discussing is also taken from the scriptures, but it seems to be more experiential than just retelling stories or myths.

3

The Jealous God Realm

The realm of the gods provides a background of the different experiences of meditative absorption, and also materialistic absorption in the world of sensual pleasure. That seems to be one of the basic key points to work through in the six realms of the world. There are also six states of bardo which are related with the six realms of the world: the bardo of meditation (clear light), the bardo of birth, the bardo of illusory body, the bardo of the dream-like quality of experiences, the bardo of existence or becoming, and the bardo of death. Those six types of bardo experience could be seen in conjunction with the six realms of the world; we could almost say that each realm we are in always has the qualities of the six bardos: the qualities of birth, death, meditative absorption/ clear light, illusion, and becoming or existence—as well as the quality of *dharmata,* or a sense of space. So each realm contains the six types of bardo experience. The different realms of being—like the hungry ghost realm or the human being realm or whatever— are the background experience. And within that background, there are the natural qualities of that background, which are the six bardos. For instance, if you are in the realm of the gods, you could have a dreamlike experience or a meditative absorptionlike experience, or other bardo experience like that. So the six types of bardo experience are connected with the six realms of the world very closely. On the other hand, we could also relate how each realm is contained in each type of bardo. It could also work that way. But at this point, that seems to be too complicated, so many figures are involved.

The next realm is the realm of the jealous gods, or asuras. *Asura* is a Sanskrit word which literally means "nongod": *a* is negative, *sura* is "god," so *asura* is "nongod." It is quite likely that having had the meditative absorption of the realm of the gods, sudden disappointment comes about, the disappointment that you have been cheated, that this is not a permanent experience at all. Therefore you turn around. Your experience turns around completely, and sudden envy begins to develop, jealousy begins to develop. You realize that you haven't been given the full truth and you haven't understood ultimate freedom—although you thought what you had achieved was the ultimate freedom of spiritual absorption.

Losing faith brings a tremendously sharp sense of relativity, a sense of comparison: "If that is so, why is this not so?" It is a kind of schizophrenic experience. Often schizophrenics are very intelligent. If you are trying to help them, work with them, then automatically they interpret your intention as laying heavy trips on them, so they do not want to be helped. But if you decide not to help, then automatically they feel you are seeking comfort, that you don't want to work with them either. And if you are trying to present alternatives, then automatically their reaction is that you are trying to play games with them, which is true. It is a very intelligent state of mind, but at the same time it is such a split mind. It is so powerful that it sees all the corners, every corner. You think you are communicating to them face to face, but in actual fact they are looking at you from behind your back. That is the asura mentality of extreme paranoia, which includes extreme efficiency and accuracy at the same time. The Tibetan word for jealousy is *tragdok*. *Trag* is "shoulder," *dok* means "crowded," so *tragdok* means overcrowdedly selfish, in other words, too much shoulder to get through traffic, so to speak. It is kind of a defensive form of pride.

The asura realm, or realm of the jealous gods, is also associated with heavy wind. It has the karma family quality of speeding and trying to achieve everything on the spot, trying to make sure that your experiences are valid and that nobody is going to attack you—that kind of situation. We get to the bardo experience of that realm by too much comparison, too much comparative work. In other words, it is the extreme paranoia of trying to save yourself, trying to attain something higher and greater constantly. In order to try to attain something higher and greater, the conclusion from the jealous gods point of view is that if you watch for every possible pitfall, then you will be saved. That is the only way to save yourself.

Jealous gods come to that conclusion and then put it into action. You don't even have a chance to get ready and prepare to put it into action, into practice. You just do it without preparation. The jealous god is trying also to develop a kind of spontaneity of its own kind and feels quite free to do that. It is all too comparative. In other words, the asura realm contains lots of elements of game playing, of the gamelike quality of living situations. The whole thing is regarded as purely a game, in the sense of opponents and yourself. You are constantly dealing with me and them, me and the rest of the world, me and my friends, and often me and myself. There is a buildup of too much comparative mentality.

To begin with, you have to train yourself to be such an ambitious person; but then at a certain stage, that kind of training becomes part of your character. So you do not have to train yourself to do it but it just naturally happens. You are sort of a born jealous person, as though jealousy were part of your instinct, your state of being. There is that quality of wind or air in everybody's being; that quality of speed in everyone. The asura quality magnifies that particular characteristic, so that all corners are regarded as suspicious or threatening; and therefore one must look into it and be careful about it. At the same time, the asura realm is not quite related with hiding oneself or camouflage at all. It is very direct. You are very willing to come out in the open and to fight if there is a problem or if there is seemingly a plot against you. You just come out and fight face on and try to expose that plot. There is a kind of schizophrenic quality of coming into the open and facing the situation, and at the same time being suspicious of yourself as well.

You also begin to develop another asura characteristic: the deaf and dumb quality of refusing to accept, refusing to learn anything. If something is presented by outsiders, because everyone is regarded as an enemy from an asura point of view, they must be trying to do something. Even the most kind person trying to help you is regarded with suspicion, as though that person had some plot in mind. So the possibility of communication is completely shut off—as a result of the extraordinarily high-strung communication that has built up within yourself due to your paranoia, which blocks out whole areas of communication and spaciousness. You do not want to be helped. At the same time, you regard any help you receive, any benefits from being helped, as very precious. It is so precious that therefore you cannot accept such a situation as possible. It is *too* precious. Therefore you do not really want to admit that somebody actually could do that precious and worthwhile performance on you at all. You tend to develop such a blockage in communication because your jealousy or envy is very accurate and at the same time very paranoid. It is a sort of antenna or radar which registers everything. But you read that registration wrongly—purely in terms of enemy rather than any kind of warmth.

Therefore, jealousy or envy could be said to be dependent on coldness, the complete opposite of compassion or love, the windy, stormy quality of cold, biting cold. And the element of speed is the only refuge. That is the realm of the asuras: very cold and bleak. That kind of feeling is dominant in the asura realm. And at a certain point, when you actually arrive at that particular realm as a one hundred percent situation, it tends to develop in the same way as the realm of the gods. You begin to lose the point: who is defending whom; who is trying to protect whom? You are completely bewildered, and you begin to lose the point altogether, any kind of reference point. But at the same time, you try to maintain that harshness constantly, all the time. That is quite an interesting highly strung characteristic that one could develop, if one is inclined toward such extremes.

All of these six different realms are connected with our innate nature, or psychological being, which has the qualities of fire, water, air, earth, and space. All of these qualities are within us, and each element or quality is connected with one of these realms. So it is possible to magnify particular qualities, which is what is meant by being in the realm of the gods or the realm of asuras, or whatever realm it may be. There is no fixed concept, such as "Now you are in the realm of the gods; now you are in the realm of the asuras"—but it is the intensely extreme case of whatever comes up. In other words, we all have schizophrenic qualities, claustrophobic qualities, paranoid qualities. All the neurotic tendencies that you can possibly think of in terms of human insanity are also in us, because they are connected with the elements, as the other side of the coin.

It seems that parts of that other side of the coin could become prominent when the external situation happens to thrust us into an extreme case as a result of being unable to relate with things as they are. That is a result of not seeing things as they are, but at the same time trying to manage ourselves and grab hold of the nearest situation and make something out of it in order just to survive, in order just to maintain one's ego. And because of that, therefore, the birth of the six realms is automatically given. As the panic becomes prominent, we occupy ourselves with *something;* not knowing what to do, we grasp the nearest situation of confusion.

Therefore, basic ignorance is referred to as one of the most important conditions for giving birth to the six realms of the world. You cannot give birth to the six realms unless there is bewilderment and uncertainty. Because of this bewilderment and uncertainty, something happens. Something is floating nearby, and you try to get hold of it and it happens to be the wrong thing to hold on to—all the time.

STUDENT: Rinpoche, which one of the bardos is this realm connected with?

TRUNGPA RINPOCHE: The asura realm also has all of the six bardo types in it already. It has the quality of being dreamlike; it has the impermanent quality of experience, which happens and then dissipates, which is death; it is also trying to create new situations, which is birth; also there is the quality of absorption, which is the meditative state; and there is an occasional spacious, or clear light quality, as well. So this realm contains all six types of bardo.

S: That's not true of all the realms, though, is it?

TR: All of them.

STUDENT: You once were talking about hell, and you said that it does not have pulsations, but that it is this constant thing with no gaps.

TRUNGPA RINPOCHE: Well, it has to have a background of some kind in order to operate. It does not have a gap in the sense of changing frequencies, but you have to exist somewhere. That maintenance, or existence in itself, is within some kind of space. Otherwise we could not experience suffering at all, if there were no suffering and sufferer.

S: So even in hell there is the possibility of release?

TR: In that view of gap, there is a misunderstanding, in that gap is regarded as a release or as relief of some kind, that you will be excused from extreme situations. In that sense there is no gap. That kind of release or relief does not exist in the hell realm at all. But in order for your suffering to function, you have to have lubrication of some kind.

STUDENT: I don't know whether this is the same question or not, but I am wondering what the opening is. The asura realm has very particular mechanics, a very particular way of maintaining itself. Just what is the possibility of breaking through those mechanics? I wonder how an opening could take place there?

TRUNGPA RINPOCHE: The opening seems to take place by itself.

S: Right, but just as there would be a particular mechanics to the maintenance, I should think there would be a specific sort of shock that would cause there to be a big gap in that maintenance process.

TR: That's part of the service, so to speak.

S: Service?

TR: Yes. It comes with the service. If you fill your gas tank, somebody else automatically wipes your windshield.

S: Would you then have a possibility of clearing up your vision?

TR: A possibility.

S: The breakthrough quality in this particular maintenance process would have to do with clearing up your vision?

TR: In terms of wearing out being in the state of the asuras. You have to maintain yourself constantly, and at some stage you begin to lose your logic, you begin to lose your faith. It is the same as being in the realm of the gods: you begin to realize that your tactic, or the meditative absorption that you have developed, is not foolproof, and you begin to wonder. As long as you begin to wonder, then automatically you are providing a more spacious situation, and other doubts come into it as well. So your experience of being in the realm of the asuras begins to diminish as you go along, the same as in the other realms. It is exactly the same thing. You see, usually one experiences a definite sense of occupation, once you are in a particular realm. It is as though you have made a great discovery: you relate to that; you would like to believe that whole thing is part of your makeup; you would like to associate with that whole thing as part of you. You begin to enjoy playing that kind of game because you have found a very solid occupation. But somehow that does not last very long; it begins to diminish.

STUDENT: Rinpoche, socially how does one deal with or how does one communicate with this type of person?

TRUNGPA RINPOCHE: It seems to be very difficult to communicate with an asura. It is kind of an isolated situation of its own.

S: Is there any possibility of communication?

TR: You see, the trouble is, if you try to communicate with an asura person, asura being, each communication could reinforce their trip. Communication could be interpreted as trying to destroy them.

S: How do you deal with a student who has come to that place?

TR: Somehow that does not happen. If you are student, you want to learn something. Therefore, you are already open. So you cannot possibly be a student and also be an asura at the same time. For that matter, you cannot be a student and be in the realm of the gods, either. A student is looking for an occupation, so you cannot be a student who tends to be stuck in the six realms of the world at all. If you are really a student, if you want to learn something, you have to give something out, you have to relate to something. But if you become a self-made spiritual person or self-made businessman, whatever it may be, then it is possible that you cease to relate to yourself as a student or a learner and you regard yourself as having found some occupation. You have found an occupation within the six realms of the world.

STUDENT: Why is accuracy so apparent in this realm?

TRUNGPA RINPOCHE: That is part of an asura's way of maintaining that whole game.

S: But it seems that in all the realms there is confusion, so it is surprising that accuracy is associated with this confusion.

TR: The accuracy is part of the confusion. If you want to get really confused, you have to be accurately confused.

S: By accuracy, I suppose that you mean you have all kinds of interpretations for events.

TR: Yes. You have all kinds of possible ways of maintaining your own confusion.

STUDENT: You said one is always reaching out for something, and whatever happens to be there is the wrong thing. But if it's there at all, isn't it part of the situation and therefore right at the moment in some way?

TRUNGPA RINPOCHE: Well, it may seemingly be right at the moment, at that moment, but it is very difficult to say. If somebody is going to rob you on the spot, it seems to be right to be robbed at that moment.

S: Well, what did you mean by wrong in that sense?

TR: That sense of wrong has to do with whether something creates further confusion or whether it clears up the situation. A right situation is not supposed to create further confusion, because it is precise. If a situation presents confusion, then it is the wrong thing.

S: But isn't the alternative also there: that just as one can be confused by it, so it can also be the guru to teach you at that moment?

TR: If you are confused, you will find it very difficult to learn from it—unless you realize your confusion as it is. If you become part of the confusion completely, you will not have any questions at all to ask. But if you are partially confused, or if you are enlightenedly confused, then the confusion brings more questions. In that case you are not really confused at all; you are beginning to find a way out of it—because you ask questions, because you begin to speculate, you are not trapped in it at all.

STUDENT: What happens if what you're reaching for is not something you want to hold on to? What happens then, if you continue to be confused?

TRUNGPA RINPOCHE: Well, then you get out of the situation. I mean, you don't have to hold on to it anymore.

S: What happens then?

TR: At the beginning it is quite irritating, because there is nothing to relate with; the whole thing is very loose. Before, you had occupations—fixed and solid occupations. But it is the way out anyway, because you are not bound by anything at that point.

STUDENT: In the asura realm, it seems you are so wrapped up in its gamelike quality that you don't even realize that what you are doing is a game.

TRUNGPA RINPOCHE: That gamelike quality of comparing situations in order to maintain one's own paranoia is a way of maintaining itself. You feel you have found a very intricate way to interpret things. Things become fascinating, intricate. And seemingly you can work with those interpretations you have made: you feel that if somebody is trying to help you, you could read something into it and try to prove to yourself that that person is actually trying to destroy you.

STUDENT: Rinpoche, where is the pleasurable aspect of the realm of the asuras?

TRUNGPA RINPOCHE: The pleasure comes from the sense that you are being smart enough that you haven't been caught anywhere. You manage even to interpret those who are trying to help you as trying to destroy you.

S: What if the persons who are trying to help you really are trying to destroy you, in the sense that if you would be helped you would cease to be a jealous god?

TR: Yes. Quite possibly. That is a kind of fascination with the occupation.

STUDENT: On the reaching process, you said that you reach for the wrong thing. Is the implication there that you could reach for the right thing?

TRUNGPA RINPOCHE: If you try to reach you can't seem to do it—unless the situation is presented to you. Automatically there is some subtlety from the external situation.

STUDENT: Do all the bardo states contain grasping?

TRUNGPA RINPOCHE: Of some kind or another, yes, like the absorption of the realm of the gods and the jealousy of the asuras. There is always the attempt to grasp something.

S: How do you give up grasping, or step out of it?

TR: Well, you can't just give up grasping just like that. Automatically, you are aware of yourself giving up grasping, which means you are grasping nongrasping. So it seems that the ultimate and obvious thing is that one has to give up the person who is grasping.

S: How do you do that?

TR: By not doing anything—meditating.

STUDENT: Rinpoche, you said the asuras were associated with the karma family quality. What quality are the gods associated with?

TRUNGPA RINPOCHE: The world of the gods is associated with the buddha family, meditative absorption. Asuras are associated with the karma family. We are getting more complicated here.

STUDENT: How does one become an asura?

TRUNGPA RINPOCHE: You find yourself in it, I suppose.

S: What drives persons from other states to the asuras?

TR: Speculative and intellectual speculation, which is largely based on trying to maintain oneself constantly. If one tries to maintain oneself constantly, then one also has to look into the negative aspect of maintenance: Who is preventing our maintenance? What's the problem with it? One has to develop jealousy.

STUDENT: It sounds as if becoming an asura is one of a variety of available practices for defending yourself.

TRUNGPA RINPOCHE: Yes.

S: Are there any special characteristics of a person who might choose this tactic over others?

TR: I think it is largely based on the ambition to cover all areas. You make sure that you have the complete right to become emperor, yearning for ultimate comfort where there is not one small instant to irritate you at all and the whole thing is completely under control. It is sort of warlord-minded.

STUDENT: You talked about how all of these six realms coexist with each other and how one is predominant. Do you mean, in terms of an actual person over a period of weeks and months, that one is predominantly in one realm? Or can it even be a question of one day—that a person moves from being predominantly in the realm of the gods to the asura realm in one day? In that way it changes very quickly.

TRUNGPA RINPOCHE: It could change very quickly as well as you could be stuck for years and years. It is the same as the general idea of the bardo experience after death. The traditional estimate is that it lasts seven weeks, but it has been said that a person with strong karmic force could take his or her next birth immediately after death, or he also could be suspended for centuries and centuries. So the same thing could occur here. Those who are able to find themselves in such realms for a long time have more determination. They are more self-centered, and they have found their occupation for life. In some cases, we could say that we get ourselves into these six types of psychotic states constantly; we get into them and we come out of them all the time.

STUDENT: You said that the six realms, because of their extreme intensity, are a bardo of some sort. And then you said that each realm has the qualities of the six bardo states. I don't quite understand what type of bardo the six realms are.

TRUNGPA RINPOCHE: All of it.

S: But doesn't one predominate? Isn't there in each realm a predominance of one of the bardo states?

TR: Well, that depends on the details of the psychological state. Whether it is predominantly a dreamlike quality, or a predominantly meditativelike quality, or whatever it may be. You see, each realm has to maintain itself by the different elements, and these elements contain six types, which are the six bardos.

S: I understand that the six realms altogether are the sipa bardo. Is that correct?

TR: You could say that our human life on earth, what we are now, is the basic sipa bardo state, in general. But within that we also have psychological states: godlike, hell-like, hungry ghost—like. Characteristic psychological states pertain all the time.

STUDENT: Rinpoche, do people in different realms have a tendency to seek each other out? Do they flock together? Do they try to destroy or conquer each other? I'm wondering how they interrelate?

TRUNGPA RINPOCHE: I suppose you could have some kind of affinity, maybe; but on the other hand, if you are an asura, when you meet another asura, it would be regarded as a mockery of yourself.

S: Rinpoche, if you were an asura, would you have a more comfortable affinity to a person in another realm?

TR: That is very hard to say. It depends on the basic strength of your sense of security, how intent you are on being in that state.

STUDENT: I have a very specific, practical question. There are people with this characteristic around, and you may find yourself running into them, perhaps at work. It sounds rather hopeless, that there is no chance of communication. Yet if you are with a person who is in the asura realm, which sounds like a very dire kind of dilemma, you might want to do anything you could to communicate, to share yourself. You would like to do anything that you might be able to do to help him or her out of that realm. Is there anything you can do, or do you just simply have to recognize the hopelessness of it?

TRUNGPA RINPOCHE: It depends on how you find the means to communicate to them. It is very intricate, and you have to be extremely skillful, because you cannot attempt it several times—you have to do it accurately at once. That communication comes from your style and the style of the other person. It is feasible that you may be able to help, but quite likely it is impossible.

STUDENT: In pictures of the wheel of life, a buddha appears in each realm.

TRUNGPA RINPOCHE: Yes, you have to be a buddha—that's right.

S: What is he doing in the realm of the asuras?

TR: He is speaking their language in an enlightened way. In the iconography, the buddha of the asura realm is wearing armor and carrying a sword in his hand. That is their language.

STUDENT: Could you distinguish between a bardo and non-bardo state?

TRUNGPA RINPOCHE: It seems that in the nonbardo state, there are no extremes, but situations could be switched back and forth. It is quite loose. There are so many junctions that you are not stuck in it, but you can make your choices; whereas in a bardo state, you are completely stuck, you are trapped in between two extremes, like extreme pain and extreme pleasure. You are trapped in it: if you try to go too far, you find yourself in extreme pleasure and you don't want to leave it; but if you go to the other extreme, you find yourself in extreme pain and you don't know how to get out of it. So you are sort of trapped in that situation—like meditative absorption or the jealous god thing or whatever it might be. Each extreme case presents a prison of its own, so you have no way out of it. The nonbardo state is like the questioning mind, or the true function of buddha nature. It is the dissatisfaction that takes place in the actual realm of people: you could communicate, you have questions, you have doubts, you could make choices of all kinds.

S: Then why is the clear light a bardo state? Is that a trap too?

TR: Clear light, in this case, is a transparent situation which could be colored by all kinds of other experiences. Clear light is generally a state of no-man's-land—and it could be made into someone's territory.

S: What if it isn't colored?

TR: Clear light is also the experience of buddha nature. It even transcends buddha nature. In that sense clear light becomes an aspect of nonreturning.

S: In other words, you don't have any sense of being in such a state?

TR: You are part of it, yes. You are part of it.

S: In actual practice how do bardo and nonbardo come together?

TR: It seems that if you have found your fixed logic, your way of maintaining your ego, your occupation, then you are in a bardo state of some kind or other; whereas, if you are still searching, if you are still open—or if you are free from searching altogether—that is the nonbardo state.

S: What about the transitions between bardo states? Are there moments of nonbardo there?

TR: Well, there are occasional doubts as to whether you are actually in that state forever, whether you have actually found some answers or not. You are uncertain and your bardo state begins to shake; your conviction begins to fall apart. And as your conviction gets more and more shaken and falls apart more—then you come out of that particular extreme case. You come back to the nonbardo state. You become a student again.

S: That's the difference between searching and not searching? It seems that very often you give the message of not searching, and yet now you say that the characteristic of the nonbardo state is the searching.

TR: Yes, it is so.

S: Are you asking us to get back into the bardo?

TR: I don't think so. Quit searching.

STUDENT: Rinpoche, is the clear light comparable to the non-bardo state?

TRUNGPA RINPOCHE: It depends. The clear light seems to be like water which has no color. If you put colors into it, the clear light absorbs that color; but still the water quality, which is color-less, remains.

S: How does that relate to the nonbardo state?

TR: Because there is also a colorless quality, even while being colored. If you pour paint into water, the water still remains transparent while it is carrying the different colors.

STUDENT: Is there a state which is beyond bardo?

TRUNGPA RINPOCHE: That seems to be the final state of realization—you are not searching anymore and you are not trapped anymore.

S: Is that taking the situation as it is all the time?

TR: Yes.

S: Is it a real possibility?

TR: You have to find out.

S: Do you feel you have some answers? Should we search for them?

TR: Searching seems to be a kind of introduction, to open your mind toward something. The style of that search is nonsearch. Do you see what I mean?

S: Nongrasping?

TR: Nongrasping, yes. If you decide to search, you have questions, you have doubts—that's good. But how to answer your problems, how to find a way out of doubts is nongrasping, which is not searching.

STUDENT: How do we relate to ourselves if we find ourselves behaving like jealous gods?

TRUNGPA RINPOCHE: I suppose that you could relate with yourself as being willing to step out of the comfort of being in such a state. That is very, very hard to do, because you have found your style, which for a long time you were looking for. We want to become somebody, which automatically means we would like to have our own style, our own dignity. Everybody longs for that. We admire people who have character; we admire people who have a style of their own, and we want to become like them. So once you have found a style of some kind, whether it is a realm-of-gods style or asura style, it is quite a delightful situation in the beginning that at last you are *somebody*.

But then, if we realize it is an asura—at that point we have developed a term for it and a frame of reference for it. We have labeled it as being that particular type of samsaric realm. So I suppose we are supposed to get the message, and be willing to step out of that comfort of creating a style of our own, and be willing to get back to the confused state where we did not have any style. It is very hard to give that up.

S: Did you say that all six bardo states are a resource that someone following the style of any one of the six realms can draw upon at any moment in order to continue his particular style of maintenance?

TR: No doubt, yes. That generally happens, but that is not regarded as being stuck in a realm, necessarily. You are acting on your potentials. You are trying to pull out, rather than actually being stuck in a realm. That seems to happen constantly all the time with everyone and anyone. It is not regarded as your actually being in a realm as such, but you are exploring your possible ways of defending yourself.

STUDENT: But how does the dream state reinforce any of the realms, because dreams have a tendency to point out what the real situation is to us, to remind us of the things that we've been forgetting while we were in the human realm. So in that sense, the dream state seems to me to be trying to tug you out of whatever realm you find yourself in at the moment.

TRUNGPA RINPOCHE: Well, dreams relate to either something that you would like to happen in the future or something that happened to you already in the past. It may not be a particularly accurate picture at the moment, but it gives you tremendous room to venture around. The bardo of dreams is kind of the realm of the imagination rather than dreams per se—imagination and possible ideas. It is completely devoid of relating with the physical situation, but it is the idea of purely relating with the phenomenal situation. All these realms have an unreal quality in them as well. Because you are trying to hold on so tightly, so hard, because it is so real; therefore sometimes it becomes very loose and very dreamlike, miragelike, at the same time. That is one of the characteristics of bardo states—that confusion between seriousness and looseness. And then occasionally, one has to bring oneself back to it.

STUDENT: Perhaps if a person is in this realm, and in a meditative state or a dream state where there is that kind of looseness, there is the possibility of communicating with that person for a split second.

TRUNGPA RINPOCHE: Well, that is a very sneaky way of communicating. It could work, but at the same time, if you raise too much alarm, quite possibly they might jump back onto their solid ground and pretend they are not dreaming at all. But it is highly possible. That seems to be one of the ways the buddhas communicate with them. The buddhas of each realm communicate by using the teaching of the situation. For instance, they might be sharing the same situation at the same time—like walking on a very shaky bridge where they both have to walk carefully. So you can communicate from that.

STUDENT: Asuras seem so defensive.

TRUNGPA RINPOCHE: The asura realm in particular is very much on guard. Their ultimate fear is that this is what people do, try to get you; and they are very much on guard for that particular style.

S: Is there a way to outsmart them?

TR: I don't think so. As far as asuras are concerned, they have worked everything out very methodically. And that could be said to be the same with the other realms as well. The whole thing is worked out very methodically. You may come on as though you are using the other person as a guinea pig, but the other person is not a guinea pig at all. He or she is a professional person in the six realms of the world—so he could come back at you and use *you* as a guinea pig.

S: What about nonverbal communication?

TR: That is also very tricky. They could also reject your vibrations, or whatever you would like to call them.

S: It sounds very important to be on the side of such a person, rather than being in any way opposed to him.

TR: Well, even that makes it a very suspicious thing—you may be trying to sabotage him.

STUDENT: Rinpoche, what would you say to the technique of intensifying the paranoia so the paranoia becomes real?

TRUNGPA RINPOCHE: There has to be a balance of how to deal with that. I mean, that kind of tactic in particular could only be used once. If you misuse it once, then you fail all the rest of it. So that is an expensive thing.

STUDENT: Rinpoche, you used the term *schizophrenic* in relation to people in the asura realm. And then you also said, in one of the answers to the questions, that such a person, in order to maintain himself, is seeking to develop a character or personality or identity. Now, I think that when psychologists talk about schizophrenia, they say that one of the schizophrenic's qualities is that he doesn't have a character, he doesn't have an identity, he doesn't know who he is, and so he doesn't feel comfortable with himself. You are saying the schizophrenic person is seizing on his identity, and the psychologists are saying he doesn't have an identity. It seems to be a conflict.

TRUNGPA RINPOCHE: Well, in one sense, he doesn't have an identity in the same way ordinary people have a permanent identity as such. But he does have some kind of identity, because he is a professional at his game, and whenever he realizes he doesn't have an identity, he jumps back to his game. So he has this extremely skillful, professional kind of approach. The same thing could be said of the asura realm: fundamentally you are insecure; therefore your security is without security. That situation gives you a tremendous sense of occupation, something to do. You are kept busy at it all the time so you don't have to think of your insecurity anymore. You are kept busy constantly playing games. But at the same time, you know *how* to play games. It is obvious to you, you do not have to think or strategize anymore at all, it just comes naturally to you, spontaneously you just do it.

S: So the schizophrenic person has a deliberate quality about his seeking?

TR: Yes, and an impulsive quality—which is very confident, as far as their game is concerned.

STUDENT: What about energy? Is there only one energy, or are there different types of energies for each realm?

TRUNGPA RINPOCHE: Well, I suppose you could say there are different textures or different colors, like the different energies of the five buddha families. But all of those energies are governed by ego. Therefore the general quality of the energy is the maintenance of ego; all the effort is given to that.

STUDENT: Rinpoche, I'm trying to compare this with what you said about bardo in the seminar in Allenspark. There I got the impression that you hang out in one of the six realms, and when the experience characteristic of that realm becomes particularly intensified, you peak out in what you call the bardo. And at that point, where you peak out, there is the possibility of freaking out or the possibility of receiving something, catching on to something. Here I get the impression, on the other hand, that most of the time we go about maintaining ourselves and we sort of hang out in the bardo state; and only some of the time are we open and looser about it. So the bardo state, rather than being a place where you might possibly receive something, is a place where you are just stuck.

TRUNGPA RINPOCHE: The whole point is that you have to have a sense of extreme case. In the situation of an extreme case, there is the likelihood that you could intensify the bardo experience and switch into a nonbardo state. But that cannot really be helped by anything at all—by an external situation or by teachers or anything. You have to do it yourself. Either you do it yourself or it doesn't happen. So it is a very manual situation—you do it by yourself. On the other hand, there is the possibility that the intensification of the bardo experience could be reduced by occasional doubt and occasional gaps, and you could come back from one realm and then maybe enter into another one, or reenter the previous one. That kind of situation goes on all the time. But they are both intense situations: one intense situation brings you back; the other intense situation frees you completely. However, at this point we have not yet touched on that particular topic and on the details of relating with the different types of wisdom of the five buddha families and the different realms associated with them—in terms of intensifying the extreme of confusion, and that confusion bringing realization.

4

The Human Realm

Today we could discuss the human realm, which is associated particularly with passion. The human realm is not necessarily the literal state of human life as such. There is something to keep in mind in discussing all of these states, or realms: in a sense they are all aspects of human life, which contains six types of world, or realms, within itself. The human realm in these terms is also a certain state of mind, and we tend to get stuck in this extreme as much as in that of the asuras or the realm of the gods.

So the human realm seems to have two possibilities. One is actual human life, which contains tremendously open karmic possibilities in which we could function intelligently and make choices, in which we could study and meditate, and in which we could change the karmic situation as we evolve. But the other type of human realm, the human realm as part of the six realms of the world, is an extreme case of the human realm, which is an effect of a certain extreme chaos. From that extreme chaos, related with passion, this extreme human realm begins to develop—much the same as in human life we may develop the animal realm, the hungry ghost realm, the jealous gods realm, or whatever.

The human realm in this sense is a process of grasping, extreme grasping in which a certain amount of intelligence functions. In other words, intelligence in the sense of logical, reasoning mind functions. The reasoning mind is always geared toward trying to create happiness, pleasurable situations. And there is an immediate tendency to separate the pleasure and the experiencer of the pleasure. There is also a sense of being lost, a sense of poverty, often accompanied by nostalgia, trying to re-create past pleasurable situations as well. This is a result of an extreme dualistic split: projections are regarded as the ultimate answer to bring about some kind of comfort, and therefore you feel inadequate, as the projector. You are not strong enough or magnetic enough to draw these extremes of external pleasure into your realm. So you try your best to draw them in. Often there is a tendency to be very critical, to have a critical attitude. There is a critical attitude toward other people in this human realm; you see them as imperfect. And you begin to see your own situation as one of perfecting. Achieving ideal perfection becomes a fantastic, sensational target to reach. So there is constant striving.

The human realm is associated, in terms of the buddha families, with the padma family mentality of magnetizing. It is a selective magnetizing in which if you are to magnetize, you have to have discriminating vision: you want to magnetize the best qualities, the highest or most pleasurable situations, the most sophisticated and most civilized. That style of magnetizing is quite different from the magnetizing process involved in the asura realm, which, again, is connected with jealousy. In the asura realm magnetizing is very blind; it is not as selective and intelligent as that of the human realm. The human realm altogether contains so much selection, and also the rejection of certain things as not your style. There is a tremendous sense that you have your own ideology and you have your own style and you magnetize situations in order to enrich your basic being. That way of magnetizing has to be precise. So in this case, the human realm seems to be extremely selective and fussy. You have to have the right balance of everything.

The human realm is also accompanied by a comparative intellectual understanding of others. On the one hand, others may have your style. On the other hand, other people may not meet your taste, your style, so they could be criticized, condemned. Another possibility is that they might meet your style, and in fact be much better at your style, sort of ideal, superior to you. You wish to be one of those people who are much more intelligent than you and have very refined taste. They are leading pleasurable lives or getting the right things you would like to have, but which they actually managed to do. This could happen either in terms of historical persons, which could be said to be mythical persons at that point, or in regard to your contemporaries. You have observed them, you have seen them, you have been with them, and you are highly impressed by those who have perfected things intellectually, convincingly, from a practical point of view. You are also envious. They have gotten everything together and you would like to be one of them. This could be said to be like the jealous god mentality, in general point of view, but it is not quite so. It has the quality of grasping; this mentality is based on grasping, or trying to draw others into yourself. So it is more than just envy, it is more than jealousy. It is ambitious jealousy, or you could say it is realistic jealousy. You do not just become jealous of a person, but you would like to compete with them. So it is a very practical jealousy, an extremely ambitious kind of jealousy.

The whole process, in this case, is always one of grasping, holding on to something, holding on to high ideals. Of course, spiritually it is holding on to the higher spiritual truths of those who have achieved. And often, people who are in this realm of human beings have visions or identify themselves with Christ, Buddha, Krishna, Muhammad, or whomever. Historical characters mean a tremendous amount to you because they have achieved something. They have magnetized everything that you can possibly think of—fame and power. If they wanted to become rich, they could become so, because they have such tremendous influence over other people. Spiritually you would like to be someone like that. You have a competitive attitude toward them: you do not necessarily want to become better than them, but you would at least like to match them. And people also have visions in which they identify themselves with great politicians, great statesmen, great poets, great painters, great musicians, great scientists, and so on.

Such a competitive attitude of the human realm is overwhelming. It seems that the whole process of approaching things from that angle is based on magnetizing. That is why the human realm stresses the idea of knowledge and learning, education, collecting a wealth of wisdom of all kinds—scientific, philosophical, or what have you. It is based on intellect. The human realm is the highest point of the six realms of the world. The human realm has the greatest potential or quality of achieving, or of creating a monument of the rest of the six realms. One of the ideals of materialistic society, ambitious society, is to try to create the greatest, or the biggest, or the largest, or the longest, historical monument. Trying to break records of samsaric speed. That kind of heroic approach is based on magnetizing.

Such a heroic approach is also based on fascination, because you encounter such intellectual understanding, meeting with remarkable people. It is also based on self-consciousness, of course, as to what you do not possess. When you hear that somebody else possesses something, you regard yourself as insignificant; when you hear that somebody is significant, that impresses you. That competitiveness is the fixed state of the human realm. It is based on continual thought process which will never end because there is so much stuff going on in your mind as a result of collecting so many things, and as a result of so many plans to be made.

The extreme state of the human realm is that you are stuck in an absolute traffic jam of discursive thoughts. It is extremely busy. There is no end to it. One cannot really relate with any kind of learning or develop anything at all. Constantly all kinds of stuff churn out. All kinds of ideas and plans and hallucinations and dreams churn out constantly. It is quite different from the realm of the gods, where you are completely absorbed in a blissful state and you have a kind of self-snug satisfaction. In the case of the jealous gods also, you are completely drunk on extreme comparative mentality; you are stuck there. There seem to be fewer possibilities of thought process happening, because your experiences are so strong and they overpower you; you are hypnotized by that state. In the case of the human realm, there seems to be much more thought process happening constantly. The thinking process takes place much more actively. The intellectual or logical mind becomes so powerful that one is completely overwhelmed by all kinds of possibilities of magnetizing new things. You are trying to get hold of new situations and new ideas, along with all kinds of strategies that you might employ, as well as case histories, as well as quotations from the books you have read, as well as the overwhelming incidents that have happened in your life. The things recorded in your subconscious begin to play back constantly all the time, much more so than in other realms. So it is a very intelligent realm and extremely busy and extremely dissatisfied at the same time.

The human realm seems to have less pride than any of the other realms. If you are stuck in the other realms, you begin to find that your realm is some kind of occupation, you can hang on to it, and you begin to get satisfied with it; whereas in the case of the human realm, there is no satisfaction. There is constant searching, constant looking for a new situation to improve on the given situation.

Of course, the human realm also has the six bardo qualities in it: the fantasy or dreamlike quality, the quality of continuously giving birth, death, absorption, as well as the gap in which you can experience the clear light. All these experiences are happening simultaneously, which provides more varieties of speeding, more possible ways of speeding.

On the one hand, the human realm seems to be a rather intelligent situation. At the same time, it is the realm which is the least enjoyable, because suffering is not regarded as an occupation in the human realm, but suffering is a way of challenging yourself. So a constant reminder or ambition is created from the suffering.

STUDENT: Do all six realms have corresponding buddha families?

TRUNGPA RINPOCHE: Yes. The god realm and the animal realm are both associated with the buddha family. The jealous god realm is associated with the karma family, the human realm with the padma family, the hungry ghost realm with the *ratna* family, and the hell realm with the *vajra* family.

STUDENT: Rinpoche, what about the extreme version? You say that each one of these realms could be considered a psychotic state. What is the extreme of the human realm? This sounds like a very normal state you're describing.

TRUNGPA RINPOCHE: The extreme case is speed, trying to catch your own tail. You are so fast that you begin to see your own behind.

STUDENT: Rinpoche, is depression associated with any one of the realms in particular?

TRUNGPA RINPOCHE: If depression is connected with any of the realms, it seems to be the human realm in particular. As I've already mentioned, the least satisfied realm is the human realm, because it is intellectually highly strung and everything is regarded as tentative. There is the possibility of getting something, but one is not quite certain whether one is really getting it or not. There is a continual sense of failure all the time. So it seems that depression is dominant in the human realm.

STUDENT: Rinpoche, while you were talking, I was wondering whether there is anything statistical about this, whether in mankind in general you find rather more persons in one particular realm than the others, or whether it is pretty evenly split up? Is this human realm that you're describing one in which more people tend to fall, or would it be some other?

TRUNGPA RINPOCHE: I think you cannot know percentages as such. But it seems that the human realm is colored by all kinds of other situations, such as the realm of hell, or the hungry ghost or jealous god realms. It seems that generally there are more people involved in the other five realms than in the standard human realm. That is also associated with the cultural situation of the moment, the political situation of the moment.

S: And how about the presentation of ideas? Yours is one particular form of presentation; do you find that it seems to appeal to one type more than others?

TR: Well, that seems to be applicable to all of them. I mean, people have different makeups, as we have been talking about, they possess different buddha natures and they have their own way of viewing or understanding, in terms of magnetizing or enriching or whatever. So the presentation does not make any difference, but the presentation is sort of a neutral situation. It is there, and they adopt it according to their style. It is like the way we eat food, for instance. Some people eat food for taste, some people eat food because they are hungry, some people eat food because they feel it is part of their occupation of escape. There are all kinds of styles. There may be a hundred people in the audience watching a cinema, and each person would have a different way of regarding that particular movie: it could be seen as fascination or entertainment or expectation or educational. There are all kinds of ways of viewing it. It is the same thing with any situation. Presenting teaching is also the same; it is a very neutral thing. How people take it will vary according to how they sense that neutral situation according to their own state of being.

STUDENT: Rinpoche, is one way of getting out of this realm, or one problem of this realm, not identifying with yourself, not seeing external qualities in yourself?

TRUNGPA RINPOCHE: I think the attitude regarded as applicable to all of the realms is that if you are able to see situations clearly as they are—without being colored by what you want to see, what you like to see, what would be helpful for you to see, but just things as they are, directly and simply—then you begin to lose any ambition involved in the different realms of the world. Each realm has its own style of ambition, so stepping out is the absence of ambition, which is not colored by present confusion.

STUDENT: Rinpoche, what would be the quality of the buddha of this realm?

TRUNGPA RINPOCHE: The buddha of the human realm is a buddha with a begging bowl. It represents the mentality of poverty, which is the largest concern of the human realm. In order to relate with poverty, you have to speak the language of poverty. But by carrying a begging bowl, in fact, it is as though you always have something to put things into. In other words, the ultimate mentality of poverty is also the mentality of richness at the same time. Whenever situations need to be created you can create them, and you get it. You are in command of the whole situation. So that is extremely wealthy.

STUDENT: Rinpoche, would one's predominant buddha family have an affinity to a particular mental aberration of the six realms of existence? Would karma people have a greater psychological tendency to pick up the aberration of the asuras?

TRUNGPA RINPOCHE: Not necessarily. You have your basic character, but at the same time, the different experiences of the different realms are purely instigated from your current situation. You may use the same style as the particular buddha family you belong to, but that style could be put into practice from a different state of being at the same time—always.

S: You said the realm of the gods was basically buddha family. Would it be possible to relate to that in a vajra way?

TR: Definitely, yes. There could also be the padma quality of magnetizing, as well as all kinds of other things.

STUDENT: For a person who has not yet achieved a simple awareness of things as they are, and who has this human quality of intellect and wants to understand things—for him it takes a certain effort, just sitting here and listening to you, a certain effort to concentrate, to hear and understand what you are saying. And that effort seems to be a kind of clinging, a kind of magnetism. Now, is there something that such a person can do directly in his realm of intellect to improve the situation, or can it only be done through the whole process of meditation?

TRUNGPA RINPOCHE: Well, you see, when you talk about improving the situation, you are talking about a confusing topic. You have the basic idea of improving the situation, but you haven't gotten to the point of the cause and effect of the improvement. Whether it should come from there or here is uncertain. So in order really to deal with situations, you have to start methodically, organically. That is to say, you need to know whether the situation is the hangup, or the person who is experiencing the situation is the hangup, or the style of experiencing the situation is the hangup. That is very subtle and very, very delicate. It seems that in order to relate with a situation, you first have to let the inhibitions come through—the hidden qualities, the masked qualities, or the ambitious qualities. So the whole thing begins with not regarding apparent hangup-type situations as hangups, but letting them be as they are, and letting further hangups come through. Then the hangup coming through shows us its direction: whether it is really coming from here or there becomes quite obvious at some point. So it has to be a very individualistic style, a very personal style.

STUDENT: What is the point or circumstance at which a person in the human realm is going to change into another realm? What leads up to that?

TRUNGPA RINPOCHE: Doubt, uncertainty—which requires a circumstance of double-take. You see one situation, you are just about to get into it; then you doubt, and you look again. You are not speeding at that moment. In the process of your double-take, you cannot speed anymore because you are stopping, you are looking back again.

S: Which way is it more likely for the doubt to lead?

TR: To all of the other realms, any of the rest. It doesn't really matter. You could go up and down the realms or come back again. Doubt is a way of reducing the intensity of the human realm.

S: Would it be good to try to create the doubt, or maybe to try and do a purposeful double-take?

TR: I don't think so. It wouldn't be honest. If you know that you are doing that, therefore, you've got yourself.

S: How about other people, then?

TR: There again it is the same problem, if it is deliberate.

STUDENT: Doesn't meditation create doubt? You could say that is the purpose of meditation or at least one of the outcomes.

TRUNGPA RINPOCHE: Obviously, yes.

S: So, in a sense the question could be, the answer could be, to meditate.

TR: Not just in order to create doubt. You just meditate for the sake of meditating. You just do it. Then all kinds of disappointment comes out of the meditation.

S: Isn't it true that anybody who goes into meditation goes in for some purpose?

TR: You start with some purpose, definitely. But once you are in that meditative state, you do not have to dwell on that purpose at all. You forget why you're meditating. Altogether you are completely involved with the technique or the practice.

STUDENT: It sounds as if the human realm is the only realm we talked about.

TRUNGPA RINPOCHE: That is why it has been said that the human realm is the land of karma. It has a kind of mentality or intelligence which the other realms do not possess. Either they are too intelligent, like the realm of the gods and the asura realm, which are highly stuck, completely involved with their own scene; or else they are like the animal and the hungry ghost realms, in which things are very down, oppressive, and there is no chance of looking at it. So the human realm is the most painful and irritating realm. Therefore, it is more fertile.

STUDENT: Is the doubt that you feel in the human realm the doubt that you can ever achieve your ideal? Is this the doubt that you are talking about? I'm not sure about the doubt that takes you out of the human realm.

TRUNGPA RINPOCHE: It is doubt as to whether your occupation is valid or not, whether it is going to help you or harm you, and also doubt as to who is putting this into practice. The first doubt is doubt of the goal, the effort, or the ambition; you are uncertain whether your ambition to put things into practice is the right one or not. The second doubt is the doubt as to who is actually putting this into practice. You are beginning to develop a sense of uncertainty as to the existence of ego or not. That kind of doubt is a secondary one. It is a very profound one, that second type of doubt.

STUDENT: In the classification system we had, as we travel through the bardos, we established that leaving one and entering another is the spot to leave that game. On another level, you also said that there is this birth-death continuum. I'm wondering, does that have spaces in it as well, in going from a dream state to a birth state or something like that? I'm wondering how they intersect.

TRUNGPA RINPOCHE: These are the styles of our daily habitual pattern. For instance, in our living situation we sleep and we get up and we walk and we wash and we eat food. The situation of our existing in a realm is based on a dreamlike quality, birth, death, and gaps of all kinds.

S: So there are gaps between those?

TR: Yes, there are gaps between one occupation and another occupation.

S: So in the passage between one and the other, there are also points where we can get a flash of the whole situation.

TR: Until the intensity becomes overwhelming. The intensity becomes overwhelming, and there is a sense of irritating space where you feel you have to get on to the next one. That could possibly be a problem. Otherwise, there are obvious gaps. But those obvious gaps could become irritating, so much so that we immediately have to latch onto another gap, another topic, so to speak.

S: That's the problem with all spaces.

TR: Yes, yes.

STUDENT: You said that the other realms happen simultaneously in the human realm. Does that mean that during each moment all the realms are happening at the same time, or are they independent?

TRUNGPA RINPOCHE: It could be said that they happen in all kinds of ways, either simultaneously or in an intensified situation of one realm at a time. That depends on how much you collect different means to maintain your ego. If you have to intensify your jealousy as well as intensifying your grasp at the same time, you are in both realms, the human realm as well as the realm of the jealous gods. And if you find that is not efficient enough, sufficient enough, then you pick up other realms to help as auxiliary ways of maintaining your ego. So that could also happen. I mean, there is really no regulation of any kind. It is not a fixed thing, it could happen in all kinds of ways.

S: Are they present together or consecutively?

TR: Both.

STUDENT: Rinpoche, if a young child and his parents fall into different realms, is he hopelessly pulled into their realm, so in a sense he reflects back to you what realm you as a parent might be in?

TRUNGPA RINPOCHE: It depends on how much the child has developed a sense of himself as an independent concept. I mean, up to that point, it is possible to be pulled in in that way. Your pet animals, for instance, could be pulled into the same scene as well. That is exactly what happens when you have a national leader who is in one of the realms—the whole nation becomes part of that realm.

STUDENT: Do all of the realms develop out of each other and have a common root?

TRUNGPA RINPOCHE: The one common root is the bewilderment of ego, uncertainty. You feel you are losing ground unless you do something, so the obvious next move is to try to get into one of those realms.

STUDENT: Rinpoche, you said that the six realms can contain the bardo state as well as the gap? Is that gap the same as *dharmadhatu*?

TRUNGPA RINPOCHE: Yes. Dharmadhatu seems to be the instigator of all the problems. At the same time, it provides the basic space for all of them as well as for the enlightened state. It is all-pervading; that is why it is all-pervading.

STUDENT: Rinpoche, you spoke of this realm as being less inherently prideful than some of the others. Yet it seems to be extremely critical, and we are generally negative toward the majority of people around us in the human realm. Can you explain that problem a little further? You said that someone in the human realm is generally very critical of everyone who doesn't seem to match his or her style; and there are a smaller number of people who seem extremely attractive and whom one would like to magnetize. Yet you say that this realm is less involved with pride than the others.

TRUNGPA RINPOCHE: There is less pride in the sense of thinking you have found a definite occupation. For instance, in the case of the realm of the gods, you can dwell on your sense of absorption; and in the case of the asuras, you also have a sense of occupation, you are living on jealousy. It seems that the human realm hasn't found a fixed, definite occupation, except trying to magnetize whatever is available around you. But that is a very, very scattered situation. The situations around you are very unpredictable. They just present themselves, and you try to get hold of them, but at the same time they go on constantly. So your mind is constantly shifting between expectations of the future and memories of the past. That creates projections. So you haven't found a really definite occupation as such. That is why particularly the human realm has the possibility of receiving a teacher and being able to hear the teachings. Because you are not fixed on definite solid ground, you do not become deaf and dumb like the other realms. In a sense, it is a more open situation.

STUDENT: Is the clear light state a desirable state to be in, in the human realm?

TRUNGPA RINPOCHE: It depends on what you mean by desirable. It is not a particularly comfortable situation in the ordinary sense, but it is definitely a nonego state. The clear light experience begins with deprivation: you have lost your occupation. A certain amount of fear begins because you do not have anything to hang on to. It is complete all-pervading space, everywhere, irritating.

S: So that is how it differs from, let's say, the gap—it has an irritating quality to it?

TR: Right, yes, precisely. It is the irritating quality of the gap. You have seen the clear light state, but you are not in it properly. You just perceive a sense of clear light, rather than being in it. So clear light is the sense of desolation of complete open space. You have nothing to hang on to. Therefore, your automatic reaction, instead of getting into it, is to try to latch on to another thing that you can hang on to, which is one of the realms.

STUDENT: You said there was a choice in the human realm; but in the Allenspark bardo seminar you proved that there was no choice.

TRUNGPA RINPOCHE: That is saying the same thing in a sense. There is no real choice; you have to accept the given situation. But if you accept the given situation, then that could be said to be a choice: because you have accepted the choicelessness of that moment, you can get on to the next situation. It is up to you whether you get into it or not.

S: How is that particular to the human realm?

TR: Because the human realm has less sense of fixed occupation. It is uncertain, extremely uncertain, and filled with all kinds of anxieties, possible failures, possibilities of all kinds.

STUDENT: If you have a sense of the clear light experience, how do you go from that point to dwelling in the clear light instead of running away from it?

TRUNGPA RINPOCHE: Well, you see, that is the thing: you cannot dwell on clear light. That is what I mean by losing your handle, something to hang onto. Usually when you try to get into some psychological state, you could dwell on it, you could keep it up. But in terms of clear light experience, there is nothing to dwell on—which is an extremely foreign idea to the ego. The whole idea is that if you would like to get into that state, you have to give up all hope of getting somewhere or attaining something. You have to give up hopes and fears of all kinds.

S: If you got to the point where you gave up all hope of getting away from the sense of clear light, would that be the same thing as giving up?

TR: That is where clear light becomes part of you. If you disown the clear light, you become part of it.

STUDENT: But there is a separation, or a difference, between clear light and the bodhisattva's state. The clear light is still a bardo state, but you described the bodhisattva's state of giving up as a desirelessness and nongrasping.

TRUNGPA RINPOCHE: Well, the style of the bodhisattva path is the same, but the clear light experience is a very concentrated state. There is automatically something vivid and threatening. In the case of the bodhisattva ideal of giving up attaining enlightenment, it is more giving up as a path rather than as the full experience.

S: So in the clear light state there is still something to be irritated? You are still going in there with something?

TR: At the beginning, yes. You see, in order to merge two into one, you have to have two to begin with, as compared with one. Then the second one ceases to exist as an independent entity, you get into oneness. So you have to have two things happening in order to become one.

S: If that goes all the way, then there's only one?

TR: There is only one, yes—which is that you have nothing to hang on to. In the case of bodhisattva experience, there is still something to hang on to—which is the occupation of the bodhisattva. Bodhisattva activity is spontaneous action without purpose, without any idea of attaining enlightenment—but it is still an expression of duality. It is an occupation with no goal, no attitude.

S: You can have a goalless occupation?

TR: You could, yes. That is a very healthy situation for the bodhisattva; he or she does not experience any disappointment anymore.

S: But by definition, the bodhisattva is one who vows to renounce nirvana until all sentient beings are enlightened.

TR: That's right, yes.

S: That is not a goal?

TR: No, because all sentient beings are limitless.

STUDENT: Rinpoche, you described the embryonic situation leading to the breakdown of the realm of the gods as hope becoming fear and fear becoming hope; and in the asuras, the question beginning to become, "Who's defending whom?" What is the direction of the breakdown of the human realm and the possibility of coming to the gap?

TRUNGPA RINPOCHE: I suppose it is the repetitiousness of familiar situations being re-created constantly. At some stage you begin to lose heart and the whole thing becomes too familiar, including your games of maintaining yourself. It becomes too repetitious. That automatically invites depression as well, in the human realm. So it is sort of like familiarity breeding contempt.

STUDENT: Does the bodhisattva path ever cease to be an occupation?

TRUNGPA RINPOCHE: Yes, and at that point, the bodhisattva becomes part of the occupation. His action becomes part of the occupation—his whole being. He doesn't have to occupy himself with anything at all. He just does it.

STUDENT: Rinpoche, you spoke about the accommodation of change. Would that have to be the practice of letting go of emotions?

TRUNGPA RINPOCHE: I think so, yes.

S: And there is the possibility of change to the degree that one is able to give up?

TR: It is not a question of giving up, but it is a question of seeing beyond; it is a question of seeing that there is no direction anymore, rather than that there is no direction. The one who experiences direction does not have any interest anymore, so that kind of direction is redundant.

STUDENT: Rinpoche, I'm not exactly clear on the clear light and the bodhisattva. When you attain the clear light state, do you naturally become a bodhisattva?

TRUNGPA RINPOCHE: Clear light seems to be the meditative state of a bodhisattva, and the bodhisattva's idea of giving up is the path, or the practice, or a bodhisattva. You see, meditative experience could be said to be clear light; it does not have any aim, object or goal, because you become part of the clear light. But that does not become the permanent experience of bodhisattvas. Bodhisattvas flash back on the clear light constantly, but they still have to occupy themselves with something.

S: So the clear light is one aspect of the bodhisattva's being?

TR: Yes. And it has different intensities at different stages of the path. At the advanced stages of the bodhisattva path the clear light experience becomes more frequent—until you reach the tenth. In the beginning, it is less frequent.

S: In the tenth stage, what is the clear light experience?

TR: It is described in the books as being like visions seen in full moon light: it is not as clear as the sunlight, as buddha, but it is relatively clear.

STUDENT: It was a surprise when I found out that the realm of the gods wasn't where salvation was. Where does salvation come in?

TRUNGPA RINPOCHE: If you could talk about salvation, it seems that it is when there is no direction, the end of ambition, which is when you become completely one with your experience. Knowledge becomes one with wisdom, which is called buddhahood, or the awakened state of mind. You realize that you never needed to make the journey at all, because the journey is there already and the goal is there already. It is not so much that you are gaining something; it is not so much that you are achieving liberation, but it is more that you realize liberation is there and that you needn't have sought for it. That is the precise definition of *jnana,* which is a Sanskrit word meaning "wisdom." *Jnana* means complete oneness with your experience; you do not relate with the experiencer as such at all.

5

The Animal Realm

The experience of the different realms should follow the qualities of personality, the way or style in which individuals handle themselves—their styles of talking, the way they make telephone calls, the way they write letters, the way they type letters out, the way they read, the way they handle their eating, the way they sleep. Everybody tends to develop a style which is peculiar to them; everybody tends to develop their own kind of composure. At the same time, they are generally unaware of that situation and of the way they handle themselves. That sense of style even goes to the extent that if we are nervous or self-conscious, we still have our style of how to be self-conscious, which is quite unique from individual to individual. We may smile because we are self-conscious, or we may try to be frozen or aggressive or polite, or whatever. There is always some kind of style we are trying to follow. And we follow these styles, or ways of handling ourselves, continuously—not only in domestic situations, but also spiritually. People have their own style of meditating, their own style of trying to be good, trying to be religious, which has a very definite flavor.

In many situations, a person's particular style, or way of handling themselves, is uncertain or unknown to them. Often people become irritated when they hear their recorded voice or see video tapes or movies of themselves. If they observe themselves in that way, a lot of people find it extremely shocking. Even photographs are extremely shocking because you carry your own style in them. You may think you are better than you are or worse than you are, but when you see pictures of yourself you begin to get another point of view altogether. It is as though somebody else is seeing your style, which is extremely alien. Generally we do not like to see somebody else's point of view of ourselves. We don't like that, we find it irritating, embarrassing.

The realm that we are going to talk about today is highly connected with that style of handling our life situation. Even self-conscious people have particular characteristics that they fail to experience as though somebody else were watching or listening to them. Instead, a kind of instinct drives them into a particular aim, object, or goal—which is the animal realm. This has nothing to do with actually being reborn as an animal as such; it is the animal quality in this particular experience of our life.

Bearing that in mind, we could relate with that kind of animal instinct in ourselves in which everybody is involved with such serious games. Seriousness, in this case, does not necessarily mean the absence of a sense of humor. Even a sense of humor could be serious at this point. Self-consciously trying to create a friendly environment, a person could crack jokes or try to be funny or intimate or clever. That kind of sense of humor still has animal instinct, animal qualities. The reason seriousness is associated with the animal realm and that generally animals are viewed as symbolic representations of this particular realm is that animals don't smile or laugh, they just behave. They may play, but it is very unusual for animals actually to laugh. They might make friendly noises, or they might make certain gestures of friendliness, but somehow the subtleties of a sense of humor do not seem to exist in the animal realm. So this whole way of handling ourselves is related with the animal realm, including the attempted sense of humor in which we try to present a solemn situation as humorous.

The animal quality is one of purely looking directly ahead, as if we had blinkers. We look straight directly ahead, never looking right or left, very sincerely. We are just trying to reach the next available situation, all the time trying. Again, we are trying to grasp in a slightly different way, trying to be in a slightly different way, trying to demand that situations be in accordance with our expectations. Intelligence still plays an important part, but at the same time, there is this dumb quality, the ignorant quality of the animal realm.

The animal realm is associated with ignorance. It belongs to the same category as the realm of the gods, in terms of its other characteristic buddha family. That is, animals have buddha family qualities. They prefer to play deaf and dumb. They prefer to follow the given games that are available rather than looking at them or seeing them as they are. You might look at those games, or you might manipulate how to perceive such games, but at the same time you just follow along, you just continue to follow your instinct. When you have some hidden or secret wish, you would like to put that into practice. For instance, when there is irritation, you just put forward the irritation, no matter whether the irritation is going to hurt somebody or damage the creative situation or not. That does not seem to be a concern of the animal realm. You just go out and pursue whatever is available, and if the next situation comes up, you just take advantage of that as well and pursue it. It is like the story of the otter. An otter, who already has his prey of fish in his mouth, swims through the water. Suddenly he sees another fish swimming, a bigger, fatter one. He forgets that he already has a fish in his mouth, and he jumps the other fish—but the first fish slips away. So he loses both the first and the second fish. So if situations are unskillfully presented or unskillfully seen, then automatically you are going to meet with disappointment.

Generally, the quality of ignorance in the animal realm is quite different from primordial ignorance, or basic bewilderment. This kind of ignorance is dead honest and serious, which brings us further confusion or ignorance. You have a certain style of relating with yourself, and you refuse to see that style from another point of view. You completely ignore the whole thing. If somebody happens to attack you or challenge your clumsiness, your unskillful way of handling the situation, quite possibly you will find a way of justifying yourself. Or at least that is the approach taught in the schools: try to find your own logic to prove yourself and learn how to be self-respectable. Therefore, whatever you do is regarded as a self-respectable situation because you have only one way to go, which is to be serious and honest with yourself—in the pejorative sense. This has nothing to do with the truth at all. Actually, we don't care whether it is true or false. The false is seen as also true, and the truth is seen as something very serious. So generally falsehood is also extremely encouraging and something to be worthy of, proud of, in terms of animal realm. If you are attacked, challenged, or criticized, you automatically find an answer, in a very clever way.

The ignorance of the animal realm is not stupid at all. It is extremely clever. But it is still ignorance, in the sense that you don't see the perspective or the environment around you, but you only see one situation, one goal, aim and object. You try to mold the situation in accordance with your desire or your demand. And all kinds of excuses need to be put into the situation in order to prove that what you are doing is the right thing. They are not very difficult to find: automatically the cunning quality of the ignorance finds its own way of associating with such falsehood, whatever it may be. And at that point, even you yourself don't regard it as falsehood. That is the very interesting point about it. Whenever there is falseness or some devious way of relating with things, you begin by convincing yourself that it is the right thing. And having convinced yourself, having developed this very narrow vision, then you relate with other people, other situations, and try to convert them to your style, to your original desire. So the animal realm seems to be extremely stubborn, but this stubbornness also has a sophisticated quality to it. It is not clumsy or stupid at all. It is a way of defending oneself and maintaining this animal realm. On the whole, the animal realm is without a sense of humor of any kind. The ultimate sense of humor in this case is relating with situations freely in their full absurdity. In other words, a sense of humor, in its true nature, is seeing things clearly, including their falsehood, without blinkers, without barriers. A sense of humor could be seen as a general way of opening or seeing with panoramic vision, rather than as something to relieve your tension or pressure. As long as a sense of humor is regarded, or used as, a way of relieving pressure or self-consciousness, it is an extremely serious thing. It ceases to be a sense of humor at that point. Instead it seems to be looking for another pair of crutches.

The final crescendo of the animal realm seems to be when we try to grope our way into the next situation constantly, trying to fulfill our desires or longings, our hidden and secret wishes. We try to put that into practice quite seriously, quite sincerely, honestly and directly. In the traditional symbolism, the animal realm—this direct and extremely mean way of relating with the apparent phenomenal world of one's projections—is symbolized by the pig. The idea behind that is that the pig supposedly does not look to the right or the left or turn around, but it just sniffs along, and whatever comes in front of its nose it consumes. It goes on and on and on, without any kind of discrimination, a very sincere pig.

Often we find ourselves identified with such an image. It doesn't matter what topic or what particular situation we are dealing with. We may be dealing with all kinds of extremely sophisticated topics and intellectual concepts of the highest standard—but still, our style of working with that sophisticated world is that of a pig. It does not matter whether the pig eats beautiful, fantastic, expensive sweets, or whether the pig eats garbage and shit. Somehow, the criterion for being a pig is not based only on what the pig eats, but it is based on its style, how the pig handles itself in the process of eating.

Such an animal realm approach could be related with all kinds of situations: domestic, materialistic, or spiritual. There seems to be a crescendo of becoming completely more and more trapped. There is no way of steering to the right or the left because you are involved with such situations constantly, all the time, throughout your daily life. You are not able to look at yourself, you are unable to relate with the mirroring quality of the realms and of your life. You refuse to acknowledge that there are such things as mirrors. Mirrors that reflect your own projections do exist, but you do not relate with that at all. So the whole daily living situation—getting up in the morning, having breakfast and then doing odd things, having lunch and then also doing all kinds of things that you are interested in, eating dinner and going to sleep—goes on and on in that way. The things you put into those situations could be at an extremely high level of intelligence, the subject that you're dealing with could contain tremendous wisdom—but the style in which you handle yourself happens to be that of an animal. There is no sense of humor. There is no way of being willing to surrender, willing to open, or willing to give, at all. There is constant demand. If one thing fails, you are disappointed and you try to embark on another thing. We do this constantly, getting into one subject after another.

In discussing a similar situation, we used the analogy of a tank. A tank just rolls along, crushing everything. If there is a roadblock, the tank just goes through it with the appropriate sidetracks. It can go through buildings or through walls. It doesn't really matter whether you go through people or through objects. You just roll along. That seems to be the pig quality of the animal realm. And the animal realm seems to be one of the biggest—or *the* biggest and most outstanding—realms. We are often in that realm—to say the least.

STUDENT: Would one see a kind of naiveté in a person like that? They seem to be unaware or unconscious of their situation.

It doesn't seem as if a person in the animal realm would have a panoramic view.

TRUNGPA RINPOCHE: I think so, yes, definitely. You have developed your own style of achieving things: either playing games of one-upmanship or playing games of conning other people in order to achieve your wishful desires. There is a constant simple-minded quality. Those games are known only to you; therefore you just do it, whether it works or not. If it doesn't work, then you get into the next situation.

STUDENT: You were portraying the animal realm in terms of the stubbornness of going forward unthinkingly. But there's also the stubbornness which we speak of as "stubborn as a mule," which is that whatever way somebody is trying to pull you, you pull in the opposite way, sort of passive resistance. Is this kind of stubbornness also part of the animal realm, or is it something different?

TRUNGPA RINPOCHE: I think that is part of the whole thing, being stubborn as a mule. The mule doesn't want to go; therefore, that is his direction. He is still going forward in his way, whether you think it is a different way or not.

S: But when I find myself in this kind of stubbornness, it's not always that I have my own direction. When I get obstinate, I'm going to go in the opposite direction of whatever direction somebody else is trying to push me. So it's not that I have my own direction and therefore I am going forward. I just feel myself in a reverse gear against whatever pull exists.

TR: Well, that is saying the same thing, in a way. Whenever there is an obstacle that you are going through, you fight that obstacle in accordance with your wishes. Obstacles provide you with a new way of being stubborn constantly. That means you also develop an attitude of boycotting any situation presented to you; you have your own, so to speak, free will, or vision. That kind of vision is there all the time. So you cannot say that you are completely unprepared for new obstacles, but you have some definite logic going on there.

STUDENT: Does the animal realm have a quality of paranoia?

TRUNGPA RINPOCHE: I think you could have extreme paranoia in the animal realm. You experience the paranoia of not being able to achieve what you want, in accord with the ideal situation you would like to see. Therefore, the only way of achieving your ideal goal is to try to push further, as much as you can. So paranoia creates stubbornness at this point.

S: Rinpoche, how does this paranoia differ or compare with the paranoia in the asura state?

TR: In the asura state there is a tendency to try to fill all the gaps constantly. It is not so much going forward in the asura state; instead there is a quality of spreading. You look for security by trying to spread all over the situation and control it by extending yourself in terms of the relative logic of jealousy, envy. The animal realm is not so much concerned with conquering, but it is very simple-minded and very monastic—if one could use such a word. You would like to achieve your aim and object, and you just go along with that. We could say it is austerity.

STUDENT: Rinpoche, what is the buddha family associated with this realm?

TRUNGPA RINPOCHE: It seems that it belongs to the central family, the buddha family, the same as the realm of the gods. It is extreme earthiness, extreme nonparticipating in any frivolous situation trying to con you, but just going straight. It is very earthy, like a rock rolling down from a steep mountain; you are just willing to go straight through.

STUDENT: Rinpoche, there seems to be something unavoidable about the cycle of this realm. I mean, you do have to make some sort of decision about style: you're not going to eat one way; you are going to eat another way. You have to make a choice. But it seems as if you are always in this realm; there doesn't seem to be any escape. In that way it seems different than the other realms.

TRUNGPA RINPOCHE: The choice of style is largely based on the particular obstacle. It is like the way animals handle their bodies as they are walking across the countryside. If somebody is chasing you, and if the person who is chasing you cannot climb up, you climb up. It is not necessarily intelligent, but it is following the physical setup of your existence. You do it. If you are a bird and if some other animal without wings chases you, you just fly. That is not particularly a cunning quality of birds at all. You haven't thought that up; it is not that you haven't come to that same conclusion before, but you always come to that same conclusion. So in that way, obstacles provide a way of how to be stubborn.

STUDENT: Rinpoche, what moves you out of the animal realm? What sets up the problem that moves you out of that realm?

TRUNGPA RINPOCHE: Well, it seems that there has to be some kind of distrust in the present given style of how you try to achieve your stubbornness. So you try to transcend your stubbornness. Again, as in the other realms, it seems that if there is a slight doubt that your stubbornness may not work, you might try different ways of handling your body, your earthy situation. In the iconographical symbolism, the buddha of the animal realm carries a book of scriptures in his hands. If you are going to read a book or read scriptures, you cannot have a stubborn mind, because you cannot rewrite the book on the spot. You have to attune yourself to the book and to what has already been written by somebody. So you have to give up your stubbornness if you are going to read that particular book. The image of buddha holding a book means that you have to tune yourself into new situations and try to learn from the other experiences that are being expressed, other ways of thinking—which is a way of stepping out of the stubbornness.

One point is that if a particular teaching is powerful and true, you cannot interpret, because it is so overwhelmingly true. I mean, if it is sunshiny and daytime, you cannot possibly deny that and try to prove it is nighttime, because it is obvious. There is light and the sun is shining and all the other qualities of daytime are obviously there, so you can't prove it to be nighttime or try to argue. That kind of teaching always seems to have relevance in dealing with your actual given situation, rather than viewing it as something that you can change. If the teaching is presented to you in its living quality, then you cannot deny that living quality.

STUDENT: When you speak about following the necessities of your physical possibilities, it sounds as if there is a strong element in this realm of the wisdom of accepting what is inevitable.

TRUNGPA RINPOCHE: There seem to be two ways of acceptance. One way is accepting that the obstacle is there and trying to tune yourself in accordance with the obstacle and present your stubbornness. That is one kind of acceptance, a tremendously faithful way of relating with the current situation so that the current situation provides you with guidelines as to how to be stubborn. The other way seems to be the acceptance that fundamentally stubbornness doesn't work, and you have to learn to open somehow or other.

STUDENT: Each time you expound on a realm automatically I think, "How the heck can we get out of this realm?" Can we be relaxed and notice that we're in a certain realm, and then do something about it? We could develop some strategy to kick us out of that realm immediately, but if we are in the animal realm, our strategy would probably be an animal strategy. So how can we get around this?

TRUNGPA RINPOCHE: Well, it depends on how advanced your plan is: if you are planning to pursue your same trip or if you could step out of this current problem of the inconvenience of being in the animal realm. In other words, you could be planning to try to step out of the animal realm so that you could become a super animal, so that you would have somewhere to pursue your previous occupation. Or else you could have a dead-end attitude, just wanting to get out of this particular realm and then letting things develop. That approach is usually referred to as very impractical by conventional society. According to conventional society you should not struggle; and if you are going to struggle, you must have an aim and object and goal. But on the other hand, it could be said to be the most practical way of looking at things at all, because you do not captivate yourself again and again by using the same ways.

Particularly in the animal realm, which is extremely involved with ignorance, the absurdity of yourself is not seen. Instead you take pride in it. You carry out your strategies as though nobody knows; as though nobody knows your tactics. At that point, particularly with the animal realm, there is a need for watching yourself being absurd or silly. It is the same analogy as we discussed earlier on: seeing your own photograph and hearing your own voice. Some kind of self-conscious, critical attitude to oneself is necessary, because the animal realm contains pride. That is why the animal realm and the realm of the gods have some common qualities. Both have survived on the pride of not watching yourself or what is happening at all, but just purely dwelling on succeeding constantly, on and on and on.

STUDENT: When I look at an animal, a cat, or even a pig, it has that quality of directness that you described. It always strikes me as almost a state of enlightenment, in the sense of being simply what it is. For instance, a cat always seems to respond precisely to the situation in its catlike way; I would even say the same thing about a pig. You say that an animal doesn't look around, that it has this blinder quality; but looking around implies a watcher, or an ego, so it seems almost as if animals are in an egoless state. It begins to sound very much like a state of enlightenment.

TRUNGPA RINPOCHE: Well, it doesn't necessarily have to be a cat or pig, but this kind of animal style is also in ourselves as well.

S: But it has this quality of simply being what we are.

TR: It is being what you are, but that is precisely the point— there are two ways of being what you are.

S: How does ego fit into the animal realm then?

TR: The ego of the animal realm is just simply being quite self-contained, satisfied in some sense in what you are. Therefore, whatever you do is to try to benefit yourself constantly; one doesn't even question it. In the case of enlightenment, you are being what you are, but you don't try to collect anything for yourself or try to benefit yourself or try to strengthen self-centered notions of any kind. The difference between the animal realm and the enlightenment state is that in the enlightened state acceptance and self-satisfaction take place in a spacious way, within open space, in a cosmic way; whereas the animal realm is centralized, and acceptance of its oneness happens in a centralized way. In exactly the same way, you could be extremely learned so you don't have to ask any more questions; but at the same time you could be extremely stupid so you can't even think of questions.

STUDENT: To me, cats in particular have this enlightened quality. A cat sitting with his paws together and his tail curled around has a very similar quality to a buddha statue. And generally, cats in their activities have this really beautiful flowing quality.

TRUNGPA RINPOCHE: Well, I don't particularly want to set out an anti-cat philosophy, but this way of just being what you are is quite common to all creatures or beings, so to speak: tigers, horses, birds, even wolves have their uniqueness. The way they handle themselves is miraculous—even centipedes, spiders—because they are being what they are. They can't help it; there is no alternative.

S : Do you mean that there's no space, in the sense that a human being has space and can fill it up in alternative ways; whereas animals don't have such space?

TR : Animals do not have alternatives of any kind, suggestions of any kind. They just have to be what they are. By possession of luck, certain animals are loved because of their natural quality of being what they are, and we tend to interpret that quality as that they are specially being for us. But they are just being what they are. In the same sense, in Buddhist iconography, there are very few walking buddhas. Usually Buddha is depicted sitting—quite possibly in feline fashion, if you would like to see it that way. But at the same time, he has choices of all kinds. He just decided to sit and associate with the earth, which is an intelligent choice. In the case of animals, they have no choice. They are just there.

Take, for instance, the example of vows. In taking vows of all kinds, such as the Buddhist precepts—traditionally not to kill, not to steal, not to tell lies, and so on—human beings can take those precepts or vows because human beings have very cunning minds, and they also have the choice to kill or not to kill; whereas animals or other beings do not. For instance, only particular types of human beings can take the vow of celibacy. If you are a eunuch or neutered, you cannot take the vow of celibacy because you cannot break the rule anyway; it is physically impossible. So it seems that if you have the choice of either committing yourself or not, allowing yourself into the temptation or not allowing yourself into the temptation and finding another way of relating with it—that provides the basic background.

S : So, for example, the choice not to eat meat has that quality.

TR : Yes, automatically.

S: How about plants?

TR: There seem to be lots of them.

STUDENT: You were talking about energy and space, and you said that animals have a self-centered image of space. Then you were talking about open space. In that regard, I was wondering why in Buddhist iconography the Buddha is always pictured in what seems to be a very centralized space. The imagery is always extremely centered. I mean, especially since you talk about animals having this very self-centered image of space instead of having a view of open space.

TRUNGPA RINPOCHE: It seems that pictures or representations of symbolical images reflect tremendously the artist who created them. Strangely enough, they also reflect one culture to another culture. For instance, different types of buddha images were created in different Buddhist countries. Japanese buddhas always have this quality of being like warriors, like samurai, with little mustaches and sitting very tightly, with round shoulders, round backs. Also, looking at the ancient images created in different parts of India, you can tell which part of India each image was made. Bengali buddhas, for instance, look kind of food-oriented; they have a certain facial expression, as though they just had a good meal. At the same time, buddhas created in Assam, in East India, are the most ancient images that you could find. Their facial expressions are very genteel, as though Buddha was a great scholar who knew everything, a very genteel professional look. So the imagery reflects the different styles from one country to another country.

STUDENT: Rinpoche, what is the difference between moving forward one-pointedly in the style of the animal realm and the confidence that you like to see in your students, the acceptance of oneself? You say we have to accept ourselves, make friends with ourselves, and learn to trust ourselves as we are.

TRUNGPA RINPOCHE: There seem to be two different styles of confidence: the security-minded confidence that whatever you do you are going to achieve something out of in order to benefit yourself; and confidence in the sense of carelessness, that you are allowing things to happen by themselves and not trying to secure situations of any kind. This second kind of confidence, where any associations to security do not apply any more, is the highest confidence. In fact, it ceases to be confidence at that point, because you don't have a target or criteria of any kind.

STUDENT: You talked about doubt as being a way out of these realms. I don't see how to reconcile that with having confidence.

TRUNGPA RINPOCHE: If you have a short glimpse of doubt as to your animal realm struggle, that this may not be the right style of pushing yourself; then at the same time, there is also confidence, that you don't need a comforter anymore. If the doubt is overwhelmingly powerful, you may find that security does not apply. Security is an important point for you—if you give up that sense of security, then you develop the confidence that you do not need security anymore. In other words, there is a sort of trust in the doubt, and that in itself becomes a sense of security.

STUDENT: Rinpoche, it sounds to me that seeking after personal comfort and removing yourself from a potentially harmful situation are both paranoid actions, motivated by ignorance. Is this correct?

TRUNGPA RINPOCHE: Ignorance is the sense of having one particular aim and object and goal in mind. And that aim and object, that goal-mindedness, becomes extremely overwhelming, so you fail to see the situation around you. That seems to be the ignorance. Your mind is highly preoccupied with what you want, so you fail to see what is.

STUDENT: Rinpoche, where is the opportunity or space to communicate with someone who is absolutely determined not to see what they're doing, and beyond that, is into justifying that they don't see?

TRUNGPA RINPOCHE: That is precisely the animal realm style of thinking: either subconsciously or consciously you ignore the whole situation, and deliberately make yourself dumb.

S: I can see that, but is there any place where you can communicate with somebody who is trapped in that situation?

TR: Well, one could try one's best to try to remind that person that such a situation is happening. Quite possibly, there may be a gap in their state of mind, their psychological state. Quite possibly they might hear the message if you are able to time it right. Otherwise, even your suggestion itself becomes reinforcement. So one has to be buddhalike, skillful—which is not impossible. It seems to be worth trying.

STUDENT: Rinpoche, it almost seems that the animal realm has a universal quality in the sense that you find an occupation in any one of the realms. The way you cope with being a hungry ghost or you habitually cope with being an asura sounds like the animal realm, because you just try to plow through everything with hungry ghost mentality or hell mentality. Do you call that the hungry ghost realm with an animal realm flavor—or what?

TRUNGPA RINPOCHE: The animal realm is in a sense less self-conscious, doing things with false conviction. The other realms seem to have some kind of intelligence, except for the realm of the gods, which doesn't have intelligence. The asura, human, hungry ghost, and hell realms seem to have some kind of self-consciousness as well. That seems to be the only difference. Apart from that, the stubbornness of all these realms could be said to have animal qualities.

STUDENT: With regard to the question that was asked earlier about the difference between stubbornness and confidence, would it be correct to say that if you are in fact working with yourself and working with the negative qualities that exist in any of these realms, such as the stubbornness of the animal realm—if you confronted it and transformed it and made it your friend, instead of a negative stubbornness, it could become a positive persistence which works for you?

TRUNGPA RINPOCHE: I think so, yes. Yes, definitely.

6

The Hungry Ghost and Hell Realms

We seem to have two realms left: the hungry ghost realm and the hell realm. First we could discuss the hungry ghost realm. Like the other realms, the hungry ghost realm is tremendously applicable apropos situations we deal with ourselves. It could be related with the idea of hunger. The Tibetan word for the emotional state of the hungry ghost, *serna,* could be said to mean "meanness" or "lack of generosity." The literal meaning of *serna* is "yellow-nosed": *ser* means "yellow," *na* means "nose." In other words, it is an extremely sensitive nose, an outstanding nose. It is like traffic patrols, dressed up in fluorescent orange shirts to raise people's attention that there is something happening. It is that sniffy quality of a dog who is looking for something to eat. Even if he comes across a piece of shit, it is a delightful thing, because he has to come up with something.

In this realm it seems that the act of consuming is more important than what you are consuming; there is a disregard for what you consume. It is related with the ratna buddha family. There is a quality of trying to expand and develop. So the consumption is also based on a sense of expanding, becoming rich. In terms of

the visual sense, hungry ghosts are presented as individuals having tiny mouths, thin necks and throats, gigantic stomachs, and
skinny arms and legs. This image is usually connected with the
struggle to get something through your mouth and swallow what
you have consumed. It is extremely unsatisfying, dissatisfying.
Given the size of your belly, you cannot possibly be satisfied at all
in filling your stomach.

The hungry ghost realm could be related with food, as symbolism, but it also could be related with the concept of food as
grasping: grasping human friendship, company, material wealth,
food, clothes, shelter, or whatever. The whole thing is related with
the hunger that we seem to have—there is tremendous hunger
involved. That hunger is extremely accurate and penetrating. You
would like to consume whatever is available around you, but there
is a slight sense of deprivation, as though you are not allowed to
do that. At a subconscious level, there is a sense that you are not
allowed to consume what you would like. You are trying to consume much more than you are meant to in terms of the size of your
mouth and the size of your neck. It becomes totally impractical:
what you are able to consume cannot fill you up, given the size of
your belly. The preta, or hungry ghost, mentality at the spiritual
level is that you would like to be entertained, because there is
constant hunger. Whatever you hear is entertaining at the time,
but it tends to become too familiar. So you are constantly looking
for new ways of entertaining yourself—spiritually, philosophically, what have you. There is constant searching, a constant grasping quality.

Fundamentally, there is a sense of poverty, disregarding what
you have. You are still poor. You are not able to keep up with your
pretense of what you would like to be. Again, there is a sense of
one-upmanship, which happens all the time. Whatever you have
is regarded as part of your pride, part of your collection—but you
would like to have something more than that. So you are constantly collecting all the time, on and on and on and on. And

when the time comes that you cannot consume anymore—when you cannot receive anymore because you are dwelling on what you have already so that what you are receiving becomes too overwhelming—you begin to become deaf and dumb.

In other words, you concentrate so much on what you want, what you would like to receive, what you would like to achieve. So much concentration is imposed on your being, your intelligence. Because you want to listen so hard, you cannot hear anymore for the very fact that you want to listen or you want to receive. You want to learn so much that you cannot hear anymore because your ambition becomes an obstacle. At that point, the deaf and dumb quality of the hungry ghost level becomes extremely powerful. You see that other people can relate: they can listen, they can understand, they can consume. Nostalgia become prominent: you wish that you were still hungry so that you could eat more. You wish that you felt poor, that you were deprived, so that you could take pleasure in consuming more and more, further and further. There is a sense of trying to return back to that original state of poverty, as much as you can. From that point of view, the mentality of poverty seems to be luxurious as far as the hungry ghosts are concerned. You would like to be able to consume as much as you can, in terms of knowledge, physical well-being, materialistic well-being, or what have you.

Finally, anything that happens in your life is regarded as something that you should consume, something that you should possess. If you begin to see beautiful autumn leaves falling down, they are regarded as your prey. You should captivate that: take photographs of it, paint a picture of it, write about it in your memoirs, how beautiful it was. Everything is regarded as something you should consume: if you hear somebody say a clever thing in one sentence in the course of your conversation, you should write it down, try to captivate that subtlety, that cleverness, that person's genius that they had such a beautiful thing to say. All the time, we are looking for something to catch in order to enrich ourselves.

There is that mentality of complete poverty. No doubt, at the same time, if any delicious international meals are being cooked in certain restaurants, we would like to take part in them, eat them, taste them, have a new adventure. The flavor is more important than the value or the heaviness of the food, or that it could fill your belly.

Preta mentality is not so much a question of filling your belly. It is based on sensuality: taking the trouble of going out and buying something, walking into a store, picking out your particular brand of chocolate or wine, and bringing it back home. You are looking forward to doing that, to taking part in that. Your purchase could be consumed purely by you. If you share it with friends, you also could watch your friends enjoying your purchase. As you open the case or the bottle or the package, even the rattling of the paper unwrapping is extremely seductive. It is a luscious feeling, opening packages; the sound of Coke coming out of a bottle gives a sense of delightful hunger. It is something very beautiful. Self-consciously, we taste it, feel it, chew it, swallow it, and then finally, we actually manage to consume it—after that whole elaborate trip that we have gone through. Phew! Such an achievement! It is fantastic. We are able to bring a dream to life, it is a dream come true.

That applies to every living situation, not necessarily food alone. Constant hunger of all kinds happens. Intellectually, you feel your lack of some kind of encouragement. In all kinds of experiences, you feel a lack of something. You are deprived of something and you decide to pull up your socks and go and pursue it, to learn and study and hear those juicy intellectual answers or profound, spiritual, mystical words. You can hear and consume one idea after another idea. You try to recall them, try to make them solid and real. In case you want to or need to, you can recall them again and again in your life. Whenever you feel hunger, you can open your notebook with your notes, or you can open a particular book written by a great person who said very satisfying things in his books. You could satisfy and resatisfy constantly, again and again. In the course of your life, when you start to feel boredom or experience insomnia, you can always open your book, wherever you are. You can read your notebooks and ponder them constantly, or re-create a playback of the video tape of your mind as much as possible. That satisfies, seemingly.

But somehow, constantly playing back situations seems to become rather repetitive at a certain stage. We would like to re-create the situation again and again, possibly making the same journey. We may search for a new situation, or try to re-create meeting that particular friend or teacher. Another introduction is an exciting thing to do. And another journey to the restaurant or the supermarket or the delicatessen is not a bad idea. So we are constantly re-creating situations again and again, as much as possible. But sometimes the situation prevents us, we are running too fast. We may be able to re-create the journey for a certain amount of time, but at a certain stage, something prevents us. Either we do not have enough money or, when we try to plan something, something else happens: our child gets sick or our parents are dying or we have to attend some other situation. We have been holding back constantly. We realize that continual obstacles are coming at us; and that much more hunger begins to arise in us. We are still suspended in the realm of the hungry ghosts. The more we want something, the more we realize that we cannot get it. Constant holding back is involved.

In terms of the hungry ghost realm, there seem to be two types of hunger. The first is basic poverty, the feeling of the lack of fulfilling your desire. The second is that when you cannot fulfill your desire because you cannot consume any more, you wish that you could be somebody else who could, somebody who *is* hungry and who could still consume. You are trying to become like one of those. You would like to take pleasure in hunger, like those other people. There is that competitiveness. That seems to be the basic quality of the hungry ghost realm.

As that builds up to an extreme, or bardo experience, you are
not quite certain whether you are really hungry or whether you
simply enjoy being hungry. If you are hungry, you can satisfy it.
But at the same time, if you satisfy your hunger, you realize that
you will not be able to enjoy your hunger anymore. You don't
know whether you should suspend yourself in hunger or whether
you should overdo it so that you could enjoy watching other people
be hungry. That kind of extreme case begins to build up. There is
uncertainty, actually, as to who is consuming and who is getting
sick of consuming. The notion of poverty seems to be prominent.

Next we could discuss the realm of hell. Basically, hell seems to
be related with aggression, ultimate aggression. That aggression
is based on such perpetual hatred that you begin to lose the point.
You are uncertain as to whom you are building up your aggression
toward, or by whom that aggression is being built up. There is
that continual process of uncertainty and confusion. Not only that,
but you begin to build up a whole environment of aggression
around you. That takes place constantly, all the time. Finally, even
if you yourself feel slightly cool about your own anger, your own
aggression, the atmosphere or environment around you begins to
throw aggression back on you from outside. So a constant sense of
aggression is involved. It is as if you were walking in a hot climate.
You yourself might feel physically cool, but at the same time you
begin to get this hot air coming at you constantly. So you cannot
keep yourself cool all the time at all, because the environment
creates heat. That kind of aggression is related with the extreme
stuffiness or stubbornness of claustrophobia. The aggression does
not seem to be your aggression, but the aggression seems to per-
meate the whole space around you. There is no space to breathe
and there is no space to act. There is no space to move at all. The
whole process becomes overwhelming.

Such aggression is so intense that if you kill somebody out of
your aggression, you achieve just a fraction of the satisfaction of
putting your aggression into practice. Somehow it doesn't help;

the aggression is still lingering around you. If you kill yourself afterward, having murdered someone already, that doesn't seem to help either, because you don't get the satisfaction of watching that you have achieved something. You could kill both your enemy and yourself by aggression, but still the aggression seems to be lingering around. There is some sense of satisfaction involved with the aggression, and that satisfaction seems to be the problem. In terms of committing suicide, you have to kill yourself—but the killer and that to be killed are still involved. Finally you realize that if you kill yourself, there's still the killer, so you haven't managed to murder yourself completely at all. It is extremely dissatisfying. One never knows who's killing whom, who could manage to eliminate whom at all, because the whole space is filled with aggression constantly.

It is like eating yourself inwardly: having eaten yourself inwardly, then the person who eats you still happens; so you continue to eat yourself inwardly and so on and so on. There is the constant onion skin of that person. If you eat the skin, then having eaten it already, there is another skin; next you have to eat that skin as well, *and* the next skin, and on and on and on. Finally, in the process of eating, you expand yourself. You get some kind of nourishment as a result of the consumption. You begin to get further strength because you have managed to eat your skin, and then you have to eat *that* skin. So constantly eating inward produces further expansion, skin of another type. So it goes on and on. It is like the analogy of a crocodile biting its own tail. Each time the crocodile bites his own tail, that crocodile is nourished, so the tail grows faster and faster and there is no end to it. That seems to be the ultimate understanding of aggression, that you can't really eliminate anything by aggression or kill anything by aggression. The more you kill, the more you are creating more situations to be killed. So a constantly growing aggression tends to develop.

Finally there is no space; the whole space has been completely solidified, without any gaps. There is no way to look back or do a double-take on your actions at all. The whole space has been completely filled with aggression. It is outrageous aggression, but there is nothing to be outrageous about, because nobody is watching. You are completely consumed in your own environment. So aggression grows constantly, on and on and on. There is not even any pleasure in watching yourself or in creating a watcher to testify to your perceptions of killing and murdering and destroying. Nobody gives you a report. But at the same time, you constantly develop an overwhelming growth of aggression, as a result of the destruction. As a result of the destruction, therefore, creation takes place constantly on and on.

Often the aggression of the hell realm is portrayed in the symbolism by both the sky and earth radiating red fire. The earth is completely reduced into red-hot iron, and the space is completely reduced into an environment of flame and fire. That is to say, there is no space to breathe the air of any coolness or coldness at all. Whatever you see around you is hot and intense, stuffy, extremely claustrophobic. So the hell realm is seen as a realm in which the more you put aggression outward to destroy the enemy and win over your opponent, that much reaction is created. When we talk about your enemy or opponent, it doesn't have to be an enemy in the literal sense. If you play a game of one-upmanship with somebody, it could be between friends—"I have experienced something much, much better than you did," or "I have heard something better than you did," "I already understand such and such a book better than you do," "I have heard the message much more subtly than you did." A constant battle goes on. It doesn't have to be a relationship between an enemy and yourself, it could be friends with friends. By putting out that kind of vibration, automatically the reaction afterward is extremely stuffy. Because you decided to overcrowd the space of the relationship, you are left with that stuffiness. So you have created your own realm in that sense, in human life.

That extreme case of one-upmanship is based on the feeling of being better, feeling that your speed is faster than somebody else's, your cunning quality is better than someone else's—your intelligence, your literary quality, your philosophical grasping, your understanding, your economical practicality, or whatever. You have a constant list of all these things, so that you can compare, "I am that, I am that," constantly. You have millions of subjects in your life to compare. Every life situation seems to be related with that sense of comparison. Everybody without fail has some genius, skill of some kind, including if they feel that they don't have any genius or skill of any kind—which in itself is genius. There are constant ingenious qualities that everybody has, and that automatically presents that much hell, that much aggression, to cover over the overcrowded situation.

You tend to overcrowd, and by doing so you are creating more hell, extending the hell realm. Basically, the hell realm is based on extending your territory to such a level that you are defending your territory constantly. You are presenting one-upmanship all the time; at an unconscious or psychological level, you are trying to nurse or protect your territory as much as you can. That seems to be the process of the hell realm—we are throwing out flames, and radiation comes back to us constantly, on and on and on. There is no room to experience any spaciousness, any openness at all. And there is the constant effort to close up all kinds of space. That is also based on a cunning quality, as in the asura realm, where we talked about jealousy. It has that quality, but at the same time, the realm of hell is much more intense: you are actually putting forth your effort at a very practical level.

The hell realm can only be created by relationships. The asura realm is not necessarily based on relationships alone; it could be based on your own psychological hangups. But in the case of the realm of hell, there are constant relationships: you try to play games with something, and dealing with another individual bounces back on you constantly creating extreme claustrophobia, so finally there is no room to communicate at all. The only way to communicate is to try to re-create your paranoia or your anger, your aggression. You thought you managed to win the war by creating all kinds of one-upmanship, by laying all kinds of ego trips on somebody else. But the result is that having done that already, you don't get any response from the other person. Seemingly, you might think that you have achieved some response, but still you are faced with your own problem: your own negativity comes back, your own aggression comes back. That manages to fill all the space constantly, so it is sort of like a gas chamber.

You are re-creating things constantly. Whenever there is a life situation in which you feel lonesome or you don't have enough excitement, you get into another situation so that you can play that game again and again. It isn't so much that there's enjoyment in playing such a game, but the realm of hell seems to be purely the sense that there isn't enough security. All the time we feel cold. If there isn't any way of securing ourselves, we become bleak and too cold; therefore, we have to regenerate the fire. And in order to regenerate the fire, we constantly have to put out that effort to maintain ourselves. The bardo state connected with the hell realm seems to be based on playing that game constantly. One cannot even help playing such a game; one just finds oneself playing that particular game on and on, all the time.

STUDENT: What kind of doubt is there in each of these realms? Where is the transition where possibly there is space to change into another realm?

TRUNGPA RINPOCHE: In terms of the hungry ghost realm, it seems that transition is based on the uncertainty as to whether you will be able to maintain your constant consumption. At the hungry ghost level, there seems to be a certain amount of pain; but at the same time, that pain is largely based on not being able to achieve what you want to be. So there is always doubt as to whether you will be able to achieve what you want or not. It is like the gap between being hungry and deprived and because of that, wanting to consume more. Although you may realize that is not very good for you, at the same time, there is the tendency to collect more, to further enrich situations. So there is always a gap: uncertainty as to whether you could achieve what you want or not. There is always that kind of paranoia or fear. So it seems that in the hungry ghost realm, fear is one of the most outstanding situations you could relate with. That fear could be the way of stepping out of it.

In terms of the realm of hell, there is not much space in maintaining yourself as such. But at the same time the spacious quality in itself becomes perpetual creation. You have to function in some kind of space. You are consumed in that hot environment of claustrophobia constantly. You are creating that all the time. There is also, on the other hand, a tendency to relate with both hot and cold. You are aware of the textures of the elements. For instance, the buddha of the hell realm is depicted by a dark gray buddha holding fire and water in his hand. That flame and water in his hand represent a sense of texture as a way of stepping out of the hell realm. You are aware of the texture of the hotness or the texture of the coldness, whatever it is. If there is a sense of texture of all kinds, then there is also doubt at the same time.

In the realm of the hungry ghosts, the buddha of the hungry ghosts holds a container filled with all kinds of food. That food seems to be a way of confusing you or liberating you. It is confusing the issue of whether you want or whether you don't want. That is the gap you can catch.

STUDENT: I don't see why a sense of texture brings a sense of doubt.

TRUNGPA RINPOCHE: Well, texture is not smooth and regular. Whenever we talk about texture, there is some pattern in the texture, as when we talk about fabric of some kind. That automatically means ups and downs and minute details. There are constant bumps or spots of texture. Otherwise, you could not experience textures. For instance, if you are being consumed in a fire and you touch an ember, there is the texture of that ember or fire coming closer and closer to you. It is sort of a pulsating quality. It is a momentary quality naturally, automatically.

S: Why does that bring doubt?

TR: Only the sense of texture can bring doubt in terms of the realm of hell. There is no greater space at all. Only the sensitivity to texture can bring doubt; only that can bring understanding. You have to perceive the texture, you have to feel it. It is like a blind person reading braille. If a person is already blind constantly, the only way to relate with reading is to read braille.

STUDENT: Rinpoche, what is the buddha of the realm of gods?

TRUNGPA RINPOCHE: The god realm buddha holds a tambura, a musical instrument, so that he can sing and play sweet music for the gods, to relate with their absorption. He draws them out of their absorption by presenting some kind of gentle seduction.

STUDENT: Rinpoche, what grasping is involved with the realm of hell? There seems to be a certain grasping with all the other realms.

TRUNGPA RINPOCHE: I suppose you could say that there is a sense of the maintenance of your perpetual continuity of being exposed to cold weather. The realm of hell is very much like living in an extraordinarily warm temperature; you have created a sort of super-central-heated house, whereas the world outside is cold weather.

S: By warmth, do you mean security?

TR: Security—which is based on your hatred, presenting your own hatred and having it bounce back on you.

STUDENT: What buddha family is associated with the realm of hell?

TRUNGPA RINPOCHE: It seems that the realm of hell is based on the vajra family. There is constant assertion; asserting yourself.

S: Is it this refusal to see the mirror?

TR: Yes, definitely.

S: Is that part of the whole activity of the aggression itself?

TR: You refuse to see the reflections, but you are fascinated by the textures, which is a different kind of thing altogether. That seems to be one of the reasons the hell realm becomes so powerful.

STUDENT: What buddha family is associated with the human realm? Did you say that it was the padma family?

TRUNGPA RINPOCHE: That's right, yes.

STUDENT: There seems to be a kind of similarity in the incommunicability of the asura realm and the hell realm. It seems that this one-upmanship game is very similar to the jealous god business. Is there a difference?

TRUNGPA RINPOCHE: Well, the difference seems to be that in the asura realm you are trying to cover your area of jealousy constantly, whereas in the hell realm you don't have to try to cover it, because your hatred has already covered that area. The only thing left for you to do is to relate with the temperatures or the textures, your aggression has become so powerful.

STUDENT: Rinpoche, you mentioned the physical characteristics of the hungry ghosts. Are there physical characteristics in each realm?

TRUNGPA RINPOCHE: The particular physical characteristics of the hungry ghosts seem to be prominent; but except for the animal realm, the rest of them seem to have the same quality.

STUDENT: Rinpoche, how is the realm of hell connected with meditation? It seems as if much of our meditation is pretty aggressive. How do we get out of it?

TRUNGPA RINPOCHE: It seems to be that way, yes. There is a sense of struggle. You really would like to apply your exertion, and you have to produce something out of the meditation you are doing. You are supposed to achieve something; you are supposed to learn something; there is some kind of duty involved with the meditation. And the more you try to put forth that kind of regimented, duty-oriented meditation, the more you end up in the hell realm. I suppose that the only way to relate with that is to regard meditation as a living situation rather than purely duty-oriented.

S: That would be a good way to avoid it, but if you find yourself there, then what?

TR: Well, then you don't regard yourself or your problem as a problem as such but as part of the general thought process, which happens automatically. Whenever any kind of ambition happens in meditation practice, it comes up in the thought process and the potential thought process, rather than anywhere else. So if you are able to see that kind of situation arising in meditation, if you regard it as thought process, then it becomes thought process. So it ceases to have a valuation of its own.

STUDENT: As a rule, does one experience all the realms before liberation comes, or how does this work?

TRUNGPA RINPOCHE: We have been experiencing them for a long time—all the time. And each of the realms has the possibility of relating with the enlightened state.

STUDENT: Isn't the feeling of hunger painful in the hungry ghost realm?

TRUNGPA RINPOCHE: It is painful and irritating, but at the same time there is a sense of hunger as a kind of occupation, which is a very optimistic and hopeful experience. For instance, if you are going to get your dinner at twelve o'clock, you begin to enjoy your hunger at eleven o'clock, knowing that you are going to get your dinner at twelve o'clock. So in that way you could consume more food.

STUDENT: Rinpoche, where does the quality of clear light fit into the hungry ghost realm and the hell realm?

TRUNGPA RINPOCHE: I think that all the realms have that quality in them, because clear light comes up in terms of subtle gaps of all kinds. In the hell realm, clear light happens in experiencing the textures of the pain, which automatically has to have some kind of space. In the hungry ghost realm, there is constant yearning and looking for ways to try to fulfill your desire. That effort of trying to fulfill your desire also has this gap or spacious quality in it. There is clear light principle automatically.

S: Is this the relationship to enlightened gap that you mentioned?

TR: Yes.

The Sequence of Bardos

There are six types of bardo experience connected with the six realms: becoming, birth, dream, death, isness, and meditation. A seventh bardo, the bardo of illusory body, points to the fundamentally shifty quality of experiences. Sipa bardo, which is the bardo of existence or becoming, stems from the current situation being manipulated by extreme hope and fear. So the birth of each realm is given by sipa bardo.

From that, because birth has been given already, that brings about another birth, or kye-ne bardo. The birth of kye-ne bardo is connected with manifesting that becoming process further. The bardo of becoming is more of a force of energy. But that energy has to materialize and function within some particular context or situation. So you have kye-ne bardo.

Birth and death are connected with the quality of circulation, which relates to birth and death together. Birth and death have to be regarded as definite events: birth is an event and death is an event as well. Those events could function according to their own nature. The continuity between birth and death is largely a survival process; that which builds a bridge between birth and death is the struggle for survival. The struggle for survival is based on administration, the maintenance of whatever solid characteristics you may have. Such maintenance is not necessarily physical maintenance alone, at all. If you want to maintain yourself, to begin with you have to have the politics or the philosophy of the maintenance. That philosophy and politics of maintenance introduces itself into domestic situations based on past experience bringing present experience, and present experience being dependent on what will be, or the future. So you have a past-present-future dwelling process. And both the past and the future could be said to be imaginary worlds. That is *milam* bardo, or dream bardo.

Dream bardo does not necessarily mean the quality of dreaming literally, but it has the style of imagination, or trying to instigate some activity. It has the quality of constantly trying to set the wheel in motion, constantly flowing. In order to set the wheel in motion, you have to have concepts and ideas, and those concepts and ideas are purely imaginary. It is a kind of guesswork in that sense—trying to achieve something as you speed along or trying to destroy something as you speed along. It is like the analogy of a cowardly soldier who runs away and throws rocks behind him, hoping that his enemies could be killed in the process of his escape. Without aim or direction, he just hopes that some particular rock he throws behind him, over his shoulder, will land on his enemy's head. In the same way, the dream bardo has a quality of going along hoping things will develop in accordance with your wishes. It is not so much just dwelling on something. It is more like imagination being put into practice by another imagination. And that imagination speaks its own language, because you have created the projections. So in the end a whole solid world is built. It is like the bouncing backward and forward of an echo in a cave: each echo throws back its sound and the whole thing builds up into a crescendo. So the dream bardo seems to be the dream *of* dreams: on the ground of dreams, the dream bardo exists as a further dream.

Then you have death, or *chikha* bardo. Death is the end of all those dreams, because your expectations, attempts, or desire to watch your own funeral party are impractical. You realize you cannot take part in your own funeral party; you cannot attend your own funeral. So there is a sense of the failure of continuing your existence. When you realize that failure to continue your existence, the dream begins to end. "I am really going to die, so I might as well regard myself as a dead person"—that is the end of the dream. Because it is the end of the dream, therefore you cannot relate with the mind-body physical situation at all. It is overwhelmingly loose and unclear. Death is the end of vision, the end of expectations, and the end of continuity. Death is, therefore, one of the outstanding experiences in the bardo. You cannot continue anymore; and not only that, but you realize that the games you developed through the dream bardo have not been all that realistic. One begins to realize the impermanent quality of all situations. In fact, the very idea of going from one experience to another experience is also seen as impermanent, as a continual death process. Then— because it is the end of all kinds of dreams, because you have experienced the living quality of the impermanence, the transitory nature of all beings—you begin to ask questions. That is where chönyi bardo begins to develop.

Chönyi is a Tibetan word which literally means "dharmaness," or "isness": *chö* means "dharma"; *nyi* means "isness." In Sanskrit it is called dharmata. The word *dharmata* is similar to the word *shunyata*. *Shunya* means "empty"; *ta* means "-ness"; so *shunyata* means "emptiness." Likewise, *dharmata* means "dharmaness," "the isness of all existence." The bardo of dharmata is the awareness of the basic space in which things could function. In other words, a complete comprehension of the process developed through the bardo experiences is based on a pattern of relating with space. This process cannot function or happen as it is if you do not relate with space. So one tends to develop a certain sense of spaciousness, a sense of lubrication. Lubrication could develop because of that accommodating quality. And that lubrication, or dharmata experience, is what has been referred to in Evans-Wentz's work as the clear light. In this sense, clear light is lubrication, accommodation, letting things follow their own course.

That brings us into the next situation, which is the bardo of meditation. Now that you have experienced birth and existence and death and everything, you begin to have a definite experience of what is called samten bardo, which is the meditative state in the bardo experience. The meditative experience of the bardo state is therefore based on the realization of the lubrication, or dharmata, as an object, as a particular situation. Essentially it is that wisdom becomes knowledge; jnana (wisdom) becomes prajna (knowledge). In other words, complete experience becomes knowledge. Complete experience has been perceived by criteria of some kind, by a certain perspective or view. Jnana has been seen as a learning process, as something we study. So jnana has become prajna. This is like the difference between somebody meditating and somebody studying the experience of meditation as a case history or as archeological intrigue.

The meditative experience of samten bardo is the microscope with which you could examine the clear light experience. It is also a way of accentuating the blackness and whiteness of the experience which happens within that accommodating open space. In other words, samten bardo, the meditative state of bardo, is not necessarily the practice of meditation as it traditionally has been taught; but it is seeing the clarity of situations as they are. For instance, if you realize you are imprisoned in the hungry ghost realm, you begin to realize the sharp edges of hungry ghost experience, as well as the space in which the sharp edges could exist in hungry ghost experience. And the same thing applies with any of the realms.

Samten bardo is a kind of watcher which transmits its message to the observer, as opposed to the watcher. So you have a double watcher in that case. You have one watcher who is like the spokesman who relates from one situation to another situation; you also have the person who appointed that watcher to his occupation, his job, his duty. In other words, you have intuitive insight, which has the ability to digest experiences; but at the same time, in order to digest experiences, you have to point them out to somebody who collects your food. That which is collecting the food is the watcher. And the food is being passed on to the central authority who appointed the watcher. This is extremely subtle. It is almost nonwatching—a perceiving entity, so to speak. So you have two types of intelligence there: crude intelligence and subtle intelligence. Crude intelligence is the watcher, the analyst: subtle intelligence is the intellectual, analytical conclusions transformed into experiential understanding. Those are the two types of intelligence—which is the samten bardo experience of the meditative state.

It seems that that kind of experience leads inevitably to the bardo of the after-death experience, which is called *gyulü* bardo. *Gyulü* means "illusory body," "body of illusions," so gyulü bardo is the bardo of illusion. That brings us to the point where finally we are suspended in the extreme experience of our life situation: the hell realm, hungry ghost realm, animal realm, human realm, or whatever. We realize that we are suspended: we haven't really been born, we haven't really died, we haven't really been dreaming at all. We haven't been experiencing clear light in a realistic way either, in actual fact. All of those situations are expressions of suspension between one experience of extremes and another. That sense of suspension seems to be the basic quality of bardo. You are in between, in no-man's-land. You are between extremes, and you realize that that in itself is an extreme situation. If you are in the realm of the gods, for instance, you realize that there is really no need to maintain yourself. Instead your path has been taken over by the inevitability of that natural, organic, mechanical process.

I suppose the conclusion that we come to in this seminar is that the six realms are largely based on the six types of bardo experience. That enables us to relate with the realms not purely as suffering or as dwelling on something. In order to dwell, you have to play games with that occupation. For instance, if you are born as a human, you have to grow up; you have to have some occupation and lifestyle; you have to feed yourself; you have to experience old age; and you also have to experience illness and death. Human life—all of life—contains those developments. The six realms and the six types of bardo experience are similar: in each realm you have birth, you have death, you have suspension of those experiences, you have dreams. You experience that your life consists of both space and objects, form and emptiness, simultaneously—or maybe side by side. I hope I haven't confused anybody by such a shocking conclusion.

STUDENT: Rinpoche, to what use can we put the things that we have learned in this seminar?

TRUNGPA RINPOCHE: What do you think? Do you have any idea?

S: I've thought of them as giving a sort of a matrix by which we can be aware of our own patterns of behavior.

TR: Yes. Well, it is the same as the presentation of the four noble truths. Suffering should be realized; the origin of suffering should be overcome; the cessation of suffering should be attained; and the path should be seen as truth. It is the same kind of thing. You see, one of the problems or one of necessities of hearing the teaching is that we generally have a confused picture, completely unmethodical and chaotic. We can't make heads or tails of what is actually happening, what is the process, or what is the situation. But in this case, we are putting that confusion into a pattern. Confused nature has a pattern. It is methodically chaotic.

So this seems to be a way of seeing those patterns as they are. It seems to be a necessity of learning that you begin to have a sense of geography, a road map of some kind, so that you can relate with such patterns. That brings more solidity and confidence. So you don't have to look painfully for some kind of stepping stone;

instead, a stepping stone presents itself in your life. You have the confidence to start on the first thing that is available within your experience—if you know the geography or road map of developmental psychological structures.

STUDENT: Rinpoche, it seems that it is the energy of the situation that determines the realm of existence. Is it the same order of energy that determines the bardo state?

TRUNGPA RINPOCHE: I think so. You see, the bardo states are the constituents of the realms, so they all have to function within some basic space or energy.

STUDENT: Are there predominant bardo experiences for each of the realms?

TRUNGPA RINPOCHE: Well, we could look at it that way, as we did in the Allenspark seminar on the six realms. That is another way of looking at the whole situation, seeing each state of bardo as being connected with a different realm. But at the same time, each realm should have all the bardo experiences. In the human realm, for instance, in our lives as human beings, we have the experience of all six bardos happening to us all of the time. And the other realms could be seen in the same way. From this perspective, no particular extreme, or bardo, is related with any particular realm, necessarily. But each realm contains birth, death, spaciousness, watching and observing yourself, having a conclusion of yourself.

S: How could all six bardos be going on at the same time?

TR: The reason the six bardos could function simultaneously is because within these six types of bardo experience, the constituents, or the styles, are always the same.

STUDENT: In the meditative state there are two kinds of intelligence: one is crude, which is the watcher; the other is more subtle, a perceiving kind of intelligence. Is that watching, or feedback, basically a healthy thing?

TRUNGPA RINPOCHE: None of the six bardos or realms are being evaluated as unhealthy or healthy. We are just purely presenting a picture of them as they are, their general makeup. For instance, we are not discussing whether having a head is a healthy thing or having arms is a healthy thing.

S: There's no sense in evaluating?

TR: No. It is a neutral situation, and basically mechanical. Maybe it is misleading to call samten bardo meditation, the meditative state. It isn't meditation in the sense of the practice of sitting meditation or awareness practice or the cultivation of jhana states. It is a natural function.

S: But when you refer to self-consciousness, I usually have the feeling that it is not such a good or healthy thing to always be so self-conscious.

TR: Well, you see, the self-consciousness we are talking about is quite different from the watcher in the actual practice of meditation. It is related with the basic mechanism which perceives and which works things out. It is that which makes you aware that you are sitting and meditating. In a very, very minute and very subtle way, you have some understanding that you are actually meditating, whether crude self-consciousness applies or not. Even if you transcend crude self-consciousness, you still have the sense that you have overcome the crude self-consciousness; that still goes on. That is the basic perceiver. It is a mechanically necessary situation.

STUDENT: You spoke at times about stepping out of the bardo states, and about doubt being the point at which you would just step out. Are any of these six states connected with that sense of doubt?

TRUNGPA RINPOCHE: All of them have to exist in some kind of basic space. So all of them have equal possibilities of stepping out of intense bardo experience. They each exist in a particular fashion, a particular form—but these forms could exist only in relation to space.

S: What is space?

TR: Space is where they could be accommodated; it is the basic environment where these six types of bardo could exist. The very idea of the existence of such experiences automatically brings up the natural function of the space where they could exist as well.

STUDENT: Does the clear light that you talked about exist in space?

TRUNGPA RINPOCHE: The experience of clear light exists in space, and when clear light ceases to become an *experience,* then that itself *is* space. When we talk about the bardo of clear light, it is still bardo, because it is experienced as bardo. Space has been perceived as space, seen as space.

STUDENT: Can somebody who is in the realm of hell actually say they are? Can they make that statement? Or in any realm?

TRUNGPA RINPOCHE: I think so, definitely, yes. That is where you are. You have an intense experience going on. You cannot just miss that altogether; it exists very solidly there.

STUDENT: Rinpoche, what's the big difference between me and a *tülku?*

TRUNGPA RINPOCHE: You are one. *Tülku* means a person who has been reborn. *Tül* means "manifestation," *ku* means "body"; so *tülku* means "body of manifestation." Everybody is a tülku.

S: In the appendix of your book *Born in Tibet,* you describe the birth and death process of the tülku as not the same as for the ordinary persons.

TR: Well, I suppose that is *a* tülku as opposed to *the* tülku.

S: What do you mean when you talk about *a* tülku?

TR: That's yourself.

S: I'm talking about tülkus in the sense that, for instance, people say the Dalai Lama is supposed to be a manifestation of Avalokiteshvara, the bodhisattva of compassion. In other words, there is a force operating other than the karmic force.

TR: Those things are highly colored by the wishful thinking of the congregate. It doesn't mean that the Dalai Lama is the one and only tülku of Avalokiteshvara. His character, his basic makeup, contains that compassionate quality.

S: Is that by accident or by will?

TR: It seems to be both. If you try to create something by will, you have to use accidents as a way of channeling yourself.

S: Considering the various principles, you could, for instance, identify with the bodhisattva of compassion. Is that so?

TR: I suppose so, yes. Each person has his or her own particular buddha family. And obviously somebody could decide to proclaim their relationship with their buddha nature, that they are what they are. Somebody could even become Avalokiteshvara.

STUDENT: I'm not really clear about the bardo states. Did I understand you to say that the bardo states coexist simultaneously when a realm is present?

TRUNGPA RINPOCHE: That's right, yes, as the mechanics or the context of the realms. In order to exist you have to be born, you have to die, you have to have dreams, all kind of things. So that is what it is. And in this particular context of bardo, the highlights of one's experience are divided into six types.

S: Should I not be satisfied with my experience until I am able to realize that these coexist and that my feeling of one succeeding the other is just a partial view?

TR: They automatically present themselves to you, you can't miss them. They are such powerful experiences in every way: birth and death are very obvious.

S: Yes, but sequentially, not coexisting.

TR: Not necessarily. They all exist simultaneously in the sense that birth means death—and it also means dream, and clear light, and the bardo of meditation. If you make a pot, for instance, you have to have clay, you have to have water, you have to have heat. So those elements exist simultaneously within one pot. It is the same kind of thing.

STUDENT: Where did this information about the bardos and the realms come from? Was it brought to Tibet by Padmasambhava and Tilopa?

TRUNGPA RINPOCHE: Historically, the basic idea developed out of the Pure Land school in Tibetan Buddhism, which was particularly strong in the study of death and bardo experiences.

S: Is that the devotional school?

TR: Not in the popular sense that it exists today in Japan. Instead it is the idea of studying your death. Amitabha's realm is regarded as a way of relating to your after-death experience in terms of limitlessness—*Amitabha* means "limitless light." Many sutras of Amitabha talk about the death experience being connected with the living experience as well. In addition to the Pure Land teachings on death, there are also tantric expositions of hallucinations and mental objects becoming overwhelming in life, as in the visions of the bardo experience described in *The Tibetan Book of the Dead*. In these two teachings—the Pure Land school and certain tantric texts—the experience of the living world is seen as a pattern of solid, colorful situations. What we are discussing seems to be an amalgamation of those two principles working together, which was presented particularly by Padmasambhava. These teachings are also related with the exposition of the twelve *nidanas,* the twelvefold causation of the samsaric chain reaction, the process of samsaric development. So it is a further amalgamation. In a sense you could say it is an amalgamation of the *abhidharma* experience of psychological patterns and the mystical experience of tantric awareness of deities, which are seen as types of emotions, or of human ego mentalities. Death is seen as being birth; after-death is the same thing as life. You live in the birth-death process constantly. That is the experience of the Amitabha sutras, which are an amalgamation of all these put together and which developed this particular formula.

It seems that these principles were in the teaching already when Buddhism developed in Tibet, but they were brought forth in particular by a teacher called Karma Lingpa, who lived around about Gampopa's time. He introduced in particular how to relate with the dying person in terms of the living person. I think Karma Lingpa was probably the instigator, or the one person who brought into living form the practice of the teachings of bardo.

STUDENT: I have two questions: one is, why do you always arrive late? Is there any particular reason?

TRUNGPA RINPOCHE: I arrive late!

S: Thank you. The second question is, whenever you make any statement, you say it *seems* that this is so, but even then, the way you say it has such an air of definiteness about it. Why do you use that particular prefix?

TR: Well, it seems that what is presented is more like a supposition, because we can't agree on any one particular thing very solidly. If there are sixty people in the audience, they will have sixty types of experiences. So you can't make things too definite. And again, conclusions should come from individuals. It could be said to be a possible attempt to present the case without trying to preach.

STUDENT: Do you think that these same ideas or similar ideas to those you have elucidated during this seminar can be found in

Western traditions? And particularly, do you think that recent Western psychology can throw more light on it? Would it be useful to try to work with the two together?

TRUNGPA RINPOCHE: It is quite possible that these different realms have definite psychotic qualities. For instance, the realm of hell is claustrophobic, and the asura realm could be said to be schizophrenic, and the realm of the gods could be said to be religious maniacs. All kinds of things could be said about it, and I'm sure that some day it would be interesting to tie them all together in that way.

S: But most Western psychology places a very strong emphasis on the early years of life, say from birth to the age of four or five, as opposed to perhaps the idea of karma or anything like that. I haven't heard you talk too much about that formative period in a person's life. Is there a conflict there, would you say?

TR: I think there seems to be a problem there, if you purely study the case history. "Because you have had a case history of unfortunate situations, therefore you experience pain now"—that seems to be an attempt to make the study of psychological states extremely scientific. It seems to be a form of protection psychologists developed, which they don't necessarily have to do. And generally, that kind of psychological analysis based on case history is unhealthy, because you don't feel the openness or the spaciousness of the present or the future. You feel you are trapped forever and that it is a completely hopeless situation. So I think there tends to be a conflict with that approach, which is so past-oriented.

S: Isn't that true of the idea of karma also?

TR: Not necessarily, not necessarily at all. You could say the present situation is based on the past in some sense, but at the same time, you are free from the past. The present is free from the past; therefore, it could be present. Otherwise it would continue to be past all the time. And the future is an independent situation. So there is a sense of freedom happening constantly. For instance, we could say that we arrived and we entered into this hall and now we are here. That doesn't mean that we cannot get out of it, because we decided to come here. We are not stuck in this hall. It is purely up to individuals if they decide to walk out of this hall or not. It is purely up to us. So the case history is that you are already here. Whether you walked here or you came here by car does not make any difference.

STUDENT: There seems to be a link between the past and the present, since we drag characteristics of the old realm into the new one.

TRUNGPA RINPOCHE: Well, in a sense we do and in a sense we don't. We have habitual patterns that we have developed, but those habitual patterns we have developed also have to maintain themselves by means of present situations. So the present is partly interdependent with the past, but it is also partly independent of the past. All the realms could exist or function as they are in the present circumstances.

S: But it seems you are always the same.

TR: You can't be the same person constantly at all. And you can't necessarily have a fixed situation of realms at all. Even the realms have a pulsating quality. They flicker between birth, death, and the others constantly. So each realm is a very tentative world. We do develop one particular heavy, strong experience, and we tend to reinforce that experience, but that doesn't have to be the same realm all the time at all. It seems that the realms we are talking about are largely based on the different states of emotions that exist in our basic being. We can't have one emotion happening constantly, but emotions change. Each emotion transforms itself into, or becomes, a realm. So a realm in this case is not only the intense state you are in alone, but the intense environment you are in as well—which you have created.

STUDENT: Rinpoche, what is mindfulness?

TRUNGPA RINPOCHE: Mindfulness is simply seeing the accuracy or the precision of the moment, and you cannot help being right there. It is seeing or experiencing the abrupt and sharp nowness, with extremely sharp contrast, sharp edges. And awareness seems to have the quality of there being a lot of sharp edges happening simultaneously everywhere. So you are not focusing on one item alone, but there are many items, and each of them is clear and precise, coexisting in one space. So there seem to be a lot of differences between mindfulness and awareness.

STUDENT: What is the watcher?

TRUNGPA RINPOCHE: The watcher is a kind of informer who perceives and sees and comments and makes things presentable to you. So it is constantly editing all the time, the translator.

STUDENT: In your teaching you put a great deal of emphasis on meditation practice: when you meditate, how long you meditate, where you meditate. What I would like to know in particular is how you would contrast this with Zen.

TRUNGPA RINPOCHE: The meditation teachings developed in Zen and presented to the West have the quality of creating an island, so to speak. In the midst of an uncultured, if I may say so, environment, they are trying to create another civilization or culture. For instance, in a chaotic city, you have a very peaceful and quiet zendo. There is a kind of Japanese world transported or transplanted into that particular zendo environment. The difference between that and the Zen developed in Japan is that they don't have to transport or import or create an island at all, because that whole style of environment is always there. The zendo is just purely one extra room where you come to sit and meditate. So there are two ways of dealing with things: re-creating a situation or accepting the situation as it is. The eccentric quality of transplanting one culture into the midst of another culture accentuates the fascination, and also accentuates a kind of extreme militant outlook. In other words, there is the definite idea that Americans have got to become Japanese, in spite of their physical differences, which one can't help.

On the other hand, I think in regard to the essence of the teaching that has developed and the practice of meditation—as far as techniques go, there doesn't seem to be any particular difference at all between the Tibetan teachings and Zen. Particularly the Soto school of Zen seems to have a lot in common with the style of meditation that the Tibetan teachers have taught. So as far as the technique of meditation goes, it seems to be almost identical, you could say. Zen students could practice Zen and then they could come and study with us and it would be just continuing their practice, rather than their having to give up anything in their practice. They just continue with meditation as they have been doing.

There seem to be some external differences of style, in that when Buddhism came to Tibet, the Tibetans adopted Buddhism as Tibetan Buddhism rather than trying to become Indians. In fact, they did not even bother to learn the Sanskrit language or the Indian language at all. The Buddhist teachings were translated into Tibetan—including the names of places like Bodhgaya or Benares or Kushinagara and names of people like Buddha and Ananda. The names of places were translated into Tibetan words so that they did not have to feel foreign to Tibetans. They were just other Tibetan names, as though they existed in Tibet. And such people also seemed to exist in Tibet, because they had Tibetan names. So the Tibetans used their own words, but they got the sense of it. So it seems to be largely based on different ways of transplanting the dharma in terms of basic environment. There could be American Buddhism—I don't think this is a particularly ambitious project.

S : This is a question of style, of a difference in style. In Zen, the teacher always comes to sit with the students. It is important as an example. I was wondering why you don't come and sit with us.

T R : Well, that is another sort of sociological issue, so to speak. The pattern happening in the world in the time of the Buddha and Christ was that it was an age of monarchy and of extreme leadership. For instance, the teachings of Buddha spread all over the Indian continent and Asia, from Japan and China to Afghanistan and up to Mongolia and Russia. There was a tremendous movement of one person spreading his teaching, like expanding an empire. And it seems that in the twentieth century, that dictatorial or imperial style has diminished. Mussolini and Hitler attempted to re-create that, in their way, but didn't succeed. So today there is a more democratic pattern.

It seems that presently in the world there is not going to be one savior or one great guru, one savior of the world that everybody has to follow. Everything has to be individual style, democratic, an individual discovery. The same is true in the practice of meditation. Obviously somebody has to instigate the idea of meditation, but it has to be leaderless practice. So the process is decentralized.

The whole approach should not be based on one person; it should be based on the individualities of people. That seems to be a form of insurance policy for future spiritual development. If you lose a particular leader, if that person has left the country or died, you don't look for somebody else to lead your meditation, but in the same way as you've been doing it all along, you can continue to do it all the time.

STUDENT: I find it a little bit disturbing, the expectations I have from leaders or people like teachers to tell me what to do. So I find what you are saying a bit unsettling. But apart from all that, do you meditate in the formal sense ever in your life? I know from reading your book that you have in the past. My question is a personal question. Do you feel like you ever need to meditate? Do you ever do it?

TRUNGPA RINPOCHE: Well, that seems to depend on the situation—but formal sitting, in terms of imposing it on oneself, somehow doesn't apply anymore.

S: To whom?

TR: To whom. That's it.

Well, perhaps we should close now. I hope that we can relate what we have discussed in this seminar with our personal experience. I sincerely hope that it will save us further expenses, in that we don't have to go shopping and spend more money.

Appendix A
The Six States of Bardo

GOD REALM	SAMTEN BARDO meditation/clear light	eternity/emptiness
JEALOUS GOD REALM	KYE-NE BARDO birth	speed/stillness
HUMAN REALM	GYULÜ BARDO illusory body	real/unreal
ANIMAL REALM	MILAM BARDO dream	asleep/awake
HUNGRY GHOST REALM	SIPA BARDO existence/becoming	grasp/let go
HELL REALM	CHIKHA BARDO death	pain/pleasure destroy/create

Appendix B
The Cycle of the Bardos

BECOMING/SIPA

BIRTH/KYE-NE

DREAM/MILAM

DEATH/CHIKHA

ISNESS/CHÖNYI

MEDITATION/SAMTEN

ILLUSORY BODY/GYULÜ

Appendix C
Transliterations of Tibetan Terms

bardo	*bar do*
chikha	*'chi kha*
chönyi	*chos nyid*
gyulü	*sgyu lus*
kye-ne	*skye gnas*
milam	*rmi lam*
samten	*bsam gtan*
serna	*ser sna*
sipa	*srid pa*
thünmong thekpa	*thun mong theg pa*
tragdok	*phrag dog*
tülku	*sprul sku*

Notes

1. W. Y. Evans-Wentz, comp. and ed., *The Tibetan Book of the Dead* (London: Oxford University Press, 1927).

2. *The Heart Sutra:* one of the Prajnaparamita Sutras and a fundamental discourse on wisdom and emptiness.

3. Chögyam Trungpa, Foreword to *The Jewel Ornament of Liberation,* translated and annotated by Herbert V. Guenther (Berkeley: Shambhala Publications, 1971).

4. E. V. Gold, *The American Book of the Dead* (Berkeley: And/Or Press, 1975).

5. Chögyam Trungpa, *Born in Tibet* (London: George Allen & Unwin, 1966; Boston: Shambhala Publications, 1985).

Glossary

This glossary contains many of the terms appearing in *Transcending Madness* which may be unfamiliar to the readers. Please note that the definitions given here are particular to their usage in this book and should not be construed as the single or even most common meaning of a specific term.

abhidharma: The detailed investigation of mind, including both mental process and contents. *The Tibetan Book of the Dead* provides a detailed geography of the workings of mind and thus might be considered a vajrayana abhidharma text.

abhisheka: In vajrayana Buddhism, elaborate ceremonies initiating students into particular spiritual practices. More specifically, *abhishekha* refers to the meeting of minds between teacher and student, which is essential for the transmission of the teachings. Without the direct oral transmission and empowerment of a master, pursuing such practices would be meaningless.

alaya: The eighth level of consciousness, literally the "storehouse" consciousness. It is the fundamental ground of dualistic mind and contains within it the seeds of all experience.

awake: Trungpa Rinpoche used the term *awake* as an expression of unconditional wakefulness. Rather than being wakeful, cultivating wakefulness, or waking up, one simply is awake.

dawn of Vajrasattva: This phrase evokes the quality of indestructible purity that arises in the midst of confusion, just like the first light of day. Vajrasattva symbolizes the pristine purity of awareness.

five buddha families: The mandala of the five buddha families represents five basic styles of energy, which could manifest dualistically as confusion or nondualistically as enlightenment. The enlightened mandala is portrayed iconographically as the mandala of the five *tathagatas,* or victorious ones. All experience is said to be colored by one of these five energies. The central, or buddha, family represents ignorance which can be transformed into the wisdom of all-encompassing space. In the east is the vajra family, representing aggression, which can be transformed into mirrorlike wisdom. In the south is the ratna family, representing pride, which can be transformed into the wisdom of equanimity. In the west is the padma family of passion, which can be transformed into discriminating awareness wisdom. And in the north is the karma family of envy, which can be transformed into the wisdom that accomplishes all action.

herukas: Wrathful male deities.

jhana: A Pali word (not to be confused with the Sanskrit term *jnana,* or *wisdom*), referring to a state of meditative absorption. Traditionally, four such states are mentioned: desirelessness, nonthought, equanimity, and neither pain nor pleasure. In his book *Cutting Through Spiritual Materialism,* Trungpa Rinpoche describes the four jhanas, which are associated with the meditative experience of the realm of the gods, as limitless space, limitless consciousness, not that/not this, and *not* not that, *not* not this.

karma family: See *five buddha families*

kriya yoga: The vajrayana path is divided into six yanas, or vehicles. The first, kriya yoga, emphasizes purification.

mahamudra practice: The predominant formless meditation practice of Tibetan Buddhism, in which the practitioner simply lets the mind rest naturally, without contrivance or manipulation.

mahamudra / maha ati: Mahamudra refers to lower tantra, and *maha ati* to higher tantra. These two approaches to understanding the nature of mind are presented at times sequentially and at other times as complementary.

mantra: Mantras are Sanskrit words or syllables that are recited ritually as the quintessence of various energies. For instance, they can be used to attract particular energies or to repel obstructions.

maras: The temptations or distractions that practitioners encounter on the path. It is said that they go hand in hand with the degree of one's realization: the more awake one is, the more maras one attracts. Thus, immediately prior to his attainment of complete enlightenment, the Buddha engaged in conquering the attacks of the maras. These forces have been personified as the demon Mara, with her sons (aggressions) and daughters (passions).

Nagarjuna. Nagarjuna, who lived in second-century India, was a foremost teacher and philosopher of the *madhyamika,* or "middle way," school of Buddhist logic, and abbot of Nalanda, India's renowned Buddhist university.

Padmasambhava: Padmasambhava, also referred to as Guru Rinpoche, or "Precious Teacher," introduced vajrayana Buddhism to Tibet in the eighth century.

sword of Manjushri: The sword of Manjushri, the bodhisattva of knowledge, symbolizes penetrating insight which cuts completely through ego's deception.

shunyata: Literally translated as "emptiness," this term refers to a completely open and unbounded clarity of mind.

The Jewel Ornament of Liberation: A classic text by Jetsun Gampopa, outlining in clear detail the stages of the mahayana path. In it the six perfections (paramitas), or transcendent actions, are presented sequentially, culminating in *prajna paramita,* or transcendent knowledge.

prajna/prajna paramita: Prajna means "knowledge"; it has also been translated as "wisdom." As *prajna paramita,* the sixth paramita, or perfection, it is said to be the transcendent knowledge revealing the emptiness of all phenomena.

samsara/nirvana: Samsara is the whirlpool of confusion, and *nirvana* refers to the cessation of confusion, or enlightenment.

satori: In the Zen tradition, great emphasis is placed on the experience of *satori,* sudden realization.

The Tibetan Book of the Dead: This famous text, whose title literally translates as *The Great Liberation through Hearing in the Bardo,* is one of a series of instructions on six types of liberation: through hearing, wearing, seeing, remembering, tasting, and touching. Its origin can be traced to Padmasambhava and his consort, Yeshe Tsogyal. It was later discovered by Karma Lingpa, in the fourteenth century. Intensively studied in Tibet, both academically and during retreat practice, the text is often read aloud to dying persons to help them attain realization within the bardo.

Tilopa: A renowned teacher of vajrayana Buddhism in India in the eleventh century. His most famous disciple was Naropa, who through his student Marpa introduced Tilopa's teachings into Tibet.

vajrayana: The literal meaning of *vajrayana* is the "diamond path." It is also known as the sudden path, because it is claimed that through the practice of vajrayana one can realize enlightenment in one lifetime.

About the Author

Ven. Chögyam Trungpa was born in the province of Kham in Eastern Tibet in 1940. When he was just thirteen months old, Chögyam Trungpa was recognized as a major *tülku,* or incarnate teacher. According to Tibetan tradition, an enlightened teacher is capable, based on his or her vow of compassion, of reincarnating in human form over a succession of generations. Before dying, such a teacher leaves a letter or other clues to the whereabouts of the next incarnation. Later, students and other realized teachers look through these clues and, based on careful examinations of dreams and visions, conduct searches to discover and recognize the successor. Thus, particular lines of teaching are formed, in some cases extending over several centuries. Chögyam Trungpa was the eleventh in the teaching lineage known as the Trungpa Tülkus.

Once young tülkus are recognized, they enter a period of intensive training in the theory and practice of the Buddhist teachings. Trungpa Rinpoche (*Rinpoche* is an honorific title meaning "precious one"), after being enthroned as supreme abbot of Surmang Monasteries and governor of Surmang District, began a period of training that would last eighteen years, until his departure from Tibet in 1959. As a Kagyü tulkü, his training was based on the systematic practice of meditation and on refined theoretical understanding of Buddhist philosophy. One of the four great lineages of Tibet, the Kagyü is known as the "practice lineage."

At the age of eight, Trungpa Rinpoche received ordination as a novice monk. After his ordination, he engaged in intensive study and practice of the traditional monastic disciplines as well as in the arts of calligraphy, thangka painting, and monastic dance. His primary teachers were Jamgön Kongtrül of Sechen and Khenpo Kangshar—leading teachers in the Nyingma and Kagyü lineages. In 1958, at the age of eighteen, Trungpa Rinpoche completed his studies, receiving the degrees of *kyorpön* (doctor of divinity) and *khenpo* (master of studies). He also received full monastic ordination.

The late fifties were a time of great upheaval in Tibet. As it became clear that the Chinese Communists intended to take over the country by force, many people, both monastic and lay, fled the country. Trungpa Rinpoche spent many harrowing months trekking over the Himalayas (described in his book *Born in Tibet*). After narrowly escaping capture by the Chinese, he at last reached India in 1959. While in India, Trungpa Rinpoche was appointed by His Holiness Tenzin Gyatso, the fourteenth Dalai Lama, to serve as spiritual advisor to the Young Lamas Home School in Dalhousie, India. He served in this capacity from 1959 to 1963.

Trungpa Rinpoche's first opportunity to encounter the West came when he received a Spaulding sponsorship to attend Oxford University. At Oxford he studied comparative religion, philosophy, and fine arts. He also studied Japanese flower arranging, receiving a degree from the Sogetsu School. While in England, Trungpa Rinpoche began to instruct Western students in the dharma (the teachings of the Buddha), and in 1968 he founded the Samye Ling Meditation Centre in Dumfriesshire, Scotland. During this time he also published his first two books, both in English: *Born in Tibet* and *Meditation in Action*.

In 1969, Trungpa Rinpoche traveled to Bhutan, where he entered into a solitary meditation retreat. This retreat marked a pivotal change in his approach to teaching. Immediately upon returning he became a lay person, putting aside his monastic robes and dressing in ordinary Western attire. He also married a young Englishwoman, and together they left Scotland and moved to North America. Many of his early students found these changes shocking and upsetting. However, he expressed a conviction that, in order to take root in the West, the dharma needed to be taught free from cultural trappings and religious fascination.

During the seventies America was in a period of political and cultural ferment. It was a time of fascination with the East. Trungpa Rinpoche criticized the materialistic and commercialized approach to spirituality he encountered, describing it as a "spiritual supermarket." In his lectures, and in his books *Cutting Through Spiritual Materialism* and *The Myth of Freedom,* he pointed to the simplicity and directness of the practice of sitting meditation as the way to cut through such distortions of the spiritual journey.

During his seventeen years of teaching in North America, Trungpa Rinpoche developed a reputation as a dynamic and controversial teacher. Fluent in the English language, he was one of the first lamas who could speak to Western students directly, without the aid of a translator. Traveling extensively throughout North America and Europe, Trungpa Rinpoche gave hundreds of talks and seminars. He established major centers in Vermont, Colorado, and Nova Scotia, as well as many smaller meditation and study centers in cities throughout North America and Europe. Vajradhatu was formed in 1973 as the central administrative body of this network.

In 1974, Trungpa Rinpoche founded the Naropa Institute, which became the only accredited Buddhist-inspired university in North America. He lectured extensively at the Institute, and his book *Journey Without Goal* is based on a course he taught there. In 1976, he established the Shambhala Training Program, a series of weekend programs and seminars that provides instruction in meditation practice within a secular setting. His book *Shambhala: The Sacred Path of the Warrior* gives an overview of the Shambhala teachings.

In 1976, Trungpa Rinpoche appointed Ösel Tendzin (Thomas F. Rich) as his Vajra Regent, or dharma heir. Ösel Tendzin worked closely with Trungpa Rinpoche in the administration of Vajradhatu and Shambhala Training. He taught extensively from 1976 until his death in 1990 and is the author of *Buddha in the Palm of Your Hand*.

Trungpa Rinpoche was also active in the field of translation. Working with Francesca Fremantle, he rendered a new translation of *The Tibetan Book of the Dead,* which was published in 1975. Later he formed the Nālandā Translation Committee, in order to translate texts and liturgies for his own students as well as to make important texts available publicly.

In 1978 Trungpa Rinpoche conducted a ceremony empowering his son Ösel Rangdröl Mukpo as his successor in the Shambhala lineage. At that time he gave him the title of Sawang, or "earth lord."

Trungpa Rinpoche was also known for his interest in the arts and particularly for his insights into the relationship between contemplative discipline and the artistic process. His own art work included calligraphy, painting, flower arranging, poetry, playwriting, and environmental installations. In addition, at the Naropa Institute he created an educational atmosphere that attracted many leading artists and poets. The exploration of the creative process in light of contemplative training continues there as a provocative dialogue. Trungpa Rinpoche also published two books of poetry: *Mudra* and *First Thought Best Thought*.

Trungpa Rinpoche's published books represent only a fraction of the rich legacy of his teachings. During his seventeen years of teaching in North America, he crafted the structures necessary to provide his students with thorough, systematic training in the dharma. From introductory talks and courses to advanced group retreat practices, these programs emphasize a balance of study and practice, of intellect and intuition. Students at all levels can pursue their interest in meditation and the Buddhist path through these many forms of training. Senior students of Trungpa Rinpoche continue to be involved in both teaching and meditation instruction in such programs. In addition to his extensive teachings in the Buddhist tradition, Trungpa Rinpoche also placed great emphasis on the Shambhala teachings, which stress the importance of mind-training, as distinct from religious practice; community involvement and the creation of an enlightened society; and appreciation of one's day-to-day life.

Trungpa Rinpoche passed away in 1987, at the age of forty-seven. He is survived by his wife, Diana, and five sons. His eldest son, Ösel Rangdröl Mukpo, succeeds him as president and spiritual head of Vajradhatu. By the time of his death, Trungpa Rinpoche had become known as a pivotal figure in introducing dharma to the Western world. The joining of his great appreciation for Western culture and his deep understanding of his own tradition led to a revolutionary approach to teaching the dharma, in which the most ancient and profound teachings were presented in a thoroughly contemporary way. Trungpa Rinpoche was known for his fearless proclamation of the dharma: free from hesitation, true to the purity of the tradition, and utterly fresh. May these teachings take root and flourish for the benefit of all sentient beings.

Meditation Center Information

For further information regarding meditation or inquiries about a dharma center near you, please contact one of the following centers.

Karme-Chöling
Star Route
Barnet, VT 05821
(802) 633-2384

Rocky Mountain Dharma Center
4921 County Road 68C
Red Feather Lakes, CO 80545
(303) 881-2184

Vajradhatu Europe
Zwetchenweg 23
D3550 Marburg
Germany
49 6421 46363

Vajradhatu International
1084 Tower Road
Halifax, N.S. B3H 2Y5
Canada
(902) 425-4275

Many talks and seminars are available in cassette tape format. For information, call or write:

Vajradhatu Recordings
1084 Tower Road
Halifax, N.S. B3H 2Y5
(902) 421-1550

Index